Sportsmanlike Driving

SEVENTH EDITION

Sportsmanlike Driving

AMERICAN AUTOMOBILE ASSOCIATION

Falls Church, Virginia

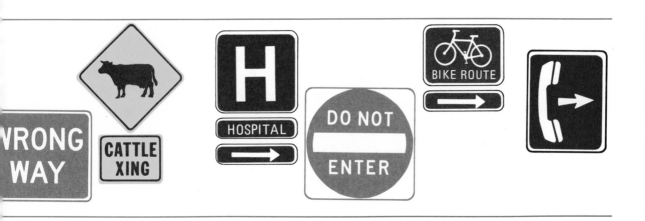

WEBSTER DIVISION, McGRAW-HILL BOOK COMPANY

New York   St. Louis   San Francisco   Dallas   Düsseldorf   Johannesburg
Kuala Lumpur   London   Mexico   Montreal   New Delhi   Panama
Paris   São Paulo   Singapore   Sydney   Tokyo   Toronto

Library of Congress Cataloging in Publication Data

American Automobile Association.
  Sportsmanlike driving.

  Includes index.
  SUMMARY: Discusses the physical and mental qualities
of a good driver, traffic regulations, road safety and
hazards, and automobile mechanics. Also gives brief
instructions for operating an automobile.
  1. Automobile driving. [1. Automobile driving]
I. Title.
TL152.5.A38   1975   629.28'3'2   74-31372
ISBN 0-07-001292-X

Editors:
    D. Eugene Gilmore
    Paul Farrell
Design Supervisor:
    Lisa Delgado
Editing Supervisor:
    Sal Allocco
Production Supervisor:
    Ted Agrillo

SPORTSMANLIKE DRIVING
Seventh Edition

Contents

Turns
Turnabouts
Driving a Car with a Stick Shift

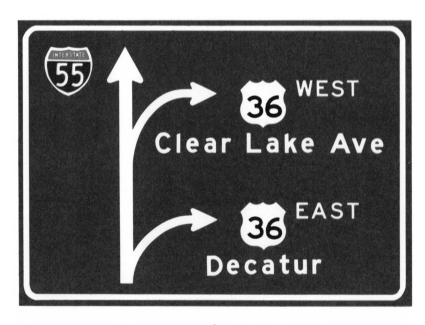

Preface

The seventh edition of *Sportsmanlike Driving*, like each edition before it, incorporates the newest advances in the field of driver education. It brings together, for beginning and experienced drivers alike, the latest ideas in task analysis, decision-making, and traffic safety for drivers. The primary purpose of this text is to provide you with the knowledge and skills you will need to become a safe, efficient user of the highway transportation system—as a driver, a passenger, a pedestrian, a bicyclist, or a motorcyclist.

To derive the greatest benefit from this course, it is our hope that you will be enrolled in a driver education program where classroom and laboratory instruction (in-car experience) are scheduled so that you can make the most of both experiences. In other words, we hope that what you discuss in class today can be put into practice in a car tomorrow and what is experienced in the car today will be discussed in class tomorrow. We realize that this will not always be the case. However, you can at least start to apply many of the concepts discussed in this book while you are riding as a passenger. (The other parts of the *Sportsmanlike Driving* program, including the *Tests*, the *Behind-the-Wheel Guide*, and *Project Workbook*, are designed to bridge the gap between your classroom and laboratory experiences.)

Your ability to physically control a motor vehicle is of obvious importance. Knowing what the various controls are and where they are located is important. However, this information is of limited value if, for example, your visibility is limited or if the driver's seat is improperly adjusted, preventing the proper use of the controls.

Equally important is your ability to process information, to decide upon the best response, and to manage the time and space available to you. It is only through the development of these skills that safe, efficient driving will be possible.

To drive well, you must also know in advance what cues to look for and how and where to look for them. You need to understand traffic laws and to be able to identify the signs, signals, and markings that provide guidelines for all motorists. You must also be able to predict the behavior of other highway users. For example, it is important for you to understand the basic handling characteristics of your own and other vehicles, including cars, trucks, buses, motorcycles, and bicycles.

As a driver, you will also have to evaluate the influence that roadway and off-road conditions, the weather, and the time of day will have on your ability to control your vehicle. In addition, you must be alert to the abilities and expected behavior of nonmotorized highway users—pedestrians and bicyclists of all ages.

What kind of driver will you be? To answer this question, still other factors have to be considered. Good driving requires more than knowledge and skill.

Certain illnesses and physical disabilities can impair your ability to drive. On the other hand, many drivers with serious disabilities drive many miles each year and have outstanding driving records.

The drinking driver is a major problem. Alcohol, like other drugs, can seriously affect a person's mind and body. Yet, many people who drink control the amount they drink if they have to drive.

Most of us, at some time, take other drugs by prescription. Some people abuse drugs or use illegal drugs. All drugs can impair driving ability. Whether to use drugs of any type and then drive is a decision only you can make.

Each of us has a personality of our own. Each of us reacts differently to different things at different times. The way we see ourselves and the behavior of others around us affects our behavior. Only you can control how you respond to irritations and frustrations. Uncontrolled behavior can be deadly in traffic. Only you can determine how you are going to drive, and you will have to make this decision each and every time you get behind the wheel.

The skills and procedures discussed in this text, together with the learning experiences in a car, can help you meet the challenges of operating a motor vehicle within the highway transportation system. What you learn will add to the freedom and pleasure that driving can provide.

Acknowledgments

The seventh edition of *Sportsmanlike Driving,* representing marked style and format changes from previous editions, was prepared under the direction of Dr. Francis C. Kenel.

Dr. Kenel received a bachelor's degree in industrial engineering and safety, a master of arts degree in vocational education and traffic safety, and a doctoral degree in traffic safety at Michigan State University. He has taught driver education, traffic safety, and accident prevention courses at both the high school and university levels.

Actively engaged in high school driver education for 20 years, he initiated and contributed to early development programs for students with learning disabilities and to the perceptual development and information processing fields as they relate to driving.

Before becoming Director of the Traffic Engineering and Safety Department of the American Automobile Association, Dr. Kenel was professor and chairman of Traffic Safety and Accident Prevention, first at Illinois State University and more recently at the University of Maryland. He was also on the Highway Traffic Safety Center staff at Michigan State University and at Sexton High School in Lansing, Michigan.

Mr. Eugene Carney, Driver Education Instructor, Bethesda Chevy Chase High School, Montgomery County, Maryland, prepared material for the chapters concerning information processing and driver decision-making.

Mr. Carney has taught driver education at Bethesda Chevy Chase High School for 15 years and driver education teacher-preparation courses at the University of Maryland. During this time, he has done extensive work in developing concepts related to time-and-space management and the strategies necessary for effective operation of motor vehicles in traffic.

Mr. John D. DeLellis, Educational Consultant to the Traffic Engineering and Safety Department of the American Automobile Association, developed the behavioral objectives and "To Think About" and "To Do" sections in each chapter. He also prepared the art specifications and the teacher annotations.

Mr. DeLellis taught driver education at North Rockland High School, in Thiells, New York, prior to joining the American Automobile Association. He is presently completing his master's degree in traffic safety education at Southern Connecticut State College. He has conducted workshops concerning driving-while-intoxicated countermeasures throughout the United States.

Special thanks are extended to AAA staff members for their contributions to the development of selected chapters:

Mr. Richard Tearle, Technical Consultant, Traffic Engineering and Safety Department, for Chapter 5, "Driving Laws" and Chapter 12, "Career Opportunities"

Mr. Dean Childs, Assistant Director, Traffic Engineering and Safety Department, for Chapter 8, "Other Highway Users"

Mr. James McDowell, Director of Automotive Engineering, and Mr. Richard Curry, Director of Environmental Affairs, for Chapter 7, "Vehicle Performance"

Mr. Charles Campbell, Director of Legal Department, for Chapter 5, "Driving Laws"

Mr. Charles Brady, Director of Highway Department, for Chapter 6, "Highway Conditions"

Mr. Sam Yaksich, Executive Director of the AAA Foundation For Traffic Safety, for review of the entire manuscript

Mr. J. Kay Aldous, Managing Director, Public Affairs Division, for review and editing of the entire manuscript.

A special thanks is extended to Mrs. Mary Fazio, Mrs. Betty Tanner, Mrs. Gladys Garoufes, and Mrs. Virginia Greene for their outstanding efforts in manuscript preparation throughout this project.

Thanks are also extended to Doctor Sister Marie Emery of the Highway Traffic Safety Center, Michigan State University, and Mr. Dennis Rowe of the Automobile Club of Southern California, for their efforts in developing the initial content outline.

Supplementary materials for the seventh edition were developed under the direction of Dr. Harvey Clearwater, Associate Professor of Health and Safety at the University of Maryland, College Park, Maryland. Dr. Clearwater was assisted by the following people: Mr. Eugene Carney, Bethesda Chevy Chase High School, Montgomery County, Maryland; Mr. Kenneth Klecan, driver education teacher, Polytechnical High School, Baltimore, Maryland; Mrs. Susan Klecan, driver education teacher, Western High School, Baltimore, Maryland; Mr. Robert Lazarewicz, Unit Administrator, Driver Education; Mr. Richard Guyer, Traffic Records Analyst, Maryland State Department of Transportation, Baltimore-Washington International Airport.

Thanks also are due to those who gave assistance to the six previous editions of *Sportsmanlike Driving.*

You and the Highway System 1

After reading this chapter, you should be able to:

1. Discuss how the term *sportsmanship* applies to driving.
2. Name the three elements that make up the highway transportation system.
3. Describe how these three elements interact.
4. Discuss how failures in the system occur and how they can be prevented.

The reasons for wanting to get a driver's license and drive vary from one person to another. Generally, however, people want to drive so that they will have greater *mobility,* or freedom of movement. Driving gives people a wider choice of places to live, work, and travel.

When you get a driver's license, you will become a *highway user* in the broadest sense. In addition to using the roadway as a bicyclist and pedestrian, you will have the right to operate a motor vehicle. As a licensed operator, you will have to accept responsibility for the safety of yourself and others. You will also have to obey a system of rules and regulations found in few activities outside of organized sports.

Driving and Sports

Driving is sometimes referred to as a "team" operation. Due to the great size and complexity of our highway system, stress is placed on the need for team effort and sportmanship. In fact, driving and sports are similar in several ways:

1. *Team cooperation in trying to reach a goal.* Highway users have to cooperate with one another, just as the members of a winning team

1

A driver's license will give you a wider choice of places to live, work, and travel.

2

Highway users have to cooperate with one another to achieve one goal: the safe and efficient movement of people and goods.

must cooperate. In sports, the goal is obvious: to win a game, a series, a match, or a title. Winning, when applied to all highway users, means the safe and efficient movement of people and goods.

2. *Regulated facilities.* Both driving and sports take place on regulated facilities, and both highway users and athletes must act according to sets of rules. In sports, the facilities are playing areas of a certain size and design. For highway users, the facilities are the roadways, sidewalks, and parking areas regulated by signs, signals, and markings.

3. *Equipment.* In sports, equipment must meet certain design and construction safety standards. The same is increasingly true of cars, trucks, buses, and motorcycles.

There are also, however, important differences between driving and sports. The immediate goal of an athletic team is to win a game. Highway users, on the other hand, have many different immediate goals, and these goals often come into conflict. Each day, millions of

New highways must meet certain design and construction safety standards.

drivers, bicyclists, and pedestrians each try to get to and from different points. Their paths often cross, and their goals are often in conflict. Some drivers think only of their own immediate goals. Once they have gotten to wherever they want they say "I made it," without regard for the goals or the safety of other highway users.

As a driver, you will be involved in an activity that you will probably take part in for the rest of your life. You are not, like an athlete, preparing for a game or a series of games. In addition, you will be able to enter or leave the roadway without giving notice. In sports, players cannot enter or leave a game unless they give notice of their intentions.

Still other factors make driving different from, and more complex than, a sports event. In organized sports, players' performances are constantly evaluated. Players who do not perform well are dropped from the team. In contrast, drivers have to demonstrate only a minimum of skill and decision-making ability to keep their licenses. Drivers are not carefully evaluated throughout their driving careers. Permission to drive can be taken away only if a driver is physically disabled or consistently fails to drive as required.

To solve these problems, it is extremely important for every driver to extend the rules of sportsmanlike behavior to their ultimate. Emphasis must be placed on *cooperation* rather than competition. As a driver, you must make every effort to drive safely. This means that you must know about and obey the laws that regulate driving. You must also learn to look for and adjust to the errors of other highway users. In short, *sportsmanship* in driving means assisting every other driver to become a winner.

4

Because of the size and complexity of our network of roads and highways, drivers must cooperate with each other.

Drivers must also cooperate with other highway users, including pedestrians and bicyclists.

The responsibility for safe and efficient movement on our highways rests with you, the individual user.

Stated simply, then, the responsibility for safe and efficient roads and highways rests with you, the individual highway user. This responsibility is yours whether you are a pedestrian, a cyclist, or the operator of a motor vehicle.

To reduce the possibility of committing errors and contributing to highway failures, particularly as a motor vehicle operator, you must understand the purpose and function of the major elements of the highway transportation system and the manner in which failures may occur.

The Highway Transportation System

The *highway transportation system* is made up of the vehicles, highways, and human beings that play a part in reaching one goal: the safe and efficient movement of people and goods throughout this country. The system is large and complicated, and it does not always work safely and efficiently. Before you begin to drive, you should understand the three elements that work together to make the system.

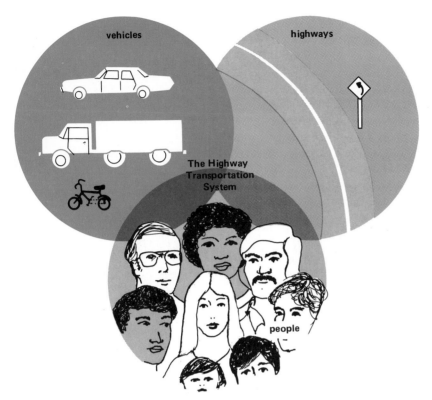

The three major elements in the highway transportation system are vehicles, highways, and people.

1. *Vehicles* (machines). There are now more than 120 million cars, trucks, buses, and motorcycles and over 70 million bicycles that provide movement within the system.

2. *Highways* (environment). There are more than 3.7 million miles of roadway and nearby off-road areas found in virtually all parts of this country.

3. *Human beings* (both drivers and pedestrians). Nearly everyone in our population of more than 210 million can be counted as a pedestrian. Many of these 210 million people also drive the more than 70 million bicycles presently in use. In addition, over 120 million people are licensed motor vehicle operators.

The way in which these three elements work together determines how safe and efficient the highway transportation system is. When any one element fails, the system will fail.

MOTOR VEHICLES IN THE SYSTEM

The highway transportation system is designed and operated to move people and goods by way of vehicles. The vehicles include bicycles, small and large motorcycles, and subcompact, compact, intermediate, and large automobiles. In addition, you will find small and large trucks

7

Vehicles of different size and performance capability often share the same highways.

and buses. When they are produced, all of these vehicles must meet certain minimum safety standards. They do not, however, "handle" the same way. In other words, each type of vehicle has a different *performance capability*. The various types of vehicles accelerate, brake, and steer differently. They also differ in the ways they protect passengers in the event of an accident. For example, a large truck cannot accelerate as quickly as a compact car, and a motorcycle does not offer the same protection (in the event of a crash) as a large station wagon.

The *maintenance* (upkeep) of vehicles is the responsibility of the individual owners and operators. It should therefore come as no surprise to find that the quality of maintenance varies from nearly perfect to dangerously bad. Before you buy and drive a car, you should be sure to check its condition. It is up to you, the individual driver, to maintain your vehicle in the best possible condition.

Performance capabilities vary greatly from one type of vehicle to another. This illustration compares the stopping distances of several types of vehicles.

motorcycle

car

panel truck

tractor–trailer

When the brakes are applied at 30 mph . . .

the vehicles would travel this far before coming to a full stop.

As you might expect, the wide varieties in the performance capability and the maintenance of vehicles in the highway transportation system can cause trouble. Vehicles of greatly different sizes and speeds, for example, often use the same roads at the same time. Drivers have to take these differences into consideration when they use the highway transportation system.

HIGHWAYS IN THE SYSTEM

A vast network of roadways reaches into the smallest communities of this country. Without this network, our nation would be an entirely different place to live. Highways permit us to travel to and from school, work, shopping, and vacations. Even more important, they permit the delivery of supplies from one part of the country to another. In natural disasters like earthquakes and floods, highways could be used for evacuating large numbers of people. It should be obvious that highways make important contributions to the health and welfare of our nation.

The roadways in the highway transportation system range from six-lane Interstate Highways to gravel-covered rural roads.

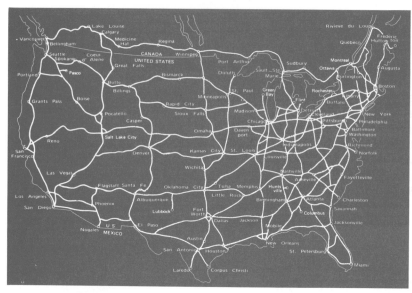

The Interstate Highway System forms a network of modern highways that link together most of the large cities in this country.

The improvement of the roadway system within the United States has been dramatic since 1947. This has been particularly true since the enactment of the *Federal Aid Highway Act* of 1956. This act provided the funds for over 40,000 miles of the Interstate System, which today links together nearly all cities that have populations of 50,000 or more. Highways in the Interstate System must meet certain minimum design and construction standards. They must have, for example, 12-foot-wide lanes, a limited number of entrances and exits, wide and firm shoulder areas, and guard rail protection. However, these standards do not remove all hazards from the Interstate System.

The federal government also provides states with money for building and improving state and local highways. As you move from the Interstate System to state and local highways, you will find more hazards on and near the roadways. For example, lanes will usually not be as wide and there will be many more entrances and exits. You will therefore have to adjust your driving to meet these conditions.

To assist drivers, signs, signals, and markings provide information about driving rules and potential hazards. Environmental factors, like curves in the road and the condition of the pavement, can limit drivers' vision and their vehicles' traction.

In other words, failure of the highway transportation system can be caused by weaknesses in the highways themselves. A highway's design or condition may lead directly to an accident. In addition, bad highway designs and roadway conditions can increase the seriousness of errors made by drivers.

PEOPLE IN THE SYSTEM

In their roles as users of the highway transportation system, human beings are the single greatest cause of system failure. Failures on the part of highway users occur for many reasons. Sometimes individuals do not have the information they need to make realistic decisions. For example, a two-year-old child attempting to cross even a lightly traveled street does not know how to judge the hazards involved. Without experience, the child simply does not have the information necessary to make a realistic judgment. Highway users can cause system failure in other ways. A driver could panic and "freeze" on the brake pedal, unaware that steering control of a vehicle is lost when the brakes are locked.

There are more than 120 million licensed drivers and many more pedestrians and bicyclists in the highway transportation system.

11

Nine out of ten drivers consider themselves to be better than average.

Perhaps a more common cause of failure in the system is that people assume that they will be all right as long as their behavior is legal. As a result, they do not anticipate that the actions of other highway users may put them in hazardous situations. They fail to look for important visual cues that tell them what other highway users may do. Lacking this information, they cannot determine realistic options for themselves: they do not know how they would respond if an emergency should arise.

Evidence of the seriousness of the breakdowns in the highway transportation system can be seen in the number of deaths and injuries and the amount of property damage that occurs in the system each year. In spite of the overwhelming evidence—that most of the failures in the system result from drivers' errors—nine out of ten drivers consider

controls speed

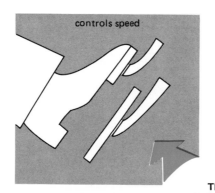

controls position

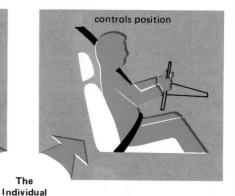

The Individual User

communicates

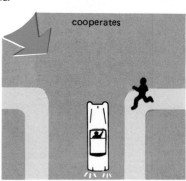

cooperates

The individual driver, by communicating, cooperating, and controlling speed and position, can often prevent failure in the highway transportation system.

12

themselves to be better than average. In no other routine activity do so many participants rate themselves so highly. Yet, in no other routine activity is an error in judgment or action so likely to have such serious consequences.

The purpose of this text is to help you prevent such failure in the highway transportation system. Even when a breakdown in the system is caused by vehicle failure, highway conditions, or a person's error, drivers must do all they can to reduce the seriousness of the consequences.

The greatest potential for improvement of the highway transportation system lies in how well highway users interact with one another. How well they communicate their intentions to others, maintain their equipment and physical well-being, and adjust their needs and goals for the benefit of all highway users will, in the end, determine the safety and efficiency of the system.

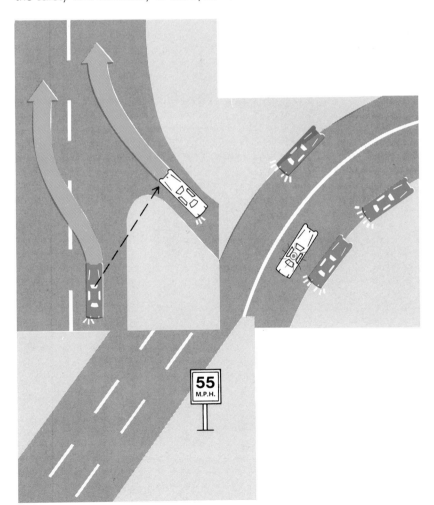

The greatest potential for improvement of the highway transportation system lies in how well highway users cooperate with one another.

To Think About

1. Describe some of the benefits of having a driver's license.
2. How is driving similar to organized sports? How is it different?
3. How does the word *sportsmanship* apply to driving?
4. What is the purpose of the highway transportation system?
5. How does the highway transportation system affect the way we live?
6. How can the performance capability of a vehicle affect driving?
7. How can vehicle maintenance affect a driver's performance?
8. What are some of the reasons for failures in the highway transportation system?
9. Where is the greatest potential for improvement in the system? Why?

To Do

1. Develop a brief list of local, state, and national organizations that are trying to improve the highway transportation system. Report on how each is trying to improve the system.
2. Survey five people who drive and five who do not. Ask them about which quality is more important for a driver—driving skills or attitudes toward driving. Can you draw any conclusions from your findings?
3. Describe how the highway transportation system plays an important part in the movement of people and goods in this country.
4. Observe traffic at an intersection near your own home. Report to your class on how drivers do and do not cooperate with each other and with other highway users.

Preparing to Drive 2

After reading this chapter, you should be able to:

1. Name the seven driving systems that will help you operate a motor vehicle.
2. Explain why it is important to wear safety belts.
3. List basic predriving checks and procedures and explain their importance.

The purpose of this chapter is to introduce you to the control systems, switches, information gauges, and safety devices that will help you more effectively operate a motor vehicle. You will have to use some of this information as soon as you begin to drive. Before you enter the driver education car for the first time, review the appropriate sections of this chapter. Once you have had some driving experience, the procedures outlined in this chapter will serve as a reference for checking and correcting predriving procedures.

Driving Systems

Whether or not you hold a driver's license, you are probably somewhat familiar with the switches, gauges, controls, and safety devices that assist a driver in the operation of a motor vehicle. These systems allow you to control the car's movement, check the car's condition, protect yourself and your passengers, make yourself comfortable, prevent theft, and communicate with other drivers. Do you know the location and function of each instrument, switch, and control device? If you are not sure, you will want to learn about them as quickly as you can. When you drive, you will have to steer and maintain speed, without taking your eyes from the road, as you reach for, locate, and adjust various instruments.

PROTECTIVE SYSTEM

These devices offer you protection from possible injury in the event of an accident or a sudden emergency maneuver. Certain protective-system components, such as airbags, impact-resistant bumpers, and side-bar door beams, are not controlled by the driver or passenger. Other components, such as safety belts and head restraints, are.

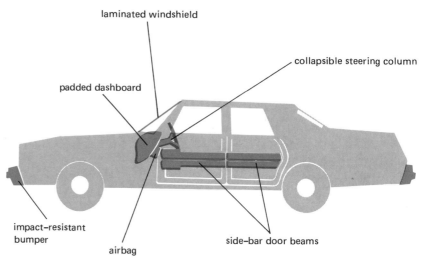

Some parts of the protective system are built into a car, and do not have to be adjusted by the driver.

Safety Belts. In a lap-and-shoulder combination, safety belts restrain the driver and the right front-seat passenger. These belts lessen the possibility of their being thrown into the dashboard or windshield or out an open door or window. In case of an emergency situation, lap belts will also help you to maintain control by keeping you behind the steering wheel.

In 1973 or older automobiles, it is usually necessary to manually adjust both the lap and shoulder belts for proper fit. The lap belt should be adjusted to fit snugly across the hips. The shoulder belt should have just enough slack to allow you to place your fist between the belt and the center of your chest. Center front-seat passengers and rear-seat passengers are provided only a lap belt.

Some cars are equipped with an *ignition interlock system* which requires the front-seat passengers to buckle up before the engine will start. Some other cars are equipped with a simple safety-belt warning light and buzzer to remind drivers to buckle up. (It has been determined that if drivers are not reminded, fewer than 30 percent of them will use belts regularly.)

Head Restraints. Fixed or adjustable head restraints are designed to help prevent *whiplash* (neck injury). When you are riding in the front seat of a vehicle having an adjustable head restraint, adjust the device high enough to make contact with the back of your head, not with the base of your skull. Failure to make such an adjustment may cause serious injury in case of a collision.

COMFORT SYSTEM

These devices make driving more comfortable and pleasant. If used properly they will also help reduce fatigue, thereby assisting you in driving more efficiently. The manner in which they are used may even help you to respond to emergency situations.

Seat Adjustments. One of the most critical parts of the comfort system is the seat adjustment. With proper adjustment, you can effectively operate the control system. In adjusting the seat for best control, you should be positioned high enough to see over the steering wheel and hood so that the ground approximately 12 feet in front of the car is visible. At the same time, your foot should rest comfortably on the accelerator and have easy access to the brake pedal (and the clutch pedal, if you are driving a manual shift car). Additionally, you should grasp the steering wheel with one hand at the 9 o'clock position (imag-

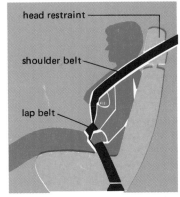

The safety belts and head restraint must be adjusted by the driver. You should be able to fit your fist between the shoulder belt and your chest.

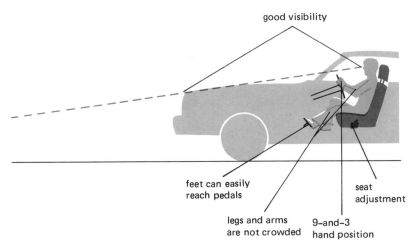

It is important to properly adjust the position of the driver's seat. This will aid visibility, will make you more comfortable, and, most importantly, will improve vehicle control.

ine the face of a clock) and the other at the 3 o'clock position. If the seat is properly adjusted, you should then be able to turn the steering wheel a full 180 degrees (a half circle) left or right and then turn 360 degrees (a full circle) in the opposite direction without changing your hand positions on the wheel.

In a car equipped with a full-range power seat and adjustable steering wheel, many drivers will be able to make the necessary adjustments without much difficulty. You may, however, need pedal extensions or seat cushions. It is important to remember that such devices, if needed in a laboratory unit or in a driver education car, are just as necessary in your own or your family's car.

Air Conditioner.   An air conditioner adds to your comfort by reducing the temperature and humidity in the driving compartment. Used properly, an air conditioner may increase your level of alertness by reducing fatigue and drowsiness brought on by hot and humid weather conditions.

Heater and Defroster.   These are designed to maintain your comfort by providing heat in the driving compartment and by defogging the window. It is important that you not keep the car too warm, however, because this can cause fatigue.

Cruise, or Speed, Control.   This device allows you to accelerate to and then maintain a given speed by pressing a button on the steering wheel or at the end of the turn-indicator arm. By touching the set button you can reduce the selected speed; by tapping the brake pedal you can release the device completely. This device can aid in reducing fa-

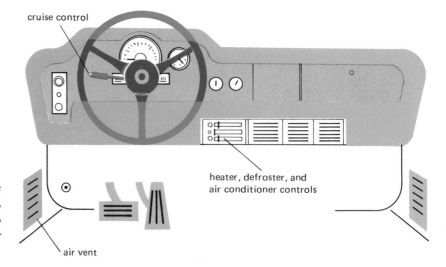

cruise control

heater, defroster, and
air conditioner controls

The locations of the other parts of the comfort system vary from one vehicle to another. Find out where each control is located in the car you drive.

air vent

tigue while driving on an open highway. At times, however, drivers become less alert when they use such a device. They sometimes fail to adjust the speed properly, and they drive into situations that suddenly require a quick response. The speed control can be an asset, but it does take practice to learn how to use it properly.

Air Vents. These are usually located on both the driver and passenger sides. They allow outside air to flow into and circulate through the compartment. The amount of air is regulated by use of the air-vent controls.

CONTROL SYSTEM
These devices allow you to start and stop the car and to control its speed and direction.

Grasp the steering wheel firmly in the 9-and-3 position.

Steering Wheel. You control the direction of the front wheels with the steering wheel. When you drive, your hands should be in the 9-and-3 position, with both hands firmly on the wheel and your upper arm resting against your rib cage. This reduces fatigue and permits the most efficient handling for steady, straight steering, for moderate turning, and for responding to emergency situations requiring hard, rapid steering.

Accelerator or Gas Pedal. The speed of the car is controlled by the amount of gasoline that flows into the engine. This flow is determined by how far you press down the accelerator. For best control, the sole of your right foot should rest on the pedal, with the back of the heel resting on the floor at the base of the accelerator. To increase speed, press the pedal gently with the sole of your foot. High-heel and platform shoes present problems in speed·control and in the movement of the foot from the accelerator to the brake. It is best not to wear them while driving. The best alternative is to keep a pair of shoes in the car for driving. If necessary, drive in bare feet rather than wear improper footwear. You should, however, check your local traffic ordinances, for while no state has a law making it illegal to drive barefoot, certain cities may have such laws.

Shoes with platform soles or high heels can get caught between the gas pedal and the brake pedal.

Foot-Brake Pedal. This pedal is used to slow or stop the car, depending on the amount of pressure you exert. There is normally some "play" in the foot-brake pedal. As you press the brake gently, you will find that the pedal moves about an inch or so before it begins to take hold.

Power-assisted brakes make braking easier by increasing the pressure far beyond that actually exerted by your foot. Power brakes do not, however, shorten the stopping distance over regular hydraulic brakes. Through use, you will probably adapt to one type of brake.

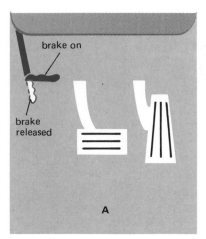
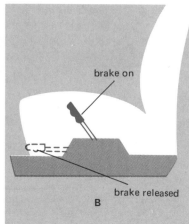
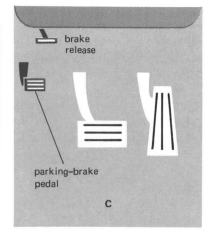

The parking brake may be controlled with a lever under the dashboard (A) or to the right of the driver's seat (B). It may also be controlled with a pedal and release lever under the dashboard (C).

Remember when changing to a car with a different type of brake system that you will have to learn again to adjust and apply pressure as necessary.

A majority of drivers prefer to brake with the right foot, feeling that this ensures that pressure is completely off the accelerator. Other drivers find it quicker and more comfortable to use left-foot braking, keeping the left foot resting on the floor near the brake and ready for use. If you select left-foot braking, avoid pressing both the brake and the accelerator pedal at the same time or driving with your left foot resting on the brake pedal. The former practice results in excessive brake wear; the latter is very confusing to drivers following you, since your brake lights would constantly be on.

Parking Brake. This brake is also known as the *hand brake* or, rather inaccurately, as the "emergency brake." It comes in one of three forms: as a small pedal located to the left of the foot brake, as a hand-operated lever located below the dash, or as a lever between the driver and front-seat passenger. The parking brake is basically used to keep the car from rolling when parked or to hold it steady when starting on a steep upgrade. It operates on the rear wheels and is independent of the foot brake.

Selector Lever and Quadrant. Cars equipped with an automatic transmission have a selector lever and quadrant which enable you to choose gears and to tell at a glance which gear the car is in. An indicator on the quadrant moves as you move the lever. The symbols on a standard quadrant are as follows:

20

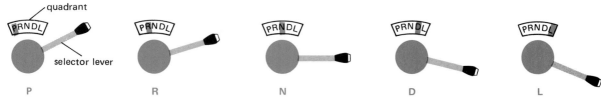

You can choose gears with the selector lever. The quadrant tells you which gear your car is in.

P (park). Automatic transmission gears are disengaged and the rear wheels locked. Generally, the car should be started with the gear in this position.

R (reverse). For backing up; you may have to lift the lever slightly toward you and then down toward the floor to shift into this gear.

N (neutral). The gears are disengaged and the wheels are not locked. As a result, your car may roll downhill if you leave it in neutral and do not set the parking brake. You may want to start your engine in this position if your car stalls while moving.

D (drive). This is the basic forward gear position. Because of a fast idle, the car may start to move when you shift into *D* even if you do not have your foot on the gas pedal. For this reason, it is wise to have your foot on the brake as you shift.

2 and *1* or *L.* These are low drive positions, for maximum power at slow speeds. You would use these positions for driving in mud, sand, or snow, for climbing a very steep grade, for helping to hold the car back when driving down a long steep hill, or for pulling a trailer on a hill.

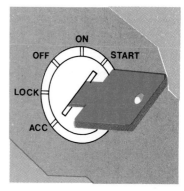

By turning a key inserted in the ignition switch, you can turn on and off the engine and the electrical system.

Ignition Switch. By inserting a key and turning this switch to *start,* you set off an electrical impulse that starts the engine. The other switch positions, in counterclockwise order, are *on, off, lock,* and *accessory (acc.) On* activates gauges, such as the gas gauge, allowing you to read them without starting the engine. *Off* stops the engine, but does not enable you to remove the ignition key. *Lock* locks the steering wheel, ignition switch, and the automatic transmission in *park.* This is the only position which allows you to remove the ignition key. *Accessory* allows you to operate electrical equipment, such as the radio, without starting the engine.

VEHICLE-CHECK SYSTEM
These devices enable the driver to check the operating condition of the car while it is running. They are the lights and gauges on the dashboard.

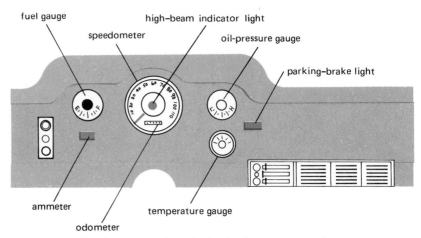

fuel gauge

high-beam indicator light

speedometer

oil-pressure gauge

parking-brake light

ammeter

odometer

temperature gauge

The location of each device in the vehicle-check system varies from one car to another. Learn where each device is in the car you drive.

Speedometer and Odometer.   The speedometer shows, in miles per hour or kilometers per hour, how fast the car is moving. When driving, you should glance at this indicator from time to time to determine the rate of speed at which you are traveling. The odometer shows the total number of miles or kilometers the car has been driven.

Ammeter.   Also known as the alternator light or gauge, this device tells whether the battery is being charged or discharged. If more electricity is being drawn than is being generated, the gauge will indicate *D* (discharge) or the alternator light will be on. If the battery is being charged, the gauge will indicate *C* (charge) or the alternator light will be off. The ammeter will indicate discharge when the ignition is on and the engine is not running, or when the engine is running too slowly for the alternator to charge the battery. A constant discharge warning light or meter reading alerts you to possible trouble in the electrical system.

Temperature Gauge or Warning Light.   This indicates whether the engine is at its proper operating temperature. Overheating of the engine may be either the cause or the result of fluid leaking from the engine's cooling system. This can lead to serious engine damage.

Oil-Pressure Gauge or Warning Light.   This indicates the pressure at which oil is being pumped to the moving parts of the engine. If the light is on, the pressure is low. The gauge or light does not show the *amount* of oil in the engine, but rather the operating pressure. If the oil-pressure light comes on, stop as quickly as you safely can.

Fuel Gauge. This gauge generally has markings showing the approximate amount of gasoline in the fuel tank. The markings usually read as follows: E (empty), $\frac{1}{4}$, $\frac{1}{2}$, $\frac{3}{4}$, and F (full).

Parking-Brake Light. Not all cars are equipped with these lights. When one is present, it flashes on if the engine is turned on while the parking brake is set. This is to remind the driver to release the brake. Some late-model cars also have a light that indicates when the fluid in the brake system is low.

High-Beam Indicator Light. This light is sometimes located near the center of the speedometer. It goes on when you put on the car's high-beam (bright) lights.

VISIBILITY SYSTEM

These devices are designed to help the driver see as much as possible, regardless of the weather or the time of day. It is essential for you as a driver to be able to see the road ahead and the areas adjacent to your intended path of travel.

Headlights. It is important to use headlights for nighttime and most bad-weather driving. High-beam headlights should be used only when no other car is close in front of you, passing you, or approaching from the opposite direction. The beams may be changed back and forth by pressing with your left foot a button located on the floor or by operating a switch located on the steering column. When you see an approaching car, switch to low beam to prevent blinding the other driver.

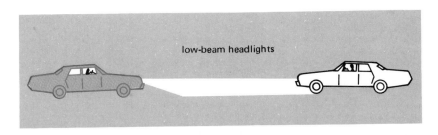

low-beam headlights

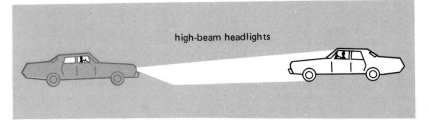

high-beam headlights

High-beam headlights can temporarily "blind" other drivers. Use low beams as you approach oncoming vehicles, as you are being passed, and when you are close behind another vehicle.

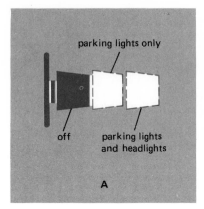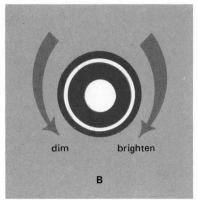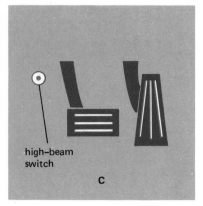

By pushing or pulling the headlight switch, you can turn on and off the parking lights and the headlights (A). By turning the switch you can adjust the illumination of the gauges on the dashboard (B). The high-beam headlight switch is often located on the floor, to the left of the brake pedal (C).

When you turn on your headlights, you will see that the dashboard also lights up so that you can see the quadrant, speedometer, and other dials and gauges. The brightness of the dashboard light should generally be kept low so that it does not interfere with seeing outside. It can be controlled by turning the knob on the headlight switch.

Rear-View and Side-View Mirrors.   These mirrors will enable you to see, up to a point, cars beside you and to the rear. When properly adjusted, the two mirrors can eliminate most, but not all, blind areas. Rear-view mirrors can also be adjusted for day- and nighttime driving.

Wiper-Washer.   Most cars have two-speed windshield wipers and a spray nozzle. Water from the spray nozzle (mixed with an antifreeze solution in winter) enables the wipers to clean dirt from the windshield.

Sun Visors.   These can be adjusted to keep much of the sun's glare from your eyes. They should not, however, be set in such a way that they block your vision. For example, they should not prevent you from seeing overhanging traffic lights. Just as important, the sun visors should not be used as a glove compartment for the storage of objects, which may easily fall and distract you.

Defroster.   A defroster is used to clear the inside of the front and rear windows of moisture or frost. When used with warm air, the defroster prevents frost from collecting on the inside. It also melts ice or frost that may have gathered on the outside of the glass.

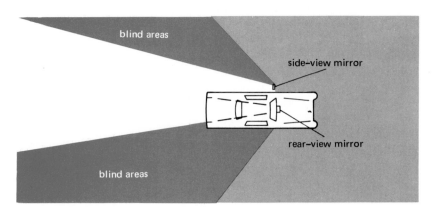

Mirrors do not eliminate all blind spots to the rear.

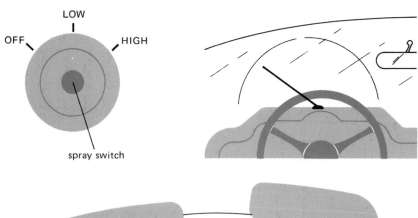

To clean a car's windshield well, wiper blades must not be worn or dirty.

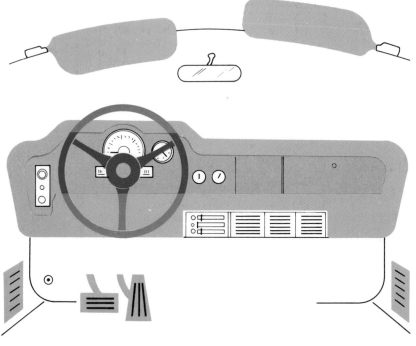

Be sure that you adjust the sun visors so they do not block your vision.

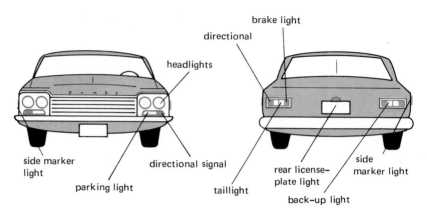

The lights in the communications system play an important part in letting other highway users know where you are and what you plan to do.

Interior Dome Light. This light goes on automatically when a front door is opened. It can also be turned on and off by turning the headlight switch. This light should not be used when driving at night because it interferes with seeing outside.

COMMUNICATIONS SYSTEM

These devices let other drivers know where you are and what movements you intend to make.

Parking Lights. These are designed to identify parked vehicles. They are not intended to illuminate the road in front of you. When daylight begins to fade, use your headlights. They not only help you see but make you more visible to other drivers and pedestrians.

Horn. A horn is a warning device that should be used to alert other roadway users of possible conflict. A gentle honk will usually be enough to attract the attention of animals, pedestrians, or drivers, and it reduces the possibility of startling them into some unexpected action. Excessive use of the horn is illegal in many areas.

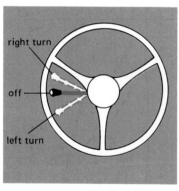

To activate the directional signals, push the lever in the direction you want to turn.

Directional, or Turn, Signals. You can let other drivers know that you intend to change direction—either turning or changing lanes—by using a directional signal. The signal control activates a blinking light at both the rear and the front of the car. To activate the turn indicator, push the directional-signal lever in the direction that you will turn the wheel: up for right and down for left. The lever should turn off when the wheels straighten out after a turn. In most cars, you can hear the click of the directional signal. If it continues to flash after you have completed your maneuver, turn it off manually.

Warning Flasher. Usually operated by a separate switch on the steering column or dashboard, this switch causes all four directional signals to flash at the same time. This signal, which you would use only when the car is stopped, provides a warning to other drivers that a vehicle is stopped either on or off the road. The flashing red light simply alerts others to your presence and reduces the possibility of a collision. The directional-signal light on most American-made cars will not operate when this four-way emergency-flasher system is on.

Taillight Assembly. This assembly has several components, including: a brake light, which goes on automatically when you press the brake pedal; the taillight, which is activated as soon as you put on your parking lights or headlights; and *white* back-up lights, which go on when you shift into *reverse*.

Rear License-Plate Light. This light goes on automatically with your parking lights or headlights and is required by law to aid in vehicle identification.

Side Marker Lights. These lights are also controlled automatically by the headlight switch. They help drivers on intersecting streets to see you.

ANTITHEFT SYSTEM
These devices make it more difficult for someone to steal or break into your car.

Ignition Buzzer. This sounds when the key is in the ignition switch and the driver's door is open. The buzzer serves two purposes: it saves you the inconvenience of locking your keys in the car, and it acts as a reminder to remove your keys when you leave the car, thereby reducing the possibility of theft.

The warning-flasher switch is often found on the steering column.

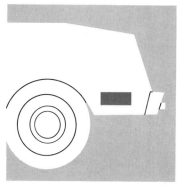

Side marker lights help other highway users see your car.

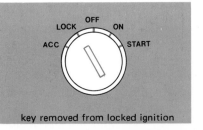

key removed from locked ignition

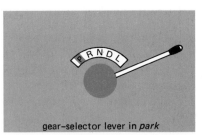

gear-selector lever in *park*

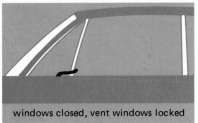

windows closed, vent windows locked

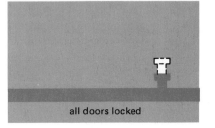

all doors locked

Before you leave your car, make sure it is secured against possible theft.

Steering-Column Lock. When you turn the ignition key to the *lock* position, this device automatically locks the steering wheel in place. When this lock is engaged, neither the steering wheel nor the gear selector lever, in an automatic transmission vehicle, will move until the key unlocks them.

Door Locks. These locks keep people out and serve as a safety device to keep you and your passengers inside the vehicle in the event of a collision. This safety factor is achieved by reducing the possibility of the door accidentally opening.

Predriving Checks and Procedures

In addition to learning the location and function of the various controls and devices, you should develop the habit of performing certain checks every time you get ready to drive. People who simply get into a car and immediately drive away are demonstrating a lack of concern for themselves and their property and for the welfare of other people. A checklist of predriving activities that should be performed every time you use your car will better prepare you for safer and more enjoyable driving.

OUTSIDE CHECKS

As you approach your car, check for small children or for objects like broken bottles and posts that may be under your car or in the path you intend to take. Before entering the car, check the headlights, windshield, taillights, and rear windows for cleanliness and breakage. Take notice of any car-body damage, visually check the tires for inflation, and note the position of the front wheels. This last check is very important to remember, because if the front wheels do not point straight ahead, the car will immediately move left or right when you start to move. To avoid sidewise movement that could result in a collision, instant corrective action would be required. If you will be driving a long distance, take time to check under the hood before starting. This should include checking the water in the battery, the windshield wiper fluid, the coolant in the radiator, and the engine oil level.

Preparing to Enter. When your car is parked at the curb, it is important to check carefully for approaching vehicles and to be sure that drivers see you before you walk into the street. Unlock the door, enter, and close and lock the door as quickly as possible. You may not have thought of it before, but car doors extend 3 to 4 feet into the roadway when fully opened. They may force other drivers to swerve to avoid hitting you. This could place you and them in a hazardous position. A

28

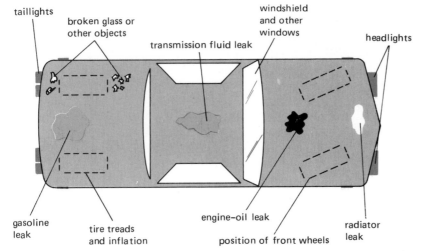

taillights

broken glass or
other objects

windshield
and other
windows

transmission fluid leak

headlights

gasoline
leak

tire treads
and inflation

engine–oil leak

position of front wheels

radiator
leak

*Make an outside check before you enter a car. Look for leaks, for damage to the
car, and for any obstructions. Also, note the position of the front wheels. Are they
straight or turned?*

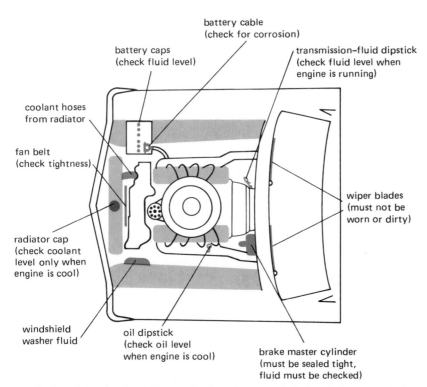

battery cable
(check for corrosion)

battery caps
(check fluid level)

transmission–fluid dipstick
(check fluid level when
engine is running)

coolant hoses
from radiator

fan belt
(check tightness)

wiper blades
(must not be
worn or dirty)

radiator cap
(check coolant
level only when
engine is cool)

windshield
washer fluid

oil dipstick
(check oil level
when engine is cool)

brake master cylinder
(must be sealed tight,
fluid must be checked)

*Under-hood checks should be made often, but especially just before you start on
long trips.*

29

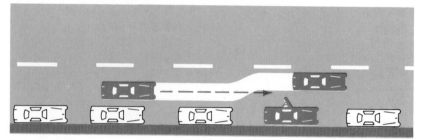

Be sure to check for traffic before leaving a car parked on the street. Otherwise, you may force another vehicle to swerve.

relatively simple solution to this problem, if you drive a car equipped with bench seats and a shifting lever mounted on the steering column, is to enter the car from the curb side.

Preparing to Leave. Just before you leave a parked vehicle, make sure that the gear selector lever is in the appropriate position (*park* in a car with automatic transmission, *reverse* in a manual-shift car). Also make sure that the parking brake is set. Turn off all accessories, close all windows, and make sure that all doors are locked after all passengers have gotten out.

If you are exiting on the street or traffic side, you must again take care to avoid endangering yourself or other roadway users. A good habit to develop is one that is sometimes referred to as "Look, Latch, and Leap." *Look:* first check in your side-view mirror for any traffic approaching on your side of the road. This includes bicycles and motorcycles, as well as cars and trucks. Then look over your shoulder to double check. *Latch:* open the door only if it is safe to do so, be aware of any traffic around you. *Leap:* step out and close and lock the door

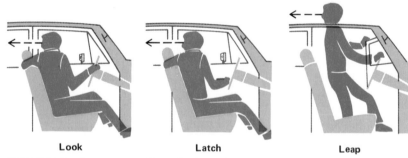

Look	**Latch**	**Leap**
First use both mirrors, then look over your shoulder.	Open the door when safe; keep checking traffic.	Step out and quickly close the door, still checking traffic.

If you exit on the street side, move quickly and keep checking traffic, first in the mirrors, then over your shoulder.

30

again as quickly as possible to get clear of traffic on the street. Far too frequently drivers swing the door open, jump out of the car, and then look to see if anything is coming.

INSIDE CHECKS

Once you are inside the car, you should develop a standard routine for preparing to drive. The location of devices and controls can vary from one make and model to another. The owner's manual for a particular model may therefore suggest procedures slightly different from those described here. The important thing, however, is to establish the correct routine and to follow it. A generally recommended routine would go like this:

1. Place the key in the ignition switch.
2. Check to see that all doors are locked.
3. Adjust the seat and the head restraint.
4. Adjust the rear- and side-view mirrors for visibility and to the daylight or nighttime position, as needed.
5. Check the inside of windows to see if they need to be cleaned or defrosted.
6. Check to see that books, packages, and other objects will neither block your view nor shift about in the event of a quick stop.
7. Check the ventilation and adjust the air vents, windows, or air conditioner as needed.
8. Fasten your safety belts and remind passengers to do the same.

Now you have been introduced to the location and purposes of the various controls, the information, comfort, and safety devices, and the predriving checks. You should practice making the recommended checks and adjustments in your family's or a friend's car before you report for your first driving lesson. In addition to this, you can begin to observe more closely the performance of other drivers. This will help you become familiar with basic driving maneuvers.

To Think About

1. Describe the different parts of the comfort system. How will their proper use assist a driver?
2. What are some of the advantages of the 9- and-3 hand position for steering?
3. What are some of the things you can learn by glancing at the gauges and dials in the vehicle-check system?
4. How does each part of the visibility system help improve visibility?
5. How can a driver use the communications system to warn other drivers of a conflict?

6. What are some of the advantages of making regular predriving checks?
7. Why is it important for drivers and passengers to wear safety belts?
8. What precautions should a driver take before getting out of a car parked on the street?

To Do

1. Interview ten drivers. Ask them if they always wear safety belts and why or why not. In your opinion, do factors such as driving experience, age, and type of vehicle influence their answers? Report the results of your survey.
2. Develop a list of vehicle safety devices found in the visibility, communications, and protective systems of a new car. Describe the purpose of each device. What safety devices does a new car have that a ten-year-old vehicle might not have?
3. Observe the way drivers enter and leave cars parked on the side of a street. How many of the drivers exit on the traffic side? How many of them check traffic as they exit?

Basic Maneuvers 3

After reading this chapter, you should be able to:

1. Describe good tracking and braking skills and discuss common tracking and braking errors.
2. Name four kinds of lateral maneuvers.
3. Discuss how to determine time gaps for making turns at intersections.
4. List and describe three kinds of turnabouts.
5. Explain the major differences between vehicles with automatic transmissions and vehicles with manual transmissions.

In Chapter 2 you read about the various vehicle *systems* that help you to drive a car effectively. In this chapter you will read about the basic *maneuvers* you will perform when you drive.

The procedures described in this chapter apply to cars with automatic transmissions, since that is the type of car you will probably drive at first. A separate section on driving a car with a stick shift is included at the end of this chapter.

Be sure to study these procedures before you report for your first driving lesson—whether it is in a simulator or in a car.

Starting Your Car

Once you have performed all the predriving checks (both inside and outside your car) and have made all the necessary adjustments, you are ready to start the engine and prepare to move. Again, it is important that you follow a set of procedures:

1. Make sure that the selector lever is in the proper position—*park*—and that the parking brake is set.

Make sure you are in *park*.

Make sure the parking brake is set.

Press the gas pedal to the floor.

Place your left foot on the brake.

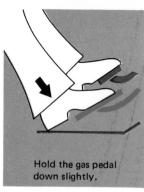

Hold the gas pedal down slightly.

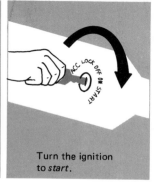

Turn the ignition to *start*.

Shift into the gear you want.

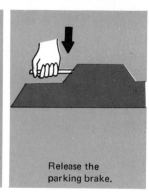

Release the parking brake.

Starting your car.

2. Preset the automatic choke by pressing the gas pedal to the floor and then releasing it.

3. Place your left foot on the brake, press down firmly, and hold it until you are ready to move.

4. Press the gas pedal down slightly and hold.

5. Turn the ignition switch to *start*, release the key as soon as the engine is running, and ease off the pressure on the gas pedal.

6. With your left hand, grasp the steering wheel. With your right hand, shift the gear-selector lever to *drive* or *reverse*, depending on which way you want to move.

7. With your left foot still on the brake pedal, release the parking brake.

Tracking

Tracking means effectively keeping your car on a desired path of travel by smoothly providing the necessary steering corrections. Beginning drivers are frequently insensitive to slight or gradual changes in position of the car. As a result, they often wait too long to respond. In essence, you will have to learn to track smoothly by steering to points ahead, selecting them on the basis of traffic conditions and where you want to go.

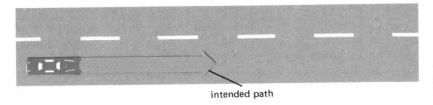

intended path

Look well ahead as you drive. Steer to a point in the center of your intended path.

TRACKING IN A STRAIGHT LINE

When driving in a straight line or steering through a moderate curve, you should place both hands on the upper half of the steering wheel (the left hand near 9 o'clock, the right hand near 3 o'clock) to provide the best steering control. Because you may lack sensitivity to gradual changes in position, you may allow the car to "wander" within your lane. When you first correct steering errors, you may tend to overcorrect and turn the steering wheel too far. This will cause the car to wander more. The degree of steering adjustment needed to make the necessary corrections for smooth tracking on a straight roadway are small but critical. These adjustments will become automatic as you learn to look further ahead to establish a path of travel.

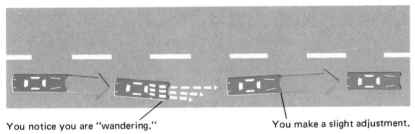

You notice you are "wandering."   You make a slight adjustment.

Make steering corrections as soon as you notice your car moving off your intended path.

To gain a better understanding of this process, observe and question a driver when you are riding. You might ask questions like these: Where in the path ahead is the driver looking? What are the factors that influence where the driver positions the car within a lane? What factors influence the choice of a particular lane? Notice the amount of steering wheel movement necessary for correction or for maintaining lane position.

TRACKING ON TURNS

Tracking effectively through a turn requires much greater steering adjustment than is required for simple lane positioning. The exact amount of correction and the timing of that correction are determined by looking through the intended turn to the point in the intersecting street that you want to reach.

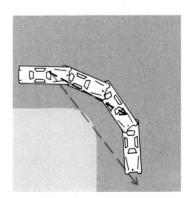

Look through your intended turn to the point you want to reach.

35

As you turn, allow extra clearance for the rear wheels. They will not follow the same path as the front wheels.

In driving through a turn, there are several other factors that you also must consider. First, the back wheels do not follow the same path as the front wheels, as they tend to do in straight-line driving. Rather, they have a smaller turning radius. As a result, you must allow extra room on the side in the direction you are turning to avoid hitting objects with the rear wheels or rear of the car. Second, a different steering technique than that used for straight-line tracking is required. To provide the degree of steering correction needed to turn a corner, it is recommended that you use what is commonly referred to as the *hand-over-hand steering* method. This method of steering through turns provides maximum steering control. You should begin with your hands located on the upper half of the steering wheel in the normal 9-and-3 o'clock position.

The desired steering correction is achieved by grasping the steering wheel tightly with the hand that is opposite the direction you want to turn. With this hand, push the steering wheel up, around, and down in the direction you want to turn. At the same time, release the other hand from the wheel and bring it up and across to grip the wheel on the far side. That hand then pulls the wheel up, across the top, and

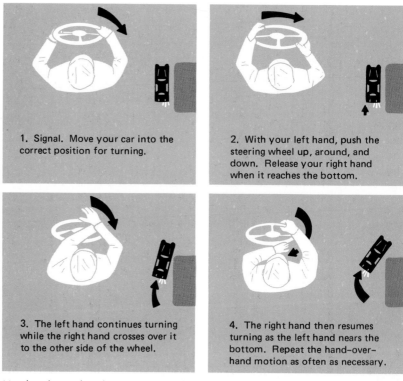

1. Signal. Move your car into the correct position for turning.

2. With your left hand, push the steering wheel up, around, and down. Release your right hand when it reaches the bottom.

3. The left hand continues turning while the right hand crosses over it to the other side of the wheel.

4. The right hand then resumes turning as the left hand nears the bottom. Repeat the hand–over–hand motion as often as necessary.

Use hand-over-hand steering to make turns. This is an example of a right-hand turn made with hand-over-hand steering.

36

down on its own side. These movements are continued as often and as rapidly as necessary to bring the car to the desired direction. It is also essential that you grasp the wheel from the outside; that is, with the knuckles of each hand outside the rim of the steering wheel.

RECOVERING ON TURNS

When the front of your car reaches a point approximately halfway through a turn, start to recover, or return the wheels to their straight-ahead position. Having selected another point in the path ahead, you can return the steering wheel to the straight position by one of two methods. The first method is simply to reverse the procedure described as hand-over-hand steering. A second method is to maintain constant contact with the wheel while allowing it to slip through your hands. This is called *controlled slipping*. It is accomplished by maintaining continuous contact with the steering wheel while allowing it to slide through your hands. You simply tighten your hold on the wheel at the point at which the wheels are directed toward the point to which you want to go. Controlled slipping is generally more difficult for beginning drivers to accomplish, especially in cars equipped with power-assist steering or in cars traveling at very low speeds. At first, you may want to use the hand-over-hand steering method to recover.

Backing and Turning. Turn your head and body until you can see through the rear side windows in the direction you wish to travel Grasp the steering wheel with both hands at the 9-and-3 position, just as you would for turning while moving forward. Select the point to which you want to steer.

HOW TO STEER WHEN BACKING

There are two major factors related to steering when backing-up that tend to cause drivers some difficulty. First, you move the steering wheel in the direction you want the car to go. When backing up, however, the rear of your car becomes the front. It is the rear of your car,

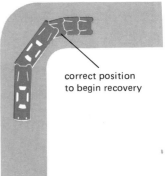

recovery begins here—too late

correct position to begin recovery

Start to recover about halfway through a turn.

When backing, position yourself so that you can see where you are going. Do not rely on mirrors.

backing in a straight line

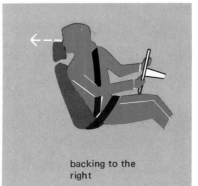

backing to the right

backing to the left

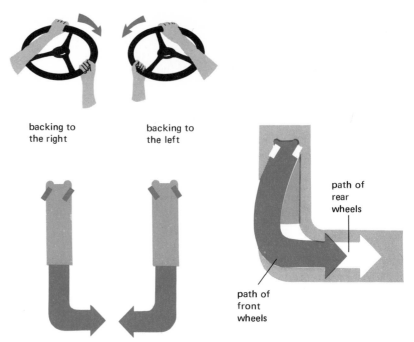

backing to
the right

backing to
the left

path of
rear
wheels

path of
front
wheels

To back to the right, steer clockwise; to back to the left, steer counterclockwise. Remember that in either case, the front wheels will make a wider curve than the rear wheels.

therefore, that will move in the direction the steering wheel is turned. Second, the rear wheels of a car always follow a path inside those followed by the front wheels. This means that when backing and turning, the front of your car will appear to swing out in the direction opposite to which you are turning the steering wheel. As a result, two high-hazard points develop in turning: the rear side in the direction you are turning and the opposite side in the front.

Backing in a Straight Line. Turn your head and body to the right until you can see clearly through the back window. Brace yourself by placing your right hand and arm over the back of the seat or by grasping the center console or passenger seat. Then grasp the top of the steering wheel with your left hand and select the point to which you want to steer.

To maintain steering control when backing, remember that if you wish to go back in a straight line or to make slight adjustments, you simply move your left hand and the steering wheel slightly left or right in the direction you wish the rear of the car to move. To change direction when backing, as in a turnabout or when parallel parking, you maintain control best if you turn the steering wheel hand over hand in the direction you desire the back of the car to travel.

38

Keep Your Speed Slow. A third critical factor to remember is to keep your speed slow. Since steering requires less effort and is more abrupt when backing-up, it is essential that you carefully control your speed of travel and steering wheel movement, particularly if room to maneuver is limited.

TRACKING TO THE REAR

Tracking to the rear tends to be a problem for beginning drivers. As with tracking through a turn, the problem arises out of difficulties related to where to look, steering control, and speed of travel. To avoid making errors, keep the following in mind whenever you attempt a backing maneuver.

How and Where to Look when Backing. Compared to the view you have through the windshield, your view through the rear window is quite limited. Head restraints and passengers can restrict your view even more. Attempting to back while looking into a rear-view mirror compounds the problem. To overcome these difficulties, position yourself correctly and look in the direction you wish to move.

Braking

Braking requires both a sense of timing and the regulated application of pressure to the brake pedal to bring the car to a smooth stop. You may at first have braking problems that arise from:

1. A lack of awareness of when to start applying the brake pressure.
2. A failure to control the amount of pressure you apply to the pedal.

Application of the exact amount of foot pressure needed to bring a vehicle to a stop will depend on a number of factors, such as the vehicle size, the speed of travel, the space available, the roadway surface, and the type of brakes. The ability to apply just the right amount of pressure, therefore, depends largely upon practice.

Observe the braking procedures used by experienced drivers. This can help you determine when to brake and how to stop more smoothly. For instance, at what point does the driver, when traveling at various speeds, release the gas pedal and start to apply brake pressure when preparing to make a routine stop? If you observe closely, you will probably see that the driver, regardless of speed, applies pressure gradually, as needed, until the car slows almost to a stop. At this point the driver should ease up slightly on the brake pedal and then reapply pressure as needed to avoid a jerky stop. While the braking procedures used to stop on ice or under other emergency conditions are somewhat different, timing and application of controlled brake pressure remain the most critical factors.

To slow down smoothly, apply brake pressure gradually.

Lateral Maneuvers

You are now ready to move onto the roadway. If you are starting from a roadside parking space, you will want to make a move from the parking space into the traffic lane. This movement, either forward or to the rear, is called a *lateral maneuver* because it involves *sideways* motion into or across the traffic flow.

Lateral movement is basic to many different kinds of traffic maneuvers. If you move to the left or right within a lane, you are *adjusting your position* within a lane. If you move to another lane, you are *changing* lanes. These are two of the most common lateral maneuvers. Others include merging onto an expressway, exiting from an expressway, pulling off a road and onto a shoulder, parallel parking, and passing.

ELEMENTS OF A LATERAL MANEUVER

The execution of all lateral maneuvers requires the same basic procedures:

1. Check the path ahead or behind to see that it is clear and that there is enough room to maneuver.

The elements of all lateral maneuvers are the same.

1. Check your path.

2. Check mirrors.

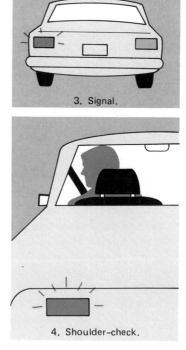

3. Signal.

4. Shoulder-check.

5. Perform the maneuver.

2. Check the mirrors to determine whether traffic is closing from the rear or in the next lane, and whether traffic is close enough to present a hazard.

3. Signal your intention to move left or right.

4. To be sure a lane is clear, check over your shoulder in the direction you plan to move.

5. Execute the maneuver when safe.

Whenever you make any kind of lateral maneuver, you must give special attention to three factors:

1. Speed adjustment, through the use of either the accelerator or the brake

2. The amount of steering required

3. The amount of time or space needed to enter or leave the traffic stream

ENTERING A ROADWAY FROM THE CURB

Entering a roadway from a parallel parking space is a common lateral maneuver. Some of the situations you may have to deal with are illustrated here.

The most simple situation is shown in *A*. The driver is about to enter a roadway when there is little or no traffic. Speed is controlled by a 25-mph limit. Entering the roadway requires slight steering and acceleration.

A

In situation *B*, a truck parked close behind the car makes it necessary for the driver of the car to move forward and check traffic to determine if there is enough space to enter the roadway. The speed limit is 30 mph, but there is room to accelerate and little steering is required because of the clear path ahead.

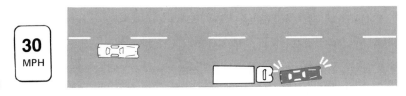

B

Situation C requires accurate perceptions and judgments. Space to maneuver is limited by cars parked ahead and behind. The driver's

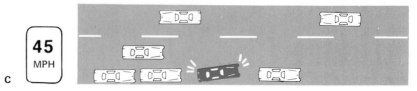

c

own speed must be closely controlled. Traffic can now move at 45 mph, and so the gap in traffic must be much greater to allow the driver time to clear the car parked ahead and to accelerate into the traffic lane.

The same perceptions and judgments of time and space apply to all maneuvers, but they are especially critical in positioning your car on the roadway. This is true whether you are positioning within the lane, changing lanes, or entering into or exiting from an expressway. The important difference between these maneuvers and entering the roadway from a parked position parallel to the curb is learning to control or manage the space around your car when there is more traffic traveling at a high rate of speed. Ways to improve your visual habits and decision-making abilities will be discussed in Chapter 4.

CRITERIA FOR LATERAL POSITION

There are several actions you can take that will help you to select the best position for your car within a stream of traffic.

Basic to your selection of a position in a stream of traffic is to place your car so that you have the greatest possibility of seeing and being seen. While the importance of this concept to your selection of lanes may be obvious, it is just as critical when selecting a position relative to cars ahead and behind. Since your greatest chance of having a collision is in front of you, it is critical that you maintain a large enough gap between your car and vehicles ahead in your lane. This gap is called *following distance*. While a following distance of one car length for every 10 mph is sometimes recommended, many drivers have difficulty making such judgments. Since distance can be converted to time at any given speed, a more simple procedure is to keep some number of seconds between your car and the vehicle ahead.

2-SECOND FOLLOWING DISTANCE

In normal traffic under good weather conditions, a time gap of 2 seconds works well for following other cars. If your car is properly positioned in a lane, a gap of 2 seconds allows you to see around the car ahead, to change lanes quickly if necessary, or to brake to a stop if the car ahead brakes suddenly. The 2-second rule will hold true, however,

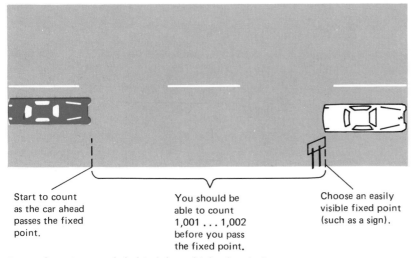

| Start to count as the car ahead passes the fixed point. | You should be able to count 1,001 . . . 1,002 before you pass the fixed point. | Choose an easily visible fixed point (such as a sign). |

Stay at least 2 seconds behind the vehicle ahead of you.

only if you can respond to whatever caused the lead driver to slow down. When you are following a vehicle that blocks your vision, such as a van or a large truck, you have to increase your following distance to at least 3 seconds.

At this point you may be asking how you can determine a time gap of 2 or 3 seconds. Actually, it is easy, and you can practice the next time you ride in a car. As the rear of the car ahead in your lane passes a fixed object—such as a tree, a sign, or even the shadow cast by an overpass—start to count "one-thousand-one, one-thousand-two." If the front of your car reaches the fixed object before you complete a count of one-thousand-two, you are following too closely. Whenever roadway or weather conditions are not ideal—such as on a rough road or in a light drizzle—you need to increase your following distance to at least 3 seconds. If there is ice or packed snow on the road, a gap of 5 or 6 seconds is better.

THE 4-SECOND RULE

The 2-second following rule works well if you have to stop because the driver ahead of you brakes suddenly. It does not apply, however, if the roadway ahead is suddenly blocked by a collision or a vehicle stopped across the lane. Under these conditions, the time needed depends on your speed. As you can see by looking at the table, it is possible to brake to a stop in approximately 2 seconds from a speed of 30 mph. However, you would need nearly 4 seconds by the time you reach 60 mph.

Therefore, if at highway speeds your path were suddenly blocked, normal following distances would not give you time enough to stop. You would have to have an *escape route* to stay out of a collision.

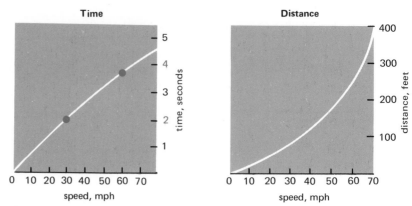

As your speed increases, so does the time and distance required to brake to a stop. The graph on the left shows the time needed to stop; the graph on the right shows the distance needed to stop.

In view of this, when you select a position in a stream of traffic, you must be able to answer two major questions. First, on the basis of roadway and traffic conditions, where do you want your car to be 4 seconds from now? This is identified as your *immediate path of travel*. Second, where would you place your car 4 seconds ahead if your immediate path of travel were suddenly blocked? This path is identified as your *alternate path of travel*.

This 4-second gap is again determined by counting. You simply pick a point ahead and count "one-thousand-one, one-thousand-two, . . . , one-thousand-four." Remember, 4 seconds is the approximate time it will take to stop at speeds above 40 mph. So, if you are traveling over

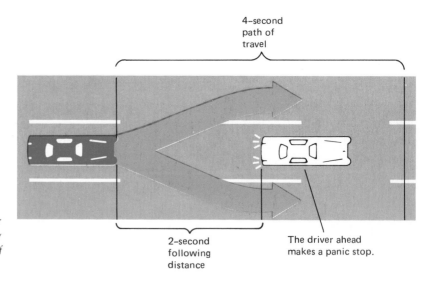

Where would you move if your immediate path were suddenly blocked? Select alternate paths of travel.

44

50 mph and your path is suddenly blocked within 3 seconds ahead, you must be prepared to steer into an alternate path.

12-SECOND VISUAL LEAD TIME

You have read about tracking and the need to make steering adjustments by looking "further ahead" along your intended path. The question now is, just how far ahead should you look? "Further ahead," as used in tracking, should be a time lead of at least 12 seconds in city driving and may be 20 to 30 seconds for expressway driving. A visual lead and search area is necessary so that you will have the information and time necesssary to choose a realistic, immediate planned path of travel. It allows you to make speed or lane adjustments well in advance of possible problems. At the same time, it allows you to identify alternate paths if an emergency should arise.

A lead time of 12 seconds may seem long, especially when driving in the city. Keep in mind, however, that at 30 mph you are traveling 44 feet per second. At this speed, your vision would take in a distance of 528 feet, or approximately one block, ahead of your car. While this distance is enough in the city, it would not be adequate on an expressway at 55 to 60 mph. If you convert 60 mph to 88 feet per second, you will see why a 12-second visual lead provides a bare minimum.

As with the 2-second following and 4-second stopping times, you can work on developing a feeling for the visual lead and search pattern by riding with other drivers. The system works the same way. Pick a reference point (a sign, a post, or an overpass) ahead and count "one-thousand-one, one-thousand-two, . . . , one-thousand-twelve." Remem-

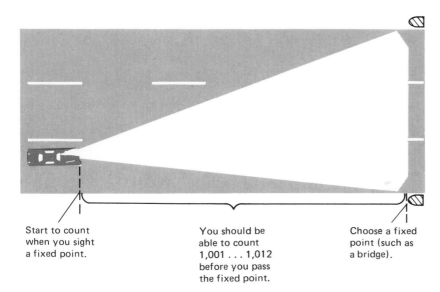

Start to count when you sight a fixed point.

You should be able to count 1,001 . . . 1,012 before you pass the fixed point.

Choose a fixed point (such as a bridge).

Look 12 seconds ahead. You can establish a 12-second visual lead time by choosing a fixed point and counting.

ber, 12 seconds is a *minimum* visual lead to work toward; it is not the final goal.

Two bad habits often affect drivers' visual leads. You should occasionally ask yourself if either of these habits is limiting your visual leads.

Staring at a Fixed Point. Staring straight ahead will not give you a safe and effective visual lead. A narrow field of vision directed straight ahead will not provide you with all the information you need to plan a path of travel. It is particularly important that you learn to *scan* the area ahead, by moving your eyes back and forth between your car and your checkpoints ahead. Look from one side of the roadway to the other. You should also periodically check to the rear. As you scan ahead, search for cues that will assist you in selecting the safest and most efficient path of travel.

Distractions. Many things—including scenery, roadside signs, or even other passengers—may distract your attention as you drive. Unless you concentrate on searching well in advance, you will have a tendency to slip into a visual lead of as little as 3 or 4 seconds. A visual lead this short means you are driving from crisis to crisis. The results of such visual habits are readily observable as drivers make abrupt lane changes or adjustments within a lane.

Now you can apply the concepts of the 2-second following distance, 4-second stopping distance, and 12-second visual lead to lateral movements in traffic. It is important to remember that you are attempting to establish the safest and most efficient path of travel: the path requiring the fewest changes of speed and lateral position. A 12-second visual lead should alert you to the possible need to make adjustments in advance and, as a result, should reduce unnecessary or abrupt adjustments.

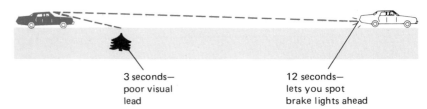

3 seconds—
poor visual
lead

12 seconds—
lets you spot
brake lights ahead

Concentrate on maintaining at least a 12-second visual lead time.

CHANGING LANES ON THE HIGHWAY

On a multiple-lane highway, changes of position within lanes, lane changes, and passing all require the same checks and precautions. For this reason we will discuss them as one maneuver.

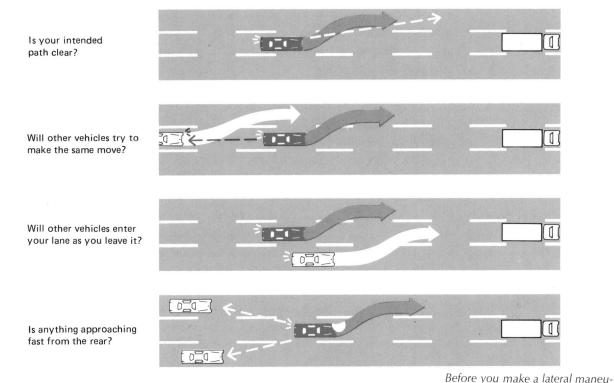

Is your intended path clear?

Will other vehicles try to make the same move?

Will other vehicles enter your lane as you leave it?

Is anything approaching fast from the rear?

Before you make a lateral maneuver, ask yourself these questions.

Assume that you have identified an object beside the road, a slow-moving vehicle, or a wide vehicle that will block your field of vision within an area 12 seconds ahead. You decide to move laterally to gain a better position. Several questions must be raised and checks made before such a move can be made. Will other vehicles, either ahead or behind, be making the same move? Is there anything now in, or approaching, the lane you wish to enter? Will other vehicles in the lane or lanes beside you try to enter your lane as you try to move out of it? Is anything approaching you rapidly from the rear? To answer these questions, you should first make sure that you maintain at least a 2-second following distance between your car and any vehicle ahead. This will leave room for you to maneuver. Then establish at least a 4-second planned path ahead. Check your mirrors and signal your intention to move. Then, just before moving, check over your shoulder in the direction you wish to move. Is there a 4-second gap in traffic in the lane you wish to enter? (A 4-second gap will allow both you and the car in the intended lane a 2-second following distance.) If everything checks out, maintain or increase your speed slightly and steer into the new lane. If your move on a multiple-lane roadway involves passing another car and returning to your original lane, simply repeat all the checks and signals. Move back into the lane you left only when you can see the front of the vehicle you have passed in your rear-view mirror.

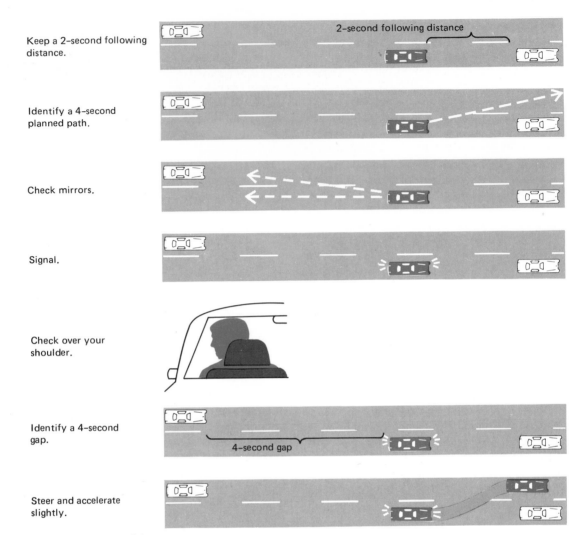

Keep a 2-second following distance.

Identify a 4-second planned path.

Check mirrors.

Signal.

Check over your shoulder.

Identify a 4-second gap.

Steer and accelerate slightly.

To make a lateral maneuver, follow these steps.

PASSING ON A TWO-LANE ROADWAY

On a two-lane road with one lane of traffic in each direction, passing another vehicle becomes much more difficult. In addition to the checking required for a lane change, you now also have to check for cars coming toward you. As a result, you must make very critical time and distance judgments. Do you have time to complete your pass and return to your lane? For instance, if you increase your speed at a normal rate to pass another car when traveling at highway speed, it will take approximately 9 to 10 seconds to complete the pass. If you and the car coming toward you are both traveling at 55 mph, the total distance traveled is about $\frac{1}{3}$ mile. This means that to pass another car when traveling at such a speed, you need almost $\frac{1}{2}$ mile between your car and the oncoming vehicle.

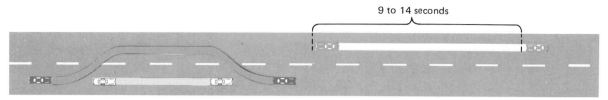

9 to 14 seconds

You would need at least 9 seconds to pass another car on a two-lane roadway. The easiest way to judge this gap is to pass only when the car in the oncoming lane appears to be standing still.

Do not try to pass in situations that limit your visual lead time.

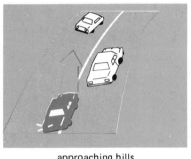

approaching hills

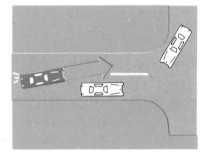

near intersections

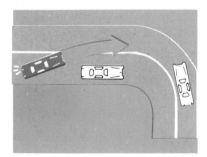

on curves

at railroad crossings

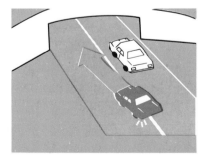

near abutments or bridges

49

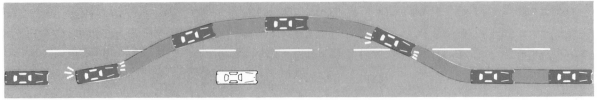

1. Complete all the checks for a lateral maneuver. Then signal.

2. Begin to move into the left lane, accelerating slightly.

3. Once you are in the left lane, accelerate firmly.

4. Once you see the car you are passing in the rear-view mirror, signal and pull back into the right lane.

Once you have determined that it is safe to pass, follow these steps.

There is a convenient guide that you can use to determine a safe time and distance gap for passing when traveling at highway speeds. When starting a passing maneuver, any vehicle coming toward you should be far enough away so that it appears to be standing still. Assuming that the road is flat and straight, the vehicle will appear to be standing still at distances of $\frac{1}{2}$ mile or more.

Learning to make the accurate time and distance judgments needed for passing can be practiced when riding with other drivers. Instead of selecting a fixed object, however, you now decide when the vehicle coming toward you has reached the nearest point that would still allow you to successfully complete a passing maneuver. At this point, you again start to count "one-thousand-one, one-thousand-two," etc. If your car and the oncoming vehicle meet before you have counted to at least one-thousand-nine, you have not allowed enough time. If you counted to a number greater than one-thousand-fourteen, you have allowed too much time and distance. Waiting for too large a passing gap will not place you in immediate danger. However, failing to pass when you have adequate time and distance may irritate drivers behind you and encourage them to attempt to pass both you and the vehicle you are following.

ENTERING INTO AND EXITING FROM AN EXPRESSWAY

The problems common to lateral movements increase in difficulty when you attempt to enter into or exit from an expressway. One of these problems arises from the fact that, in many cases, one group of cars is slowing to exit while at the same time another group is accelerating to enter. The two groups cross in what is known as a *weaving lane*.

Similar problems may arise when you attempt to enter expressways where traffic is heavy or acceleration lanes are short or curved. You may be unable to increase your entry speed to that of the expressway traffic flow. In either case, control of speed and the timing of your lateral movement to merge are extremely difficult.

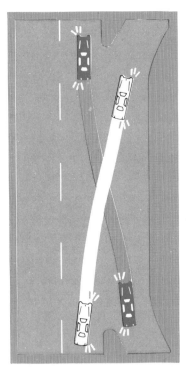

In weaving lanes, exiting and entering traffic cross each other's paths.

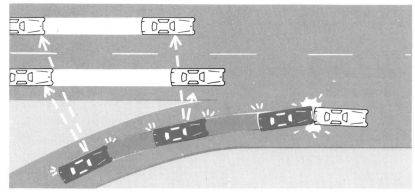

As you enter an expressway, be sure to maintain a 2-second following distance while you check to the left for a gap in the traffic flow.

Expressway Entry.   As you approach the weaving or acceleration lane, check traffic ahead and maintain a 2-second following distance. If there are other vehicles ahead of you, consider the possibility of their slowing or stopping due to traffic conflicts. If any of the drivers ahead of you at the entrance appear uncertain, increase your following distance and be prepared to stop. At the same time, signal your intention to enter the expressway.

Check to the side and over your shoulder. Watch both for vehicles signaling to exit and for an appropriate gap into which you can merge. Adjust your speed up or down to match that of the traffic flow. Continue to check traffic ahead and the gap you expect to merge into. You have to merge into the gap you have selected before you reach the end of the acceleration lane.

At some expressway entrance points, you will find either a short acceleration lane or, in a few cases, no acceleration lane at all. Signs will require that you yield to thru traffic. When these conditions exist, you will need a longer gap in traffic to enter, because you must have time to accelerate to the speed of the traffic on the expressway.

Another situation that will require very quick and accurate time and distance judgments is an acceleration lane that merges directly into the extreme left lane of an expressway. Since this lane is usually used by high-speed or passing traffic, the vehicles in it will probably be moving quite fast. This situation demands earlier and more precise decisions on your part. Acceleration will have to be even more rapid to ensure smooth merging.

Expressway Exit.   It is important that you know where you want to exit and that you position your car in advance for that exit. Will you exit from the left or right side of the expressway? Will your exit involve a simple lane change to a deceleration lane and a reduction of speed for an exit ramp? Will exiting require passing through a weaving lane?

51

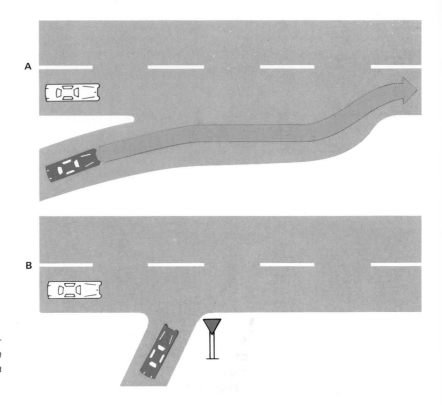

Not all expressways have acceleration lanes. In which situation does the entering car need a longer gap?

To assist you, advance guide signs are generally placed about 1 mile ahead of interchanges in urban areas. In rural areas there are signs both 1 and 2 miles ahead of interchanges. Additional signs indicate whether the exit you want is located on the left or right side of the expressway and, usually, the number of exit lanes available. This information should give you time enough to make the necessary changes in position and speed.

If you exit at a direct connection with a crossroad—such as at a diamond interchange—simply make the necessary lane changes, one lane at a time, to position your car in the far right lane. Signal your intention to exit, steer into the deceleration lane, and slow to the recommended speed. If, however, your exiting movement requires you to maneuver through a weaving area, your task becomes more difficult. Having moved to the appropriate far left- or right-hand lane, signal your intention to exit well in advance. This will alert drivers behind you and those approaching the weaving area from the entrance ramp. Maintain an adequate following distance and check for a gap in the entrance-ramp vehicles that are moving toward the weaving area. If traffic trying to merge onto and off from the expressway is heavy, you may have to slow or accelerate quickly to complete your merge out of the thru lane, to the weaving area, and onto the exit ramp.

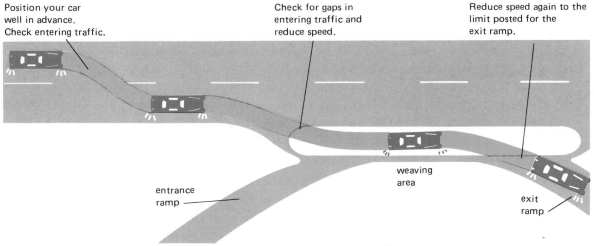

Position your car well in advance. Check entering traffic.

Check for gaps in entering traffic and reduce speed.

Reduce speed again to the limit posted for the exit ramp.

weaving area

entrance ramp

exit ramp

Exiting from an expressway through a weaving area.

LEAVING THE ROADWAY

A maneuver which requires leaving the roadway to a position on the shoulder or next to a curb can be simple or complex. If traffic is light and there is nothing parked at the side of the road, leaving the roadway may require little more than a routine lane change and braking to a stop. Parallel parking in moderate traffic is more complex, because of the limited space for maneuvering. Leaving the roadway by suddenly moving to the shoulder to avoid a collision calls for the greatest degree of awareness and vehicle control. This last maneuver will be treated in Chapter 9, which deals with critical situations.

STEERING TO THE CURB

When preparing to park along the curb, inform other drivers of your intentions. Position your car well in advance and signal your intentions to leave the road by using your turn signals, slowing, and flashing your brake lights. Care must be taken if you select a parking space just beyond an intersection. If other cars are either waiting at or approaching the intersection, position your car and slow down; but *wait* to use your turn signals until your car has actually entered the intersection. Slowing and signaling as you approach the intersection could lead other drivers to believe that you intend to turn. They might then pull out into your path.

PARALLEL PARKING

As you are looking for a parking space, make sure that you keep an eye on the traffic around you. Total concentration on finding a parking space could make you neglect sudden changes in traffic ahead or lead you to make a move without checking or signaling.

Identify a space.

Check traffic, signal, and flash your brakes to show that you are stopping.

Make sure that the space is large enough and that parking is legal.

ONE HOUR PARKING

9 AM 7PM

Position your car 2 to 3 feet from the car in front of the space, aligning rear bumpers.

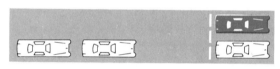

Follow these steps to get in position for parallel parking.

Once you have identified a possible parking space, use your turn signal and flash your brake lights to warn the other drivers of your intention to stop. Adjust your lane position to within 4 feet of the line of parked cars. Check to make sure that it is legal to park in the space. If it is, is the space large enough for your car? As a general rule, the space must be at least 5 feet longer than your car. If the space is long enough, drive forward and steer left or right so that you have a space about 2 to 3 feet wide between the side of your car and the parked car. Stop when the rear bumper of your car is in line with the rear bumper of the car you want to park behind. If the cars are approximately the same size, you can simply line up the backs of the front seats.

Entering a Parallel Parking Space.   From this point on, placing your car in a parallel parking space becomes a lateral movement to the rear. It is a maneuver, however, that requires concentration and good control of both steering and speed.

An important thing to remember is to keep your speed *slow*. Keep this in mind as you read through the step-by-step procedure for parallel parking:

Press down the brake pedal and shift to *reverse*.

 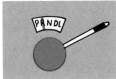

Back up, turning the steering wheel right. Keep your foot on the brake pedal.

When your front seat passes car A's rear bumper, turn the steering wheel left. Continue backing until you almost touch car B.

Shift to *drive* and move forward slowly.

Follow these steps to parallel park a car.

1. While pressing down on the brake pedal with your left foot, shift to *reverse*. Check for traffic in the next lane. (When backing, remember that the front end of your car will swing out in the direction opposite to that in which you turn the steering wheel.)

2. If parking on the right side of the street, turn the steering wheel at a smooth steady rate all the way to the right while backing slowly. (Keep your foot on the brake pedal.)

3. When the back of your front seat is in line with the rear bumper of the car you are parking behind, turn the steering wheel quickly and smoothly back to a straight-line position. Again, keep your speed *slow*. Failure to straighten your front wheels produces such a sharp angle with the curb that your rear right wheel will strike the curb. If

you turn the steering wheel too far to the left, your right front fender may collide with the left rear fender of the car you are parking behind.

4. Continue backing at this angle until your right front fender just clears the left rear fender of the car you are parking behind. At this point, your left rear fender should be lined up with the inside edge of the left headlight of the car parked in the space behind you.

5. While looking over your left shoulder, move back slowly and turn the steering wheel quickly and smoothly all the way to the left. Continue backing slowly, and stop just before touching the car parked behind you.

6. Shift to *drive* and, while moving very slowly forward, turn the steering wheel all the way to the right. Continue forward until the right front tire lightly touches the curb. At this point, your car should be centered in the space. It should also be parallel to, and within 12 inches of, the curb.

There are slight differences in step 6, depending on whether you are parked on a level roadway or on a hill. On a level surface, or when heading downhill, or when heading uphill *without* a curb, the procedure remains the same. Move your car forward slowly and turn the steering wheel all the way to the *right*.

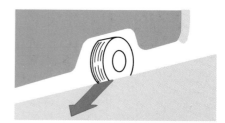

When you are parked heading uphill, turn the front wheels away from the curb.

When you are parked heading downhill, turn the front wheels toward the curb.

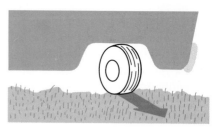

When you are parked where there is no curb, turn the front wheels away from the road.

Adjust the position of your front wheels according to where you are parked.

However, if you are parked heading uphill with a curb, you would have to change the procedure. Shift to *drive* and, while moving very slowly forward, turn the steering wheel to the straight-ahead position. Continue moving forward in a straight line until you are about 1 foot behind the car ahead and stop. Then shift to *reverse* and, while backing slowly, turn the steering wheel all the way to the left. Continue moving back slowly until the rear of the right front tire lightly touches the curb. At this point you should be centered in the space and parallel to the curb. In addition, if you have performed the maneuver correctly, your car should be within 12 inches of the curb.

Parallel parking on the left is accomplished in much the same manner. The main difference between left-side and right-side parking is that at each of the check points you turn the steering wheel in the opposite direction. Since you can see each of the check points more readily, you may find that parking on the left is easier than parking on the right.

The final step in parallel parking—turning the steering wheel to block the tire against the curb or toward the side of the road—is a safety measure. (It is required by law in some states.) This step may prevent the car from rolling downhill or into the street. Parked cars that are accidentally left in *neutral* without set parking brakes can create a hazard, especially if there is any chance that they could be struck by other cars.

Exiting from a Parallel Parking Space. To exit from a parallel parking space, first move slightly forward or back, as needed, to break contact between the front tire and the curb. Turn the steering wheel left or right until the front wheels are pointing straight ahead. Then move backward in the space until you are almost touching the car behind you. At this point, simply reverse steps 2 through 5 for entering a parallel parking space. Again, be sure to move your car *slowly* and to check for other cars as you pull out into the traffic lane immediately adjacent to the parking space.

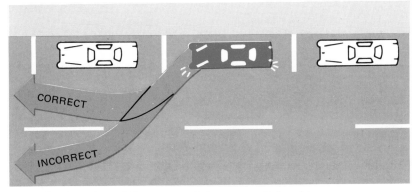

Move slowly and carefully as you exit from a parallel parking space.

Turns

The second group of basic maneuvers can be identified as *turns*. Once you have gained experience moving a car laterally, you must develop the techniques for making turns and for judging the time and space requirements necessary to make turns under various conditions. As with lateral movements, although the basic procedures remain the same, turns vary greatly in difficulty. A turning maneuver may be as simple as entering an angle parking space with no other cars around. In contrast, exiting from the same space some time later may be made difficult by closely parked cars and heavy traffic. Likewise, turns at intersections range from those made into one-way streets, where vehicle movement is controlled by traffic signals, to those made into multiple-lane, two-way streets, where there are no traffic controls and traffic is moving at a high rate of speed.

PREPARING FOR AN INTERSECTION MANEUVER

When approaching any intersection it is essential that you let other drivers know what you intend to do. Communicating is best accomplished through a combination of actions. The first step is to position your car in the correct lane, and properly within that lane, in advance. If you intend to turn, signal your intentions early. Many states require that you signal at least 100 feet ahead of a turn in town and 200 feet ahead in the country. However, 150 to 200 feet in town and 300 to 500 feet on the open highway gives drivers behind you an earlier warning of your intentions.

While approaching the intersection, check for signs which might control your movement. Is the intersection controlled by a *traffic control device*? Are turns permitted? If turns are permitted, are they limited to certain hours of the day, days of the week, or type of vehicle? Are there special lanes set aside for turning? In any case, slow to an appropriate speed by pumping the brake pedal.

As you approach an intersection to make a turn, look for information that might affect your maneuver.

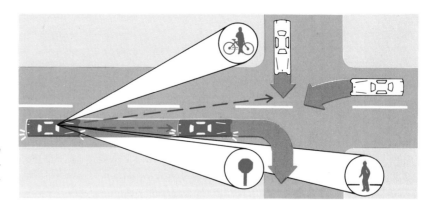

58

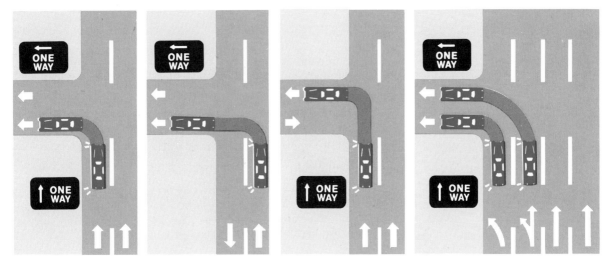

Turn from and into the correct lanes at an intersection.

While differences in the control and design of intersections exist, the following rules will apply whether you are turning from or into a one-way street:

1. Depending upon the direction you wish to travel and unless otherwise indicated, turn from the far left or far right lane of traffic moving in the same direction.

2. Unless otherwise indicated, enter the first traffic lane going in the direction you wish to travel.

3. Where turns are permitted from more than one lane, turn *into* the lane corresponding to the lane you left.

JUDGING THE TIME AND SPACE GAP AT INTERSECTIONS

Having arrived at an intersection, you must make a new set of judgments. Time and space management becomes critical if you are to drive through the intersection with the least chance of a collision, regardless of whether you are turning or driving straight ahead. The problem is particularly critical at uncontrolled intersections or at intersections controlled only by *yield* or *stop* signs. Under either of these conditions, you have to determine what is a safe gap in traffic.

Up to this point all considerations of gap selection have dealt with vehicles traveling in either the same or the opposite direction. At intersections you must learn to judge gaps in traffic when vehicles are moving at varying angles from both the left and the right.

Often, drivers wait for a longer gap in traffic from the left than from the right. This is probably because vehicles coming from the left are in the first lane that the driver must enter. Vehicles from the left *do* represent the most immediate hazard, but the greatest number of intersec-

59

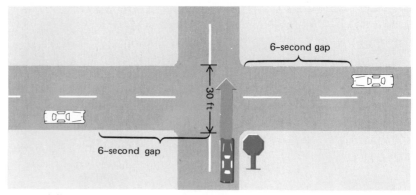

From a full stop, you would need about 4 seconds to cross an intersection 30 feet wide. You should therefore wait until there is a 6-second gap to be sure that you can get across the street without interrupting cross-street traffic.

tion collisions occur when the vehicle leaving a *stop* sign is struck from the right. As drivers move out of the path of vehicles on the left and into the path of vehicles closing from the right, they may fail to recognize the need for extra time—a larger gap—to avoid a collision.

There are general rules that will help you to decide when it is safe to start across an intersection or to make a turn. Assuming a moderate rate of acceleration, it will take you approximately 4 seconds to cross a 24- to 30-foot-wide street from a stopped position. This means, then, that you must have a gap in traffic from both directions of 5 to 6 seconds. There is no magic method of translating this time gap to distance at all speeds. However, at 30 mph, a time gap of 6 seconds equals about one-half block. Again, you can start to learn to make time-gap judgments before you get into a traffic situation as a driver. First, learn to judge time gaps for cars approaching from the right. Stand on a corner and pick a car coming from the left. As it passes through the intersection, start counting "one-thousand-one, one-thousand-two, ..." How far does it travel by the time you count to one-thousand-six? Repeat this process several times at the same location and identify the average distance that the cars travel in 6 seconds. Cars coming toward the intersection from the right, then, should be at least this far away when you start to cross the street.

When you have identified a point for cars coming from the right, use the same system to determine a similar point for cars coming from the left. These two points then provide references for similar streets and traffic conditions. You can repeat the same process where roadway, traffic, and speed conditions are different.

Time Gap for a Right-Hand Turn. In preparing to make a right-hand turn, it is again necessary that you decide the gap needed to complete a turn. Since it takes approximately 6 seconds to turn right and accel-

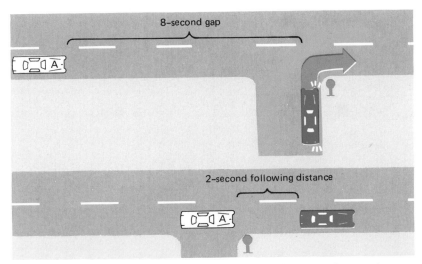

8-second gap

2-second following distance

You would need about 6 seconds just to make the right turn and to accelerate to 30 mph. Therefore, to maintain a 2-second following distance with car A, you would have to have an 8-second gap.

erate to 30 mph from a stopped position, you should not start a right turn unless the gap between you and a vehicle approaching from the left is about 7 to 8 seconds. A gap of this size will allow the approaching car to maintain a 2-second gap once you get up to traffic speed.

On the open highway, where speeds may be up to 55 mph or more, you must allow additional time to accelerate up to the speed of traffic after completing your turn. As a result, the gap time needed increases to 11 seconds or more. The way to determine this gap time is again the same. Pick a car passing through the intersection from the right and determine how far it travels in 11 seconds. The distance traveled represents the gap that you will need for vehicles traveling toward you from the left.

Time Gap for a Left-Hand Turn. The possibility of being struck while making a left turn is at least as great as that for driving straight through an intersection. In a left-turn maneuver, you are faced not only with the immediate hazard of vehicles moving toward you from the left, but also with the hazard of vehicles moving toward you from the right. Rather than driving across the far lane and out of danger, you turn into the far lane while moving at a low rate of speed. This action takes more time and, in fact, increases the gap you need. In a 30-mph zone you would need approximately 9 seconds. The 9 seconds is made up of 7 seconds needed to turn into and accelerate up to speed in the far lane and 2 seconds to allow a gap between you and the car closing from the rear.

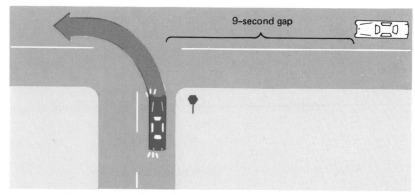

A left-hand turn requires a longer time gap. If traffic on the cross street is moving at 30 mph, you will need a 9-second gap to make the turn.

When you turn left onto a highway where traffic is traveling at speeds of 55 mph or higher, your gap needs will increase to 13 or 14 seconds. This amount of time will again allow you to accelerate at a moderate rate to highway speeds while allowing a 2-second following distance for the vehicle closing from the rear.

Now we can apply what we have discussed to making a turn at an intersection controlled by a stop sign.

RIGHT TURN

Your right signal should be on when you arrive at the intersection. Position your car behind the crosswalk or stop sign, in the far right lane, about 4 to 5 feet from the edge of the road. Remember, your right rear wheel will have a smaller turning radius than the front wheel and will strike the curb unless you allow additional room when turning. Check for pedestrians or other obstacles in your planned path of travel. Also check for cars across the intersection that may turn in the same direction at the same time. Identify a 7- to 8-second gap in traffic to your left. Move forward until your front bumper is in line with the curb or edge of the road you wish to enter. Look through the turn to that point in the intersecting street which you want to drive to. Turn the steering wheel hand-over-hand to the right while maintaining a speed of approximately 5 mph. Select another point 3 to 4 seconds ahead of your car and start to turn the steering wheel left (back to the straight-ahead position) when the front of your car reaches a point about halfway through the turn. Accelerate to the speed of traffic and make sure the turn signal is canceled.

LEFT TURN

Your left-turn signal should be on when you arrive at the intersection. Position your car next to the centerline behind the crosswalk or stop

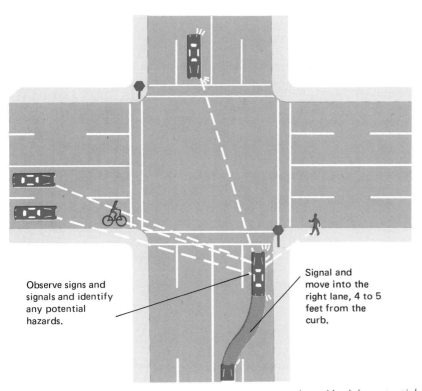

Observe signs and signals and identify any potential hazards.

Signal and move into the right lane, 4 to 5 feet from the curb.

Before making a right-hand turn, position your car correctly and look for potential hazards.

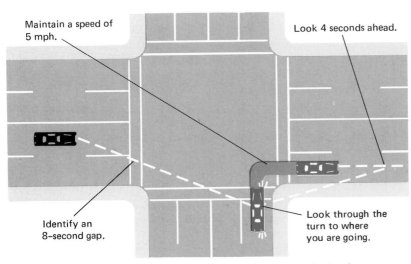

Maintain a speed of 5 mph.

Look 4 seconds ahead.

Identify an 8-second gap.

Look through the turn to where you are going.

As you make a right-hand turn, keep your speed low and look where you are going.

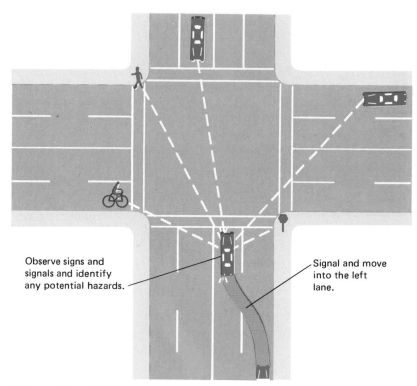

Observe signs and
signals and identify
any potential hazards.

Signal and move
into the left
lane.

Before making a left-hand turn, position your car correctly and look for potential hazards.

sign. Then check for pedestrians or other obstacles in your planned path of travel. Also check for cars across the intersection that may travel straight through the intersection or are signaling to turn right. Identify a 9-second gap to your right, and look through the turn to a point in the intersecting street that you want to drive to.

Move forward until you are about one lane width away from the center of the intersection and start to turn the steering wheel hand-over-hand to the left. Maintain a speed of 5 to 10 mph.

Select another point 3 to 4 seconds ahead of your car, start to return the steering wheel right (back to the straight-ahead position) when the front of your car enters the first lane beyond the center line.

Accelerate to the speed of traffic, and make sure the turn signal is canceled. Once up to speed, position your car in the appropriate lane.

Left Turn into a One-Way Street. If you are making a left turn into a one-way street, the procedure is similar to that followed for a right turn, in that you enter the first lane going in your direction.

64

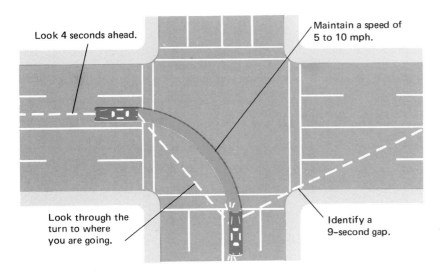

Look 4 seconds ahead.

Maintain a speed of 5 to 10 mph.

Look through the turn to where you are going.

Identify a 9-second gap.

As you make a left-hand turn, keep your speed low and look where you are going.

ANGLE PARKING

Angle parking is one of the most common turning maneuvers that you will perform as a driver. In many parking lots and on some streets it is the only kind of parking permitted. Because both maneuvering space and visibility are limited, you have to take great care in both entering into and exiting from angle parking spaces.

A general rule to follow when looking for a place to angle park is to maintain a position that gives you the greatest visibility and most space to maneuver. To satisfy this rule, keep your car 5 to 6 feet from parked cars and watch for any sign—such as brake lights or exhaust—that vehicles are attempting to back out.

Angle Parking on the Right. When you see an empty parking space, turn on your turn signal and slow to a speed of 3 to 5 mph. Move forward until you can see along the left side of the car parked to the

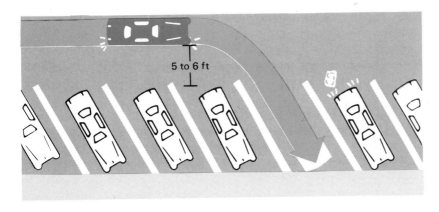

5 to 6 ft

Before you enter an angle parking space, slow to 3 to 5 mph, position your car as shown, and watch for signs of vehicles trying to back out.

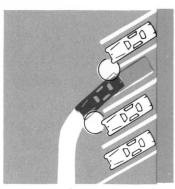

As you enter or leave an angle parking space, be especially careful of the position of your front and rear fenders.

right of the space you want to enter. Turn the steering wheel quickly, hand-over-hand, all the way to the right. As the front of the car approaches the center of the space, return the front wheels to the straight-ahead position. Remember, keep your speed slow and, when centered in the space, move forward until you gently touch the curb. When entering or leaving an angle parking space, be sure you do not hit vehicles parked on either side of you. The points on your car that require special checks are your left front bumper and your right rear fender or door.

Exiting from an Angle Parking Space.   To exit from an angle parking space, place your foot on the brake pedal and shift to *reverse*. Check for pedestrians, bicycles, and other obstacles. Move back slowly, checking your left front bumper so that you do not strike the vehicle to your left. Also check over your right shoulder for traffic. When your rear window is in line with the rear bumper of the car parked to your right, check traffic. If the lane is clear, turn the wheel all the way to the right and continue backing slowly. As your car centers in the traffic lane, straighten the front wheels, shift to *drive,* and move forward with the flow of traffic.

Angle Parking on the Left.   Angle parking on the left requires the same checks and procedures as angle parking on the right. The only differences to keep in mind are:

1. Reverse the direction of steering wheel movements.
2. Carefully check the position of your right front bumper and left rear fender to avoid striking vehicles parked on either side of the space.

PERPENDICULAR PARKING

In some parking lots, you may find that parking spaces have been marked at 90-degree angles, rather than at the typical 30 to 60 degrees. Lots marked in this way provide more parking spaces, but they also result in more vehicle damage. Again, the problems are the same—limited visibility and limited room to maneuver. It is important, when you are attempting to park in such an area, that you stay alert for cars preparing to exit from a parking space. Watch for the brake lights of and exhaust from cars that are parked.

Entering a Perpendicular Parking Space.   Once you have identified an available space on the right, signal and slow to a speed of 3 to 5 mph. Then move laterally to a position 7 to 8 feet away from parked cars on the side that you wish to turn into. When your front bumper is in line with the left side of the car parked next to the space that you intend to turn into, turn your steering wheel quickly (hand-over-hand) to the right. Carefully check for clearance of your left front bumper and

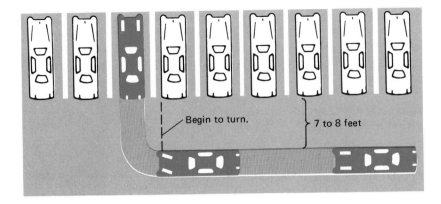

Entering a perpendicular parking space.

move forward slowly. As your car centers in the space, turn your steering wheel back to the straight-ahead position and carefully check your right rear fender to see that it does not scrape the rear bumper of the car on your right. Move slowly forward, positioning your car in the center of the space. Stop just short of the curb or the car parked in the space facing you. Then shift to *park* and secure your car.

The procedure for entering a perpendicular parking space on the left is the same, with the following exceptions. When your front bumper is in line with the right side of the car parked next to the space that you intend to enter, turn your steering wheel quickly (hand-over-hand) to the left. Carefully check for clearance of your right front bumper and move forward slowly. As your car centers into the space, turn your steering wheel back to the straight-ahead position and carefully check your left rear fender to see that it does not scrape the rear bumper of the car on your left.

Exiting from a Perpendicular Parking Space. When you exit from a perpendicular parking space, you will be faced with extremely limited visibility to both sides and to the rear. As a result, all such moves must

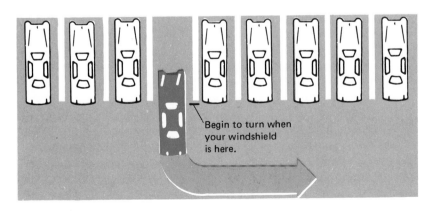

Exiting from a perpendicular parking space.

be made with carefully controlled speed. Once you have shifted to *reverse* and are moving to the rear, keep your foot poised over the brake pedal. Constantly check to the side and rear for vehicles, pedestrians, and other obstacles. Back straight out until your windshield is in line with the rear bumper of the cars parked to either side. Start to turn your steering wheel slightly left or right, depending on which way you want to back. Check carefully to make sure that your front bumper does not strike the rear of the car opposite to the direction you are turning. As your front bumper clears the rear bumper of the car beside you, check carefully to the rear and turn the steering wheel rapidly in the direction you wish to turn. Turn the steering wheel rapidly in the opposite direction to straighten the front wheels as the car centers in the lane. Stop, shift to *drive,* and move forward, remaining alert for vehicles, bicycles, and pedestrians.

Turnabouts

The last general group of maneuvers are those identified as *turnabouts*. These maneuvers, as their name implies, are used to reverse direction. All these maneuvers, when performed on a street, create hazardous situations. The amount of hazard depends on the field of vision, width of the street, number of vehicles, and speed of traffic. In many situations, turnabouts may be illegal. Keep this in mind if you are considering such a maneuver.

It is obvious that all turnabouts involve risks. You may, therefore, decide that going around the block will be faster and safer. However, since you will sometimes find it necessary to make turnabouts, you should learn the correct procedures.

TWO-POINT TURN

In the least hazardous method of reversing direction, you can back into a driveway. This is sometimes referred to as a *two-point turn*. First, signal your intention to stop. Then follow the steps listed below:

1. Bring your car to a stop 2 to 3 feet from the curb. Your car's rear bumper should be just beyond the driveway or alley that you wish to back into.
2. With your foot on the brake, shift to *reverse*. Check for traffic, pedestrians, and other objects in your planned path of travel.
3. When you are sure that the way is clear, look over your right shoulder into the driveway or alley. Back slowly, turning the steering wheel rapidly all the way to the right.
4. As the car enters the driveway or alley, turn the steering wheel to the left as needed. Stop when the front of the car is clear of the traffic lane. The front wheels should be turned straight ahead.
5. Check traffic, shift to *drive,* signal a left turn, and leave when safe.

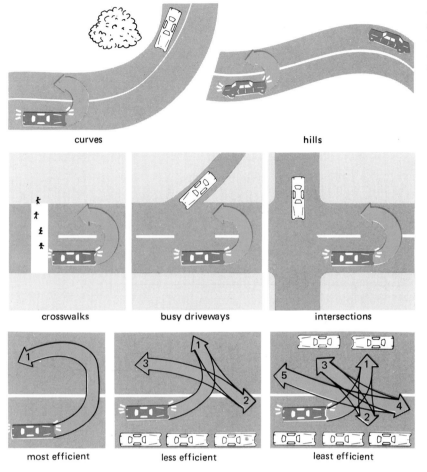

Select a location where you can make a turnabout safely and efficiently. Avoid hills, curves, and intersections, and any area where there may be obstacles.

curves

hills

crosswalks

busy driveways

intersections

most efficient

less efficient

least efficient

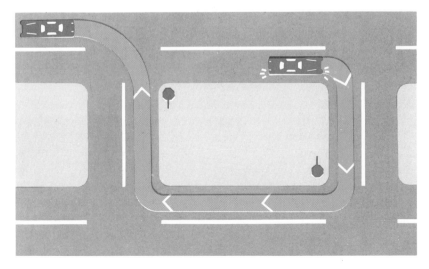

Where a turnabout is illegal or hazardous, go around the block.

You can make a two-point turn by backing into an alley or driveway. This is the least hazardous turnabout.

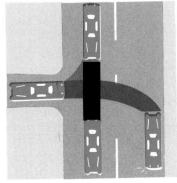

Making a two-point turn by heading into a driveway is more hazardous because it requires backing into a traffic lane.

There is another way to make a two-point turn but it is more hazardous. It requires that you head into an alley or driveway, back into the street, and come to a stop in a thru traffic lane. The steps in this maneuver are as follows:

1. Select a driveway or alley on the left that affords a good field of vision.
2. Turn on the left-turn signal, check for traffic, and turn into the driveway or alley. Stay as close as possible to the right side of the driveway.
3. Stop with the front wheels straight when the rear bumper clears the edge of the roadway.
4. Shift to *reverse*.
5. Check for traffic and look over your right shoulder into your planned path of travel.
6. While moving slowly to the rear, turn the steering wheel rapidly all the way to the right, keeping the car within the first traveled lane.
7. Halfway through the turn, start to straighten the steering wheel.
8. Stop with the front wheels turned straight ahead.
9. Shift to *drive* and accelerate to traffic speed.

U-TURN

A second turnabout, which represents an intermediate hazard, is called a *U-turn*. While this turnabout is the easiest to perform, it requires a wide street. (In addition, it is illegal in many areas.) If you must make such a turn and it is legal, pick a place where visibility is good. Other drivers must be able to see you. After giving the appropriate warnings, proceed as follows:

1. Stop your car as far to the right as possible.
2. Check for traffic from both directions, then signal.

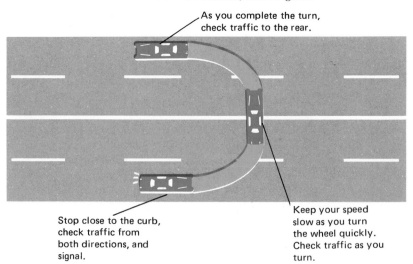

As you complete the turn, check traffic to the rear.

Stop close to the curb, check traffic from both directions, and signal.

Keep your speed slow as you turn the wheel quickly. Check traffic as you turn.

The procedure for making a U-turn.

3. When a very large gap is available from both directions, move forward, turning the steering wheel rapidly (hand-over-hand) all the way to the left.

4. As you complete the turn into the opposite lane, check for traffic to the rear and continue to signal a left turn.

5. When the lane is clear, accelerate to the speed of the traffic flow.

THREE-POINT TURN

The most difficult and hazardous turnabout maneuver is a *three-point turn*. This turn should be used only when the street is too narrow for a U-turn, there are no driveways or alleys, traffic is extremely light, and visibility is very good. This maneuver is especially hazardous because the car making the turnabout must be brought to a stop twice—each time blocking a traffic lane. If such a maneuver must be made, remember the following:

1. Be sure that you are not near an intersection, a curve, or a hill crest. If a fast-moving car appeared suddenly after you started your turnabout, you would be helpless, since you would be stopped, blocking a traffic lane.

2. Check the height of the curbs on either side. The front and rear ends of your car will extend well over the curbs during this maneuver. If the curbs are high they could damage the car.

| position 1 | position 2 | position 3 | position 4 |

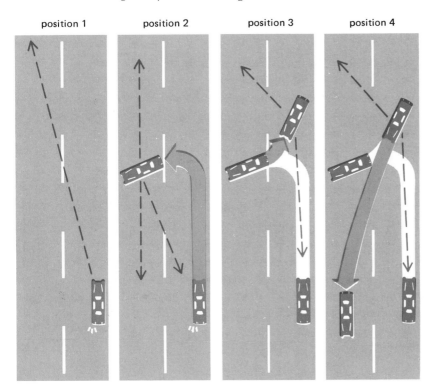

The steps in making a three-point turn.

71

3. Pick a spot without trees, telephone poles, fire hydrants, or other objects near the curb. They are hard to keep in sight while maneuvering the car, especially while backing and turning. You will also want to give as much attention as possible to both traffic lanes.

4. Move the car *slowly* and the steering wheel *rapidly.*

Once you have checked all these conditions and feel that you are ready, proceed as follows:

1. Stop close to the right-hand edge of the pavement or curb.

2. Check for traffic in both directions. Wait for a gap that is long enough to complete the maneuver.

3. Turn on the left-turn signal and check over your left shoulder before starting the turn (position 1).

4. Shift to *drive* and move the car forward slowly. Turn the steering wheel very rapidly to the left to bring the car into position in the opposite lane (position 2).

5. When the front tires are about 4 feet from the edge of the pavement or curb and the car is still moving ahead slowly, turn the steering wheel rapidly to the right and stop the car just short of the road edge or curb.

6. Shift to reverse and back slowly, turning the steering wheel rapidly to the right (position 3). Again, for the last 4 feet or so before stopping, reverse the turn of the steering wheel, moving it rapidly left. Be sure to continue looking back until you have stopped the car.

7. Move the car forward slowly, completing the turn to the left (position 4). Check traffic and proceed.

8. If necessary, repeat steps 6 and 7 to complete the turn.

Driving a Car
with a Stick Shift

Learning to drive a car with a *stick shift,* or *manual transmission,* is not difficult once you have learned to operate a car equipped with an automatic transmission. Basically, you will have to develop the skill needed to coordinate the clutch pedal with the shifting lever and accelerator. When you first start to drive a car with a stick shift, you will need longer gaps in traffic. This is because you will have to learn to use the clutch smoothly for both starting from a stop and for shifting gears. In addition, shifting does demand attention to the sound of the engine, to the car's vibration, or to a speedometer. Simply stated, you have more things to consider when you drive a car with a manual transmission. When you add shifting to the other demands of driving—steering, accelerating, braking, and choosing the best path of travel—you may be stretching your abilities.

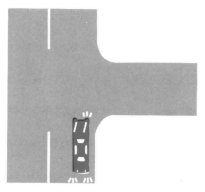 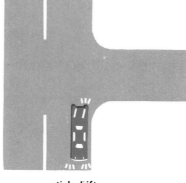

automatic transmission

1. Scan for obstacles.
2. Alert rear traffic.
3. Brake and steer.

stick shift

1. Scan for obstacles.
2. Alert rear traffic.
3. **Brake, steer, and downshift.**

The driver of a car with a stick shift has an additional task to perform in many routine situations.

Shifting requires extra time and effort. If you are driving a stick-shift car and identify a hazard ahead, act early. Give yourself the extra time you will need by shifting—either up or down—*before* you have to brake, change lanes, or make a turn. Having completed the shift, you will be able to give your full attention to the task at hand. The procedures, once you have shifted, are no different from those you would use with an automatic-transmission vehicle.

When driving a vehicle with an automatic transmission, you simply move a selector lever to a desired position and the transmission shifts itself. When driving a vehicle with a stick shift, you must change gears manually (by hand). You will want to go from low to high gear as you accelerate to traffic speed, or high to low as you slow or stop. The two controls that you must learn to use effectively are the clutch and the shifting lever.

Changing gears is accomplished by moving a *shifting lever* or *stick shift*—located either on the steering column or on the floor directly over the transmission. How often and when you shift depends on the size of the engine and the number of "speeds" the transmission has. Some cars have *three-speed* transmissions. This means they are equipped with three different forward gears and a reverse gear. Cars with *four-speed* transmission have four forward gears and a reverse. Some trucks have many more forward gears.

To move the shifting lever from one gear position to another while the engine is running, you have to press the *clutch pedal* to the floor and hold it there. The clutch pedal and shifting lever must work together. (There are times when you may use the clutch pedal alone, such as when stopping from a very low speed. You should not, howev-

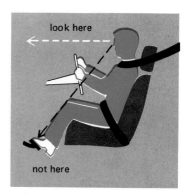

When shifting, look along your intended path, not down at the controls.

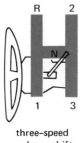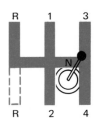

| three-speed column shift | three-speed floor shift | four-speed floor shift |

The placement of the shifting lever and the number of forward gears vary from one vehicle to another.

er, try to move the shifting lever from one point to another without pushing down the clutch pedal.)

The purpose of the clutch pedal, which is connected to the clutch, is to make or break the connection between the engine and the power train, or drive shaft, which provides the power to turn the rear wheels. When the clutch pedal is up, the engine is, in a sense, locked, or engaged, to the transmission and power train. When the clutch is disengaged, you can shift from one gear to another.

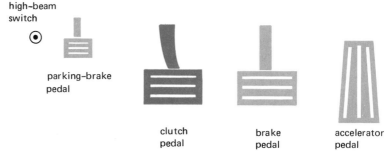

The clutch pedal is located to the left of the brake pedal.

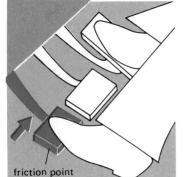

You have to get a "feel" for where the friction point is.

The secret to the smooth operation of a stick shift is developing the ability to sense where, as you bring the clutch pedal up, the clutch and the rest of the power train begin to engage. This is known as the *friction point*. At this exact point, further upward movement of the clutch pedal must be closely controlled and matched by a gradual increase in gas-pedal pressure. The additional gas is needed to generate the power required either to get the car in motion or to match the engine speed at which the power train is already rotating.

If you have learned to perform the basic driving tasks in a car equipped with an automatic transmission, you should not have dif-

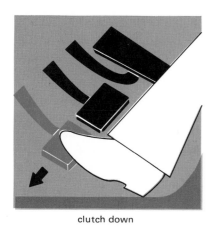

clutch down

clutch at friction point

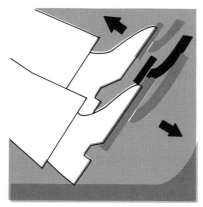

passing friction point—
additional pressure
applied to accelerator

foot is removed from
clutch pedal

Clutch-pedal and accelerator-pedal movements must be coordinated.

ficulty learning clutch control. The easiest way to develop a "feel" for the friction point is to use *reverse* gear at first. Since *reverse* provides the lowest gear available, great skill is not required to control the clutch. Once you have developed this "feel" for clutch control, learning to shift from one gear to another should be simple.

SELECTING GEARS
The purpose of the various gear combinations is to provide the range of power and speed needed for various driving conditions.

Low, or *first,* gear provides the power needed to get the car in motion or to move through mud, sand, water, or deep snow.

Second gear allows you to accelerate to speeds of 15 to 25 mph, depending on the size and type of engine and whether your car is equipped with a three- or four-speed transmission. In addition, second gear can be used for starting on ice, for driving on roads covered with several inches of snow, or as a brake when going down long or steep hills.

Third gear, if the vehicle is equipped with a three-speed transmission, is used for all speeds over 20 to 25 mph. If a vehicle is equipped with a four-speed transmission and a small engine, however, *third* gear would generally be used for speeds up to 30 to 35 mph.

Fourth gear is used when traveling at speeds above 35 mph on flat roadways. When driving on hills it may be necessary to wait until you are traveling approximately 40 mph before shifting to *fourth* gear.

GETTING READY TO DRIVE

Once you have made the necessary outside checks and entered the car, look at the location and size of the foot pedals. The clutch pedal is located to the left of the brake pedal and steering column. You will usually find that the brake pedal in a stick-shift car is smaller than the brake pedal in a car with an automatic transmission. The smaller pedal is necessary because stick shift cars have three pedals: the accelerator, brake, and clutch. Vehicles equipped with automatic transmissions have only two: the accelerator and brake.

The clutch pedal must be pressed to the floor every time you start the car, shift gears, or stop. With this in mind, make the necessary predriving adjustments. You may find it necessary to change your seat position or to use pedal extensions.

STARTING THE ENGINE

Before you start the engine, *be sure the parking brake is set.* Then, proceed as follows:

1. With your left foot, press the clutch pedal to the floor and hold it there. (If the engine is cold, press the accelerator to the floor and

Starting a car with a stick shift.

Be sure the
parking brake
is set.

Press and hold
down the clutch
pedal.

Make sure the
shifting lever
is in *neutral.*

Turn the key
and start the
engine.

release it. This sets the automatic choke, feeding more fuel to the cylinders.)

2. Make sure the shifting lever is in the *neutral* position. (Otherwise, the car will move suddenly when you start the engine.)

3. With your right foot pressing lightly on the accelerator, turn the ignition key clockwise as far as it will go. You will hear the starter begin to turn the engine. *Be sure to release the key as soon as the engine starts to run.* The key will spring back from the *start* position to the *on* position. (Never use the starter when the engine is running. If you are not sure the engine is off, press gently on the accelerator before you try to use the starter again.) With the engine running, you can remove your foot from the clutch pedal.

To stop the engine, turn the key counterclockwise to the *off* position.

PUTTING THE CAR IN MOTION

After you have started the engine, use the following procedures to put the car in motion:

1. Press the clutch pedal to the floor, while keeping firm pressure on the foot brake.
2. Shift to *low (first)* gear.
3. Release the parking brake.
4. Check the rear-view mirrors.
5. Just before you start to move, look back over your shoulder and check the blind spots. (Do this each time you start so that it becomes a habit.)
6. Signal your intention to move. Continue to look ahead through your immediate path of travel. *Do not look down at your feet.*
7. Let the clutch up slowly until it reaches the friction point. Hold it at that point momentarily.
8. Move your right foot from the brake to the accelerator and press down gently.
9. Slowly let the clutch pedal up the rest of the way.

If the car jumps forward in a jerky motion, either you have not released the clutch properly or your right foot is bouncing on the accelerator. In either case, press the clutch down at once. Practice releasing the clutch only as far as the friction point until you can make the car start to move smoothly. If you feed too little gasoline with the accelerator, your engine will stall and you will have to start it again. However, do not feed too much gas to the engine. That will cause it to "race" and damage the clutch when you release the pedal. When you have successfully performed these nine steps, your car will be moving forward in *low* gear.

Putting a stick-shift car in motion.

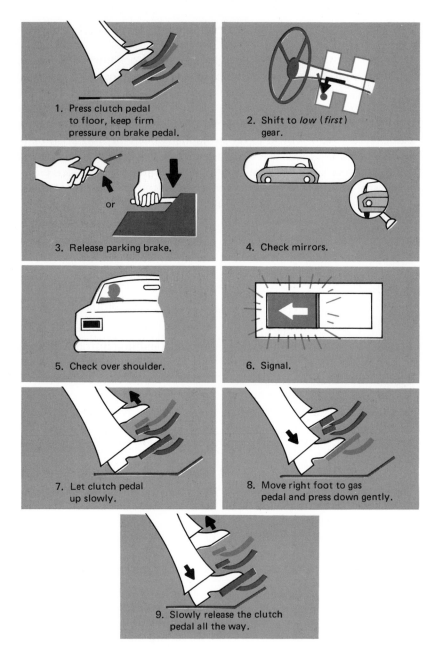

1. Press clutch pedal to floor, keep firm pressure on brake pedal.
2. Shift to *low* (*first*) gear.

or

3. Release parking brake.
4. Check mirrors.

5. Check over shoulder.
6. Signal.

7. Let clutch pedal up slowly.
8. Move right foot to gas pedal and press down gently.

9. Slowly release the clutch pedal all the way.

STOPPING FROM LOW GEAR

To stop from a low gear—either *first* or *second* at speeds less than 10 mph—follow these steps:

1. Check the rear-view mirrors for other traffic.
2. Signal for a stop with the brake lights or by hand.

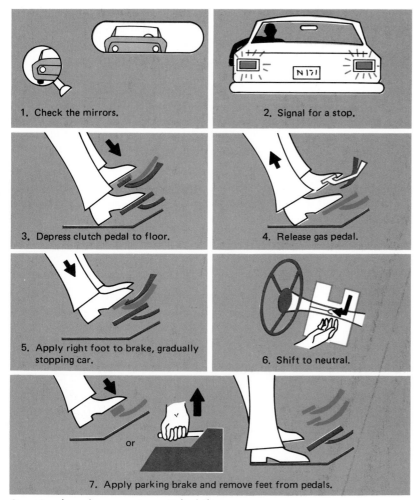

1. Check the mirrors.

2. Signal for a stop.

3. Depress clutch pedal to floor.

4. Release gas pedal.

5. Apply right foot to brake, gradually stopping car.

6. Shift to neutral.

or

7. Apply parking brake and remove feet from pedals.

Stopping from low gear in a stick-shift car.

3. Depress the clutch pedal to the floor.

4. Release your foot pressure on the accelerator. (Pressing the clutch pedal down an instant before you release the accelerator will prevent a jerky movement.)

5. Move your right foot to the brake pedal and press down gradually until the car has stopped.

6. Keep firm pressure on the brake pedal and shift to *neutral*.

7. Apply the parking brake and remove your feet from the clutch pedals.

You may find that your car moves to a stop with a jerk and a slight "nose-diving" motion. If that is the case, ease up slightly on the brake pedal just before the car comes to a complete stop. Then apply pressure again. (Do not, however, completely remove your foot from the brake pedal.) When practicing, make each stop a full stop. "Rolling through" practice stops is not the same as making smooth stops.

After coming to a stop, keep the gearshift lever in the *neutral* position until you are ready to move again. This should become a habit. It is especially important at traffic lights, stop signs, and other places where there may be pedestrians crossing in front of your car. If you keep the car in gear while you are waiting, your foot may slip off the clutch. The car would then jump forward suddenly.

SHIFTING FROM LOW TO SECOND GEAR

Once you have your car moving ahead smoothly in *low* gear, you are ready to change to *second*. Continue to look ahead through your immediate path of travel. Then, without taking your eyes from the road, follows these steps:

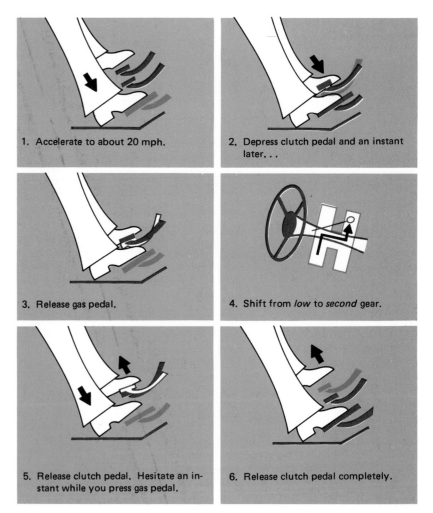

1. Accelerate to about 20 mph.

2. Depress clutch pedal and an instant later. . .

3. Release gas pedal.

4. Shift from *low* to *second* gear.

5. Release clutch pedal. Hesitate an instant while you press gas pedal.

6. Release clutch pedal completely.

Shifting from low *to* second *gear in a stick-shift car.*

1. Press down on the accelerator until the car is moving at about 20 mph. This will give the car speed enough to keep moving while the clutch is disengaged.

2. Press the clutch pedal to the floor. (This should be done an instant before you release the accelerator pedal.)

3. Release the accelerator pedal.

4. Move the shifting lever through the *neutral* position into *second*.

5. Release the clutch pedal as far as the friction point and hold it there for an instant while you press down on the accelerator.

6. Release the clutch pedal all the way.

SHIFTING FROM SECOND TO THIRD GEAR

To shift into *third* gear, have the car running smoothly in *second* gear and then, keeping your eyes on the road ahead, do the following:

1. Press down on the accelerator until the car is moving at about 25 to 30 mph.

2. Press the clutch pedal to the floor.

3. Release the accelerator pedal.

4. Shift to *third* gear.

5. Let the clutch pedal up smoothly. At the same time, press the accelerator pedal down gradually.

6. Move your foot from the clutch pedal to the floor.

Again, during step 1 of this shift, give the car enough speed—approximately 25 to 30 mph—to keep it moving while the engine is disengaged. (This speed also keeps the engine from "laboring" when it moves into *third* gear.)

STOPPING FROM THIRD GEAR

When stopping from third gear, there is a difference in the order of the steps:

1. Check the rear-view mirror for other traffic.

2. Signal for a stop.

3. Release your foot pressure on the accelerator.

4. Press on the brake pedal, slowing the car speed to about 10 to 15 mph.

5. Press the clutch pedal to the floor.

6. Continue to brake, easing up on your foot pressure slightly just before the car comes to a full stop. Then ease down on the pedal again. To prevent the car from moving, maintain pressure on the foot brake.

7. Move the shifting lever to *neutral*.

8. Apply the parking brake and remove your feet from the clutch and brake pedals.

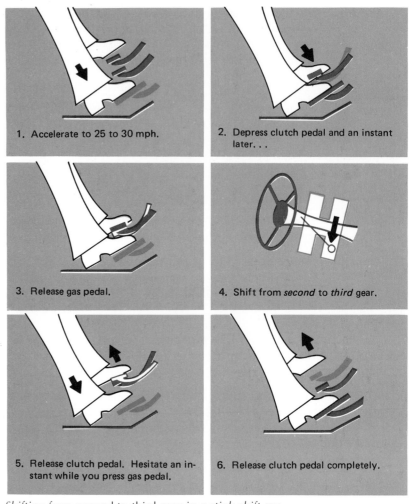

1. Accelerate to 25 to 30 mph.

2. Depress clutch pedal and an instant later. . .

3. Release gas pedal.

4. Shift from *second* to *third* gear.

5. Release clutch pedal. Hesitate an instant while you press gas pedal.

6. Release clutch pedal completely.

Shifting from second *to* third *gear in a stick-shift car.*

Notice the order of steps 4 and 5. It is the reverse of the order for stopping from *low* or *second* gear. In stopping from *third* gear, you use the foot brake *before* you press down the clutch pedal. When you take your foot off the accelerator in order to brake, the engine slows down. This helps to slow down the car. If you press down the clutch pedal too soon when you are driving in *third,* you lose the braking power of the engine.

SHIFTING FROM THIRD TO SECOND GEAR

Sometimes it is necessary to *downshift—to go from a higher gear to a lower gear.* Shifting from *third* to *second* increases the engine's power and decreases the car's speed. You would want to do this when going

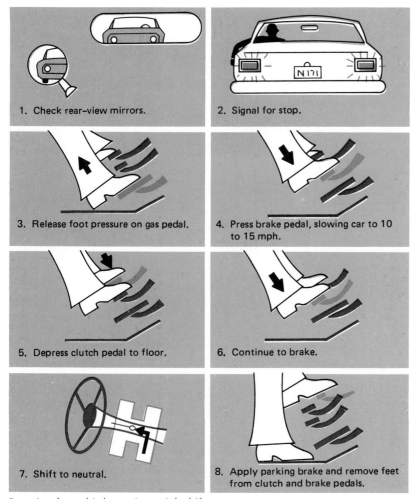

1. Check rear–view mirrors.

2. Signal for stop.

3. Release foot pressure on gas pedal.

4. Press brake pedal, slowing car to 10 to 15 mph.

5. Depress clutch pedal to floor.

6. Continue to brake.

7. Shift to neutral.

8. Apply parking brake and remove feet from clutch and brake pedals.

Stopping from third gear in a stick-shift car.

going uphill

going downhill

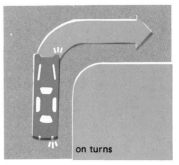

on turns

Downshifting increases the engine's power and decreases the car's speed.

up steep hills, moving slowly in heavy traffic, or turning corners. You would also want to downshift on long, steep, downhill roads, to make use of the braking power of *second* gear.

Always shift to *second* if you feel that the engine is laboring in *third* gear because the car's speed is too slow. Once you have shifted to *second,* you can increase or decrease your speed easily and quickly. Downshift from *third* to *second before* you reach a speed that is too slow for *third* gear. For example, if you are going to make a turn, complete the downshift before you reach the corner. That way, you will not have to take one hand away from the steering wheel after you have started to turn. Follow the steps listed below to downshift from *third* to *second:*

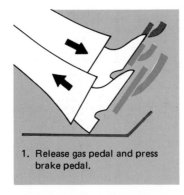

1. Release gas pedal and press brake pedal.

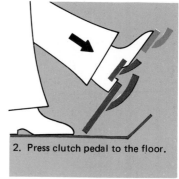

2. Press clutch pedal to the floor.

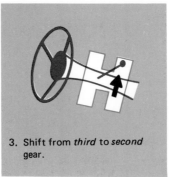

3. Shift from *third* to *second* gear.

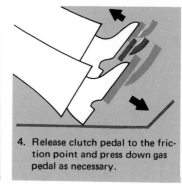

4. Release clutch pedal to the friction point and press down gas pedal as necessary.

Shifting from third *to* second *gear in a stick-shift car.*

1. If your car speed is too high for *second* gear, release pressure on the accelerator pedal and press the brake pedal.

2. Press the clutch pedal all the way to the floor.

3. Shift from *third* to *second*. (If you are going uphill, shift quickly. Otherwise you will lose momentum.)

4. Release the clutch pedal to the friction point. At the same time, adjust pressure on the accelerator pedal as needed.

Practice in downshifting from *third* into *second* will give you the "feel" of the proper engine speed.

In cars equipped with small engines and four-speed transmissions, the procedure for shifting from *third* to *fourth* or for shifting from *fourth* to *third* gear is the same as outlined for shifting from *second* to *third* or from *third* gear to *second*. The shift into *fourth* gear should occur at about 35 miles per hour.

THE EMERGENCY DOWNSHIFT

Downshifting from *second* to *low* is difficult unless you are moving very slowly. You can, however, move the shift lever into *second* gear at practically any time. When you shift from *third* to *second* to decrease your speed on a long, steep, downgrade, you will have to use

84

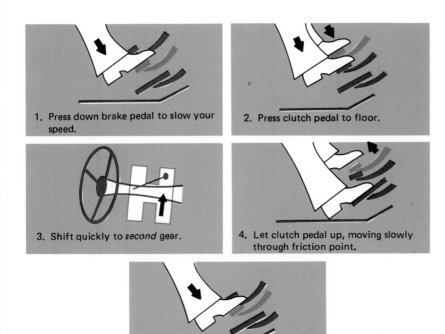

1. Press down brake pedal to slow your speed.

2. Press clutch pedal to floor.

3. Shift quickly to *second* gear.

4. Let clutch pedal up, moving slowly through friction point.

5. Brake as needed.

The emergency downshift.

your brakes. The braking power of the engine will not be enough. Follow these steps:

1. Press down the brake pedal to slow your speed.
2. Press the clutch pedal to the floor.
3. Shift quickly to *second* gear.
4. Let the clutch pedal up, moving slowly through the friction point.
5. Use the brakes as much as needed.

It is best to practice shifting up or down some place away from other traffic. Learn to perform these shifts smoothly before you attempt maneuvering in heavy traffic.

STARTING ON A HILL

Cars are likely to roll backward when stopped facing uphill. When driving a vehicle with an automatic transmission the solution is simple. You apply brake pressure as needed. When you are ready to move, you accelerate until the engine pulls slightly against the brake. Then you remove your foot from the brake pedal and move ahead. The procedure is more difficult in a car equipped with a stick shift:

1. After stopping the car, set the parking brake.
2. When you are ready to move, press the clutch pedal to the floor and shift to *first* gear.

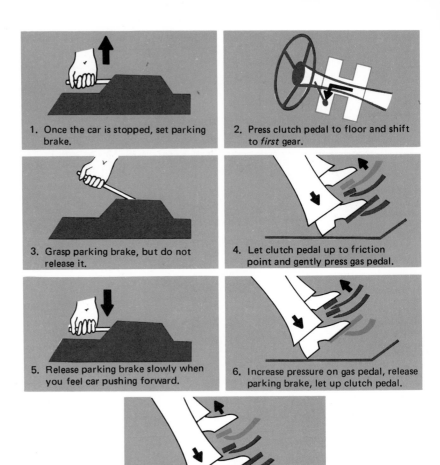

1. Once the car is stopped, set parking brake.

2. Press clutch pedal to floor and shift to *first* gear.

3. Grasp parking brake, but do not release it.

4. Let clutch pedal up to friction point and gently press gas pedal.

5. Release parking brake slowly when you feel car pushing forward.

6. Increase pressure on gas pedal, release parking brake, let up clutch pedal.

7. Accelerate in *first* gear.

Starting on a hill.

3. Keeping one hand on the steering wheel, grasp the parking-brake release without actually releasing it.

4. Let the clutch up to the friction point and press gently on the accelerator.

5. Release the parking brake slowly when you feel the car pushing forward against the brake.

6. Increase pressure on the accelerator, release the parking brake fully, and let up on the clutch.

7. Accelerate in *first* gear until you gain enough speed to shift gears.

The critical step is to accelerate enough to move the car foward the instant the clutch is at the friction point and the parking brake is released. If you release the parking brake too soon, the car will roll back. In addition, if you do not feed the engine enough gas, the car will stall. If the car stalls or starts to roll back, press the brake pedal, set the parking brake, shift to *neutral,* and begin again.

There is another method for starting on a hill. It is simple because it uses only the clutch and accelerator:

1. After stopping, shift into *first* gear. Keep your right foot on the brake.

2. Let the clutch up to the friction point.

3. Quickly move your right foot from the brake pedal to the accelerator and press down until the car "tries" to move. At this point you "balance" the forces on the car, preventing it from either rolling back or going forward.

4. As soon as you are ready to move, press harder on the accelerator and let up more on the clutch.

If you press down on the clutch while "balancing," the car will roll back. If you do not give it enough gas, it will stall. If you press too hard on the gas, the car will move forward. This method of starting on a hill is used on slight grades and for *brief* traffic stops. If it is used excessively on steep hills, it will wear out the clutch. As you can see, it takes just the right timing so that the car neither rolls back nor stalls.

STOPPING ON A HILL

Securing a car on a hill adds one more step to your stopping procedure. Before shutting off the engine, shift into *reverse* gear and set the parking brake. Release the clutch after turning off the ignition.

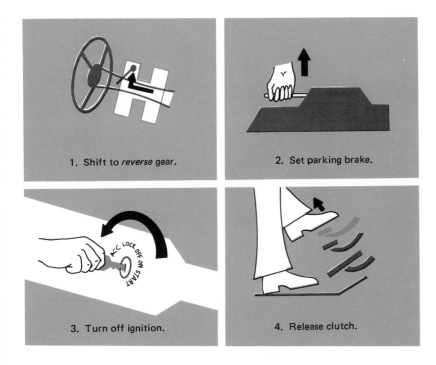

1. Shift to *reverse* gear.

2. Set parking brake.

3. Turn off ignition.

4. Release clutch.

Stopping on a hill.

The clutch and transmission working together in a stick-shift car serve the same purpose that the *park* gear position serves in a car with an automatic transmission. The power train is "locked" to an engine that is off. Even if the parking brake failed, the car would not move.

To Think About

1. What are some of the tracking and braking errors that beginning drivers tend to make? How can they be corrected?
2. Why is tracking on a turn more difficult than tracking on a straight line?
3. What is the purpose of the 4-second rule?
4. What can cause a 12-second visual lead to be cut down? How would you correct this situation?
5. How would you determine whether it was safe to pass a truck you were behind on a two-lane highway?
6. In what kind of situations would you never pass another vehicle?
7. Do you need a larger time gap to make a left-hand turn or to make a right-hand turn? Why?
8. What factors would you consider in choosing a place to make a U-turn?
9. Why are longer time gaps necessary for driving a car with a stick shift?
10. In what gear would you leave a stick-shift car when you parked it on a hill?

To Do

1. Ride with an experienced driver and make notes about the way the driver makes steering corrections. Are the corrections smooth and gradual? Does the driver tend to "wander" across the road or within the traffic lane?
2. While riding in a friend's or in your family's car, identify alternate paths of travel. Then ask the driver where he or she would go if the immediate path were blocked. Repeat the question in several driving situations. Do you and the driver always agree?
3. In an area with parallel-parked cars, observe 5 to 10 drivers entering the traffic from a parked position. How many of them fail to maintain an adequate gap to the rear? Make a record of your findings.
4. Station yourself at at intersection that is controlled with a *stop* or *yield* sign. Identify vehicles that are turning or driving through the intersection. Do the drivers wait for sufficient gaps in the cross traffic? Report on your findings.

Decision-Making and Driving

After reading this chapter, you should be able to:

1. Describe how drivers should gather, analyze, and evaluate information.
2. Explain why decision-making is such an important part of good driving.
3. Demonstrate an understanding of minimizing risks and simplifying situations.
4. Give examples of the ways in which drivers should compromise by adjusting vehicle speed and position.

We make decisions thousands of times a day. Decision-making is such a common activity that we are seldom aware of it. Only when we are forced to make important decisions are we likely to realize how difficult decision-making can be. Yet, the mental operations involved in making a simple decision (Which shoes should I wear today?) or a difficult decision (Should I go to college or get a job after graduation?) are basically the same.

Decisions on the Road

On the highway, drivers continually have to make decisions about speed and position. After such decisions have been made, the driver may maintain, decrease, or increase speed and steer to a new lane position or maintain the same path of travel. Such decisions are generally selected from among options that range from worthless to the best possible choice. If the final decision is at least among the good options, even if it is not the best one, speed and position will be adequate to handle the situation. If, however, the option selected is less than good or is totally inappropriate, the consequences will range from a momentary interruption of traffic flow, requiring other traffic to adjust,

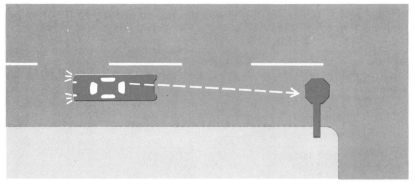

Drivers must use information to make driving decisions. Some decisions are as simple as deciding to slow down and stop as you approach a stop sign.

to a possible collision. Good decision-making, then, is the key to safe and efficient driving. It may be the single most important factor in good driving.

As a group, drivers between the ages of 16 and 25 have the best reflexes, vision, and general good health of any age group on the road. Physically, they are the best "equipped" drivers on the road. Yet, although the cars they drive and the roads they travel are no different from those used by other drivers, the drivers in this age group have the highest rate of accidents and fatalities. Why is this so? Something other than physical ability must be taken into account.

Drivers must observe and evaluate potentially dangerous highway situations before they can act. Obviously, the sooner they observe and evaluate situations, the more time they will have to adjust their speed and position. In other words, drivers must *anticipate* what may happen. They can then act to prevent or avoid hazards *before* they find themselves in crisis situations. They can make systematic decisions and choices, rather than be forced to act in an emergency.

Good decision-making in driving should aim toward one goal: achieving accident-free roads and highways. If all driving situations

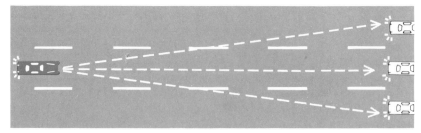

Other decisions are not so simple. As a driver, you will have to anticipate hazards. If the cars well ahead of you on an expressway begin to brake and slow down, you too should slow down and look for alternate paths.

were exactly alike, achieving this goal would be easy. We would need no more than a simple list of "dos" and "don'ts" to tell us how to act. Unfortunately, all driving situations are not alike. The wide variety of driving situations cannot be covered by a set list of "right" and "wrong" actions. What may be right in one situation could be wrong in a slightly different situation. For example, you should ordinarily slow and prepare to stop when you see a yellow traffic light ahead. However, what would you do if you approached the same light at highway speed, knowing that a large truck was following close behind? Would you suddenly brake to a stop or speed up and drive through the intersection? A simple "do" or "don't" rule does not answer the question. In this situation, you would need more information than a simple rule can give. You would have to make a decision based on the speed you were traveling, how close the truck was, traffic ahead, cross traffic, pedestrians, the condition of your car, and what you knew about the stopping distances of your vehicle and large vehicles.

Most of the decisions we make may be acceptable. However, because we are human, we do make errors, and errors, either on your part or on the part of other highway users, can cause accidents. To achieve an accident-free highway system, then, you have to do more than simply stay out of accidents yourself. You have to avoid creating situations that may cause others to have accidents. When you make decisions, you must consider the abilities and needs of other highway users. You cannot simply look out for yourself.

What, then, should you look for? And how should you look? What kind of information is important to your decision-making? What kind of information is not important? Finally, once you have the information you need, what should you do with it?

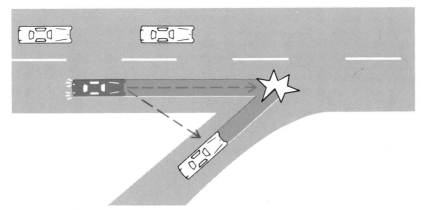

To achieve accident-free driving, you have to look out for the needs of other highway users. In this situation, you might slow down to create a gap for the car approaching on the entrance ramp.

We must gather, analyze, and evaluate information before we can make decisions. As you approach a car that you have any reason to believe will turn across your path, you should slow down.

Information Processing

Computers *process* information. That is, they gather "raw" data, analyze it according to a program, and reproduce it in a form that can be used in making decisions. In three steps, people process information in much the same way:

1. We *gather* the information by identifying things in the world around us.

2. We *analyze* the information by selecting those items that seem to bear on the problem we are faced with.

3. We *evaluate* the information by establishing the apparent relationship of one item to another, which in turn leads to conclusions. On the basis of these conclusions, we make decisions.

At times, human information processing is automatic. It may be as simple as deciding to carry an umbrella on a rainy day. When people process information, they often use what they have learned from previous experience.

In Chapter 3 we dealt with many driving tasks that will, with practice, become *habits*. These habits, such as fastening seat belts or traveling in a straight line, require a minimum of attention. However, there are times when the driving environment may become so complicated that a driver's decision-making abilities are taxed to their limits. This could cause panic.

Whether you are driving in the city, in a residential area, in the country, or on an expressway, there may be sudden changes in the traffic flow or roadway environment. You will not be able to prevent these sudden changes, but you can adjust the speed or position of your

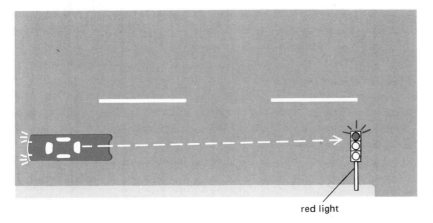

red light

Some driving situations are easy to evaluate and require simple responses that may become habits. For example, when you see a red light, you will almost automatically slow down to stop.

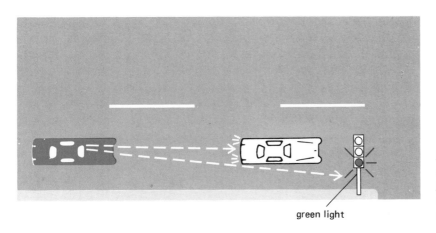

green light

Similar situations may not be so simple. If you identified both a green light and a car stopped ahead of you, what would you do?

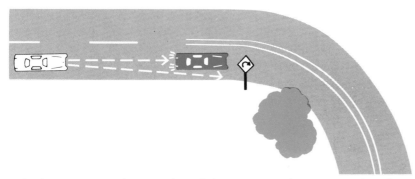

Once you have gathered the correct information, you can adjust the speed or position of your car.

vehicle. Once you have gathered the correct information—that there is an accident ahead or you are entering a heavy storm area, for example—you can decide what you have to do.

93

GATHERING INFORMATION

Safe driving decisions begin with selecting the right information. We gather this information through our senses of sight, hearing, touch, and smell. For driving, sight is the most important sense. We receive most of the information we need through our eyes. Driving performance therefore depends largely on how well we use our eyes. One of the biggest problems in driving is that there is simply too much to look at. Many of the things we can see are very important to us as drivers. Others are not important, or may even distract us from the driving task.

SEEING WHAT WE WANT TO SEE

People do not ordinarily analyze their environment. We often fail to notice things. This is because we are not looking for anything in particular. For example, we know, in general, what our own street looks like, and so we do not bother to carefully look it over each time we drive on it.

You should not get into the habit of assuming that other drivers will always behave normally. They may do the unexpected and create serious hazards. In this case, the oncoming driver turns across your path without signaling.

predicted path

real path

We tend to notice those things that are out of the ordinary. This can be a handicap when we drive, since most roadway users, both drivers and pedestrians, usually behave in predictable ways. This can make us forget that an occasional driver or pedestrian will *not* behave as usual. As drivers, we should not get into the habit of assuming that other roadway users will always act normally.

This same habit pattern may affect the way we look at controls, warning signs, and the rest of the driving environment. If we assume too much, we stop looking carefully at what is around us. Our attention may be drawn to interesting or attractive objects, and we may fail to see something that is a hazard.

DEVELOPING AN ORGANIZED SEARCH

One way to improve your decision-making ability is to try to gather and process information that will help you reach a specific goal. Try to

94

organize your search for information. Do you know what you are looking for and why you are looking for it?

If you organize your thinking, you know where and toward what to direct your search. For example, if you are driving on a crowded city street, you probably would not direct your attention to a car parked on the opposite side of the street with its trunk lid up. Instead, you would direct your attention to the pedestrians, bicyclists, and vehicles nearest your immediate path of travel. On a lightly traveled two-lane rural highway, however, the opposite might be true. The raised trunk lid might alert you to the possibility of a pedestrian crossing the roadway.

SELECTIVE SEARCH

Our minds are not able to interpret everything we can see. We must learn to *search selectively* for whatever can provide us with the information we need.

The basis for selection can be stated simply: Anything that does not relate to accident-free driving should receive brief attention and then be forgotten. In contrast, anything that has *collision potential* (that could cause an accident or interfere with your path of travel) should receive close attention.

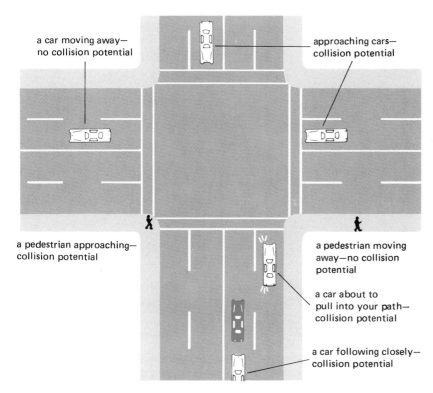

a car moving away— no collision potential

approaching cars— collision potential

a pedestrian approaching— collision potential

a pedestrian moving away—no collision potential

a car about to pull into your path— collision potential

a car following closely— collision potential

You must selectively search the traffic environment for these elements that have collision potential.

95

The scenery along a rural highway may be interesting, but it does not directly affect accident-free driving, unless it results in an area of limited visibility. When you drive on such a highway, it is more important for you to pay attention to the elements on and adjacent to the roadway itself. You must be *selective* about where you look.

SEARCHING BY CATEGORY

You can improve the way you gather information by grouping similar items into categories. The information you need to drive safely can be divided into four basic categories. As you drive, check for information in each of these categories.

Signs, signals, and markings can provide important information about the roadway environment.

1. *Signs, signals, and roadway markings.* These provide information about the road environment and are guides for behavior. The posted information that warns you of hazards, like curves or steep hills, is usually dependable and easy to understand. Compare this with information about driving behavior, however. Can you be sure, for example, that other drivers will obey speed limits or stay in the lanes that are marked on the roadway?

2. *The highway.* You have to gather information about roadway design, construction, maintenance, surface conditions, and visual obstructions. Any one of these factors may affect your ability to control your vehicle. The roadway and nearby areas must be searched for objects that have collision potential. You must also identify an alternate path of travel, should you at some time have to leave the roadway.

3. *Motorized vehicles.* The information in this category is frequently more difficult to evaluate. Cars, motorcycles, trucks, and buses dif-

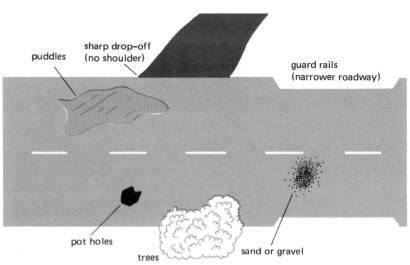

The roadway itself and nearby off-road areas must be checked for elements that may have collision potential.

fer not only in response characteristics—acceleration, steering, braking, and visibility—but also in level of maintenance, the operator's knowledge of the given vehicle's capabilities, and the individual operator's driving ability. It is essential, however, that you become aware of these differences so that in predicting the possible moves of vehicles around you, you can better prepare to adjust speed and position to accommodate that move. You will also find that operators of certain types of vehicles will tend to be less predictable in their selection of speed and position. Consideration of this type of information simply enables you to better select those vehicles in the traffic stream that you should pay more attention to.

4. *Nonmotorized highway users.* Pedestrians, bicyclists, and animals are the least protected highway users. They, too, provide information that must be constantly checked and rechecked. Be especially careful to check for them, even if they are not on the roadway itself.

ESTABLISHING A PATTERN FOR SEARCHING

Once you have an effective pattern of search, you should consciously use it until it becomes a habit. Search well ahead of your car, at least 12 seconds, looking for objects or events on, near, or approaching the roadway that might influence your selection of speed and position. Check again to determine whether your immediate path (4 seconds ahead) is clear. Has there been any change in hazards that you have already identified? Make sure that you have at least 2 seconds between you and any vehicle ahead. In addition, check the space between you and any vehicles in adjacent lanes.

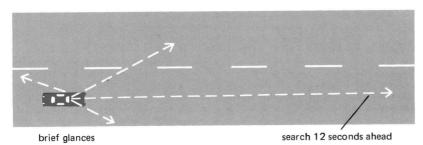

brief glances   search 12 seconds ahead

Establish a search pattern 12 seconds ahead of your car. Other checks (to the sides and rear) should be brief. Always return your attention to your path of travel.

Visual checks in any other direction should be brief, followed immediately by returning your attention to your path of travel. If a *brief* glance over your shoulder or in a rear-view mirror does not provide enough information, do not keep staring. *Always return your attention to your path of travel.* If there is no immediate problem in the path, then check the mirrors or look over your shoulder again.

If a hazard ahead forces you to slow down, check for vehicles closing from the rear. You can warn following drivers of the hazard by flashing your brake lights.

When you check the instrument panel or glance at a gauge or dial, quickly return your attention to the path ahead.

Vehicles closing from the rear or traveling beside you may create hazards, especially if you slow down or change lanes. Checking the mirrors when you may be making a stop, reducing speed, or making a lateral move allows you time to signal, making a collision less likely. A simple rule to follow is to check traffic to the sides and rear as a matter of course when anything within 12 seconds ahead indicates that you may have to slow down or move laterally.

You should also make checks of the instrument panel—you may need to know the speed at which you are traveling or what your gauges read. At any rate, be sure to glance at the gauges quickly, and immediately return your attention to your planned path of travel.

Perception

A major source of driving errors is inaccurate perception of roadway events. We *perceive* something, *decide* what to do, and then *act* on that decision. If what you perceive is incorrect, you may make a serious error. Suppose you decide that a particular speed, position, or maneuver is safe, and you act on that decision. You may want to drive safely, but if you perceive the situation incorrectly, you may make the wrong decision.

EXPECTING NORMAL EVENTS

We *expect* other drivers to behave normally most of the time. Unfortunately, we cannot *depend* on them to always behave normally. In fact, you should be ready to deal with the unusual and unexpected so that you will not be taken by surprise. Good drivers do not have a false sense of security. They know they cannot assume that other drivers will always behave correctly.

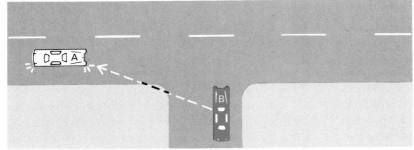

Seeing the signal of car A, the driver of car B
might predict that car A is going to turn right.

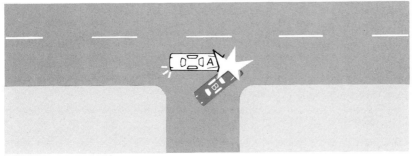

However, the driver of car A may be signaling
to pull over to the curb, and not to turn.

Drivers who perceive situations incorrectly may make wrong decisions.

PREPARING FOR THE UNEXPECTED

You cannot know for sure how other drivers will act, no more than you can predict the weather with certainty. Obviously, some things cannot be predicted and controlled.

When driving, you have to be prepared for the unexpected. Will your speed and position leave you time to adjust to the unexpected? Are you alert to *potential* hazards and conflicts? You have to consider what *might* happen, and you have to plan how you will act if it *does* happen.

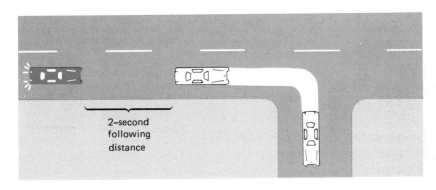

2-second
following
distance

You cannot absolutely depend on other drivers to behave normally. You have to be prepared for the unexpected. By maintaining an adequate following distance, you could cope with a driver who suddenly turned without signaling.

Interpreting information on this basis lets you *preplan* responses. You will know what might require a response and what your response options are. If you have any doubt that your own speed and position will give you time enough to respond, you can adjust them.

CLOSING MOVEMENTS

A *closing movement* is any maneuver that may lead to a collision, either between two vehicles or between a vehicle and another object. It is important to learn ways to prevent closing movements from ending in collisions. Listed here are several common situations that can create a closing movement from which you may have to escape:

1. *Possible rear-end collisions.* You are closing so rapidly on a lead vehicle that you would be unable to steer around it if the vehicle stopped. In addition, someone may be tailgating you, reducing your possible avenues of escape in an emergency.

2. *Vehicles entering your path of travel.* Vehicles parked at the curb, in a driveway, at an intersection, or approaching a merging lane might pull into your path.

3. *Possible head-on collision.* An oncoming vehicle could pull into your path either while turning or while passing another vehicle.

4. *Possible sideswipe.* A passing vehicle might cut back into your lane before completely passing you.

5. *Striking a pedestrian or animal.* A pedestrian or animal near the roadway could step or run into your path, causing you to lose control.

6. *Encountering off-road elements.* You are forced to leave the roadway. What elements would interfere with your car's path of travel?

The danger in closing movements like these is compounded when your field of vision is limited (for example, on hill crests and "blind" curves). Hills, large bushes, or signs may hide hazards of one type or another. You should be especially careful about potential closing movements when driving in fog, after dark, or in heavy rain or snow. In each case, prepare for the unexpected.

PROBABILITY AND CONSEQUENCES

In attempting to adjust either speed or position in response to objects or events that you identify as having closing potential, you must ask yourself two questions:

1. What are the chances *(probability)* that an actual collision course will develop?
2. What would be the results *(consequences)* of such a collision?

First consider the question of probability. You are driving at a speed of 55 mph on a two-lane state highway that passes through gently rolling farming country. Ahead, to your right, you notice in a fenced field several cows running toward the road. While the *consequences* of colliding with a cow under any condition would generally be severe, the *probability* that a cow will jump over or break through the fence to enter your path of travel is very slight. So, while you may slow to watch them, the cows require little attention as a collision threat. Suppose, however, that three or four wild deer are bounding across the same field and are moving toward the road. The *consequences* of striking a deer are also severe. But the *probability* of wild deer leaping the fence and continuing into your path of travel is, in fact, very high. Here, you must obviously adjust your speed to meet the threat. The difference in the level of risk, then, is in the probability that the event will occur.

Look at a different type of situation. Here, too, the matter of concern is which event is more likely, or probable. This time you are driving at 45 mph on a two-lane state highway where traffic is moderate. About two-thirds of the way up a rather long, steep hill, a warning sign indicates that a hidden country road intersects from the right. You are faced with a double problem of limited visibility. Someone may crest the hill, coming toward you over the center line or actually trying to pass, or a vehicle which you cannot see may suddenly enter from the right. We will simply conclude that both situations represent severe *consequences*. However, in evaluating the situations, it is reasonable to assume that the *probability* is greater that an oncoming car will swing out to pass as you both crest the hill than it is that a vehicle will run the stop sign and enter your path. While you must remain alert for both possibilities, your anticipation should be directed to the possibility of an oncoming car.

You will frequently be confronted with multiple potential hazards involving parked cars, pedestrians, or bicycles, as illustrated in the following example.

You are driving at a speed of 30 mph on a two-lane urban street. Coming toward you is a steady line of cars, some of which you must meet as you pass a young boy riding a bike. The boy obviously is having some problem pedaling and is slowing down. While the bike is off the road, the distance varies from 1 to 3 feet away as he weaves along. Where do you position your car? Quite obviously, both the car and the

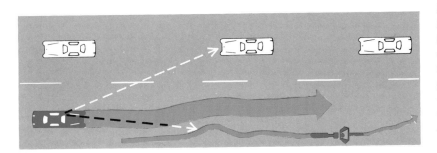

In some situations, you may have to deal with two potential hazards at the same time. In a case like this, both the oncoming traffic and the bicyclist could present hazards. Since the probability of a collision with the bicyclist is much greater, you should move closer to the oncoming cars.

bike have collision potential. The *consequences* of colliding with either one is severe. How about the *probability* of colliding? From the information you have, you should agree with the need to slow down. In addition, your position in this case should be as close to your side of the center line as you can get. There is the possibility of one of those cars crossing the center line, but the *probability* is low. However, the bike rider has exhibited every evidence of having difficulty and shows a high probability of entering your path of travel. The only thing left for you to do is to give him as much room as possible.

The ultimate problem in decision-making while driving arises at that moment when the system fails—when the probability of a collision is absolute. However, if you do not panic, consequences can usually be reduced. For example: You are driving at a speed of 55 mph on a wide multiple-lane roadway (two 12-foot lanes in each direction). Traffic is heavy in all four lanes. While maintaining an adequate following distance, you have moved to the inside lane in preparation for a left turn at a traffic light one-half mile ahead. Suddenly the left front tire of an oncoming vehicle, also traveling at 55 mph, blows out. The driver panics and slams on the brakes. The car skids, hits the left rear fender of the car ahead of you and slides straight down your lane toward you. There is no way you can brake to a stop. While you may slow a little by braking, a collision here will be head-on (maximum force); you have only one option—reduce the consequences.

All you can hope for is that any driver in the lane to your right will identify the situation and move right. With 24 feet of lane width, there is ample room for three cars in an emergency. With proper steering and control and 1½ to 2 seconds to respond, you should be able to move right and stabilize 8 to 10 feet to either avoid the sliding car or strike it at an angle. Yes, you do face the risk of a sideswipe with a vehicle on your right if that driver does not move right. But a

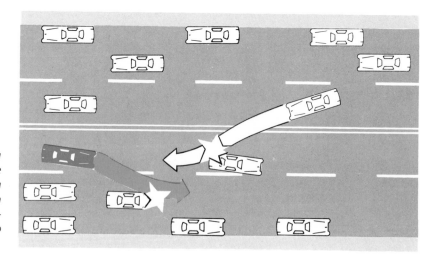

If a collision is inevitable, you may still be able to reduce the consequences. In this case, you could avoid a head-on collision (the most serious type of collision) by side-swiping the car to your right.

102

head-on collision will probably involve a much greater number of vehicles.

In assessing possible consequences of your actions, the most important thing to consider is the extent of personal injury that might result. How many people would be involved, and how seriously might they be injured?

In assessing the probability that an event may occur, the driver must consider all evidence, both for and against. But because the number of factors involved in a given situation may seem almost unlimited, mistakes will occur during decision-making. In addition, the driver will be influenced by his or her personality and reasons for driving, as well as by how much risk he or she will accept at a particular time.

Driver Decisions

With experience, all drivers develop patterns of behavior. These patterns may be good and improve one's driving, or they can lead to bad driving habits. The problem is that once people fall into certain patterns of behavior, it is difficult for them to change. For example, some people might always drive in the right-hand lane of rural, low-use highways. They may do this for years without having an accident, and

low-use highway

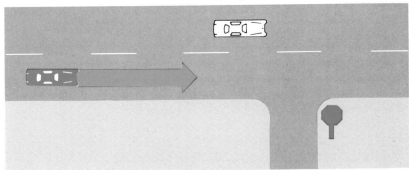

crowded highway

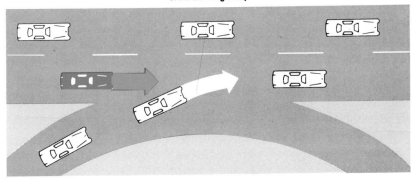

What is a good driving habit in one situation may be a bad driving habit in another, slightly different situation. For example, driving in the right-hand lane of a low-use highway may be a good idea; but driving in the same lane on a busy highway, where many vehicles are entering and exiting on the right, would not be a good idea.

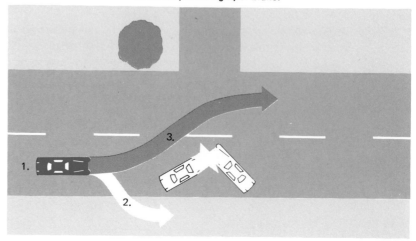

Move left, move right, or brake?

1. Will abrupt braking cause a rear-end collision? Is there time enough to warn following traffic?

2. Is there a firm shoulder onto which you can move? Will this endanger any pedestrians or cyclists?

3. Is pulling into the opposite lane safe? Will oncoming or cross-street traffic create a hazard?

Drivers must learn to choose the best option from those available in any situation. If your forward path were suddenly blocked, how would you react?

this might tend to *reinforce* (strengthen) the habit. What would happen, however, if they constantly used the right-hand lane of a very busy urban highway where there were many cars frequently entering and exiting on the right? The habit the drivers had learned on rural roads might no longer serve them well. The left-hand lane might be a more reasonable choice.

Once you have accurate information and have decided upon several options, you must determine the best from among those you have identified. This problem exists any time you make a decision: There are almost always several options to choose from. If you are unaware of the best option, your choice will obviously be less than the best.

Even a minor error in selecting an option can change a situation from manageable to unmanageable, or from safe to deadly. Under normal conditions, there is usually a wide range of speeds and positions available. Under conditions of time and space stress, however, the range of options is smaller, and the margin for error is slight.

RISK ACCEPTANCE

Accepting risks and taking chances are routine parts of everyday living. However, we rarely give them conscious thought. Most of our normal activities involve taking risks that would hardly ever lead to injury or

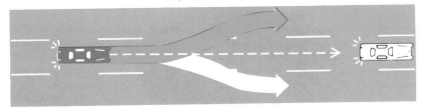

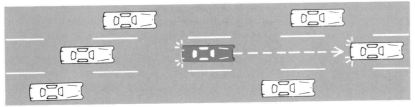

Having adequate time and space in which to maneuver will increase the number of options open to you.

other serious consequences. For this reason we accept most everyday risks. We would not, for example, stop a child from riding a tricycle. The risk involved is not serious enough, and we would want the child to get the benefits of play and exercise. On the other hand, we would not pass a car as we approached the crest of a hill, knowing that a vehicle might be rapidly approaching from the other side. The risks in this case would simply be too high.

Certain risks should be rejected by drivers. For example, if the gap in a highway traffic flow you want to enter is too small, you should wait for a larger gap. The risk involved in merging just then would be too great.

The question is, just how much risk is a driver willing to accept? In other words, what determines a driver's *level of risk acceptance?* An individual's willingness to accept risk can change for a variety of reasons. (Alcohol, drugs, and fatigue can certainly affect a driver's idea of what is and is not a reasonable risk. These factors will be discussed in Chapter 10.) We want to discuss here how a driver, under ideal conditions, judges risks.

Personal Goals and Risk Acceptance.   Driving is a social activity, and each driver's behavior must be viewed in light of its effect on others. Highways may seem impersonal, but virtually all driving decisions directly affect other people. Unfortunately, some drivers create high-risk situations. These drivers may be unaware of what they are doing, or they may simply not care that they are endangering the lives of the people around them. At any rate, we should ask why some people create high risks for both themselves and others.

What makes drivers take unnec-essary risks? Some drivers make spectacular maneuvers as atten-tion-getting devices. Others may feel that reaching their immedi-ate goal justifies any risk.

One reason why drivers may take unnecessary risks is *social pres-sure*. A driver may attempt to impress passengers, to gain their admira-tion by getting out of "close calls." Drivers who always operate vehi-cles safely stay out of high-risk situations. Therefore, they are seldom involved in spectacular maneuvers. Drivers who want attention, on the other hand, may see unsafe or high-risk driving as a means of get-ting admiration or approval.

Another reason for operating a vehicle in a high-risk manner is to reach an immediate goal. A driver who speeds may be late for work or may want to get to a party to have a good time. Another driver, faced with an emergency, may feel that getting to a destination as quickly as possible justifies *any* risk. In all these cases, the results will be the same: The drivers are more likely to commit errors, placing them-selves and others in dangerous situations.

Personality and Risk Acceptance. The way you operate a vehicle tends to reflect your basic personality and behavior patterns. People who are generally bold and aggressive tend to drive the same way. The same often holds true for those persons who are withdrawn or insecure. Unfortunately, many people sometimes use cars to express their worst emotions—to express anger, to release frustrations, or to build up their sense of self-importance.

DECISIONS AND DRIVER RESPONSE

It should be apparent that drivers can make mistakes in both gathering and processing information. In addition, they can be distracted from driving safely by both the environment around them and their own emotions. All these influences make safe driving more difficult. To overcome these influences, drivers must learn to exercise personal control.

You must learn to center your attention on those factors that will help you select the best possible speed and roadway position. To achieve this goal, you must develop three abilities:

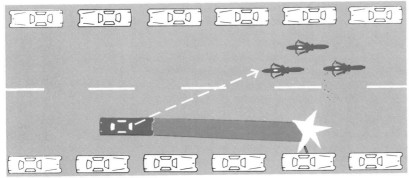

Personal control is essential to good driving. Avoid staring at distractions.

1. You should learn to adjust your position and speed so that you reduce the risk involved in any single hazard. This is called *minimizing risk.*
2. You should learn to adjust your position and speed so that you respond to the fewest potential hazards at any given time. In short, you attempt to manage the risk that you accept by *separating* hazardous elements (dealing with one hazard at a time). This is called *simplifying situations.*
3. Finally, you should realize that if you *minimize* one risk you may increase another. In addition, when you *simplify* one situation you may complicate another. You have to resolve these conflicts within the limited space of a highway. This is called *compromise.*

MINIMIZING RISK

Reducing the risk of any single roadway hazard requires adjusting your speed and road position. In the first place, this will give you *time* to respond to any event that could lead to an accident. Second, you must be able to maintain *control* of your vehicle while you are responding. Will you have enough time to respond? Will your vehicle remain under control while responding?

by braking

by communicating

You can minimize risks in several ways. The object is to keep a space cushion between your vehicle and anything that has collision potential.

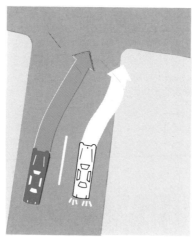

by steering and braking

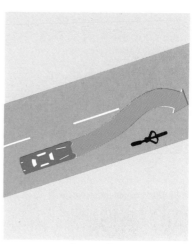

by steering

Managing Time. You have heard someone describe a traffic accident this way: "It happened so fast, I couldn't do anything about it!" The point is, there was *too little time available to respond*. Many drivers do not know that they can "give" themselves time to respond. Too often they decide on how to avoid an accident after it is too late. The value

108

of an effective visual search pattern should be immediately apparent. The sooner you realize that you may be on a collision course, the sooner you can begin to respond.

One way to increase response time is to maintain as much distance as possible between your vehicle and all hazards having *collision potential* (other vehicles, pedestrians, animals, obstacles). Keeping your distance from potential hazards is often referred to as *maintaining a space cushion*. Obviously, you should maintain a space cushion between your car and other vehicles and between your car and stationary objects, like parked cars, road signs, and walls and fences. What many drivers forget, however, is that they should also maintain a space cushion between their own vehicles and potential hazards. For example, you would want to keep your distance from a "hidden" driveway (one blocked by trees or shrubbery). You may see nothing coming out of the driveway as you approach it, but a car could easily pull out just far enough to check traffic. This could block your path. The obvious solution is to have a good space cushion before you even see such a car. If a left lane is available, move to it before you are near the driveway. If there is only one lane in your direction, keep as close to the center line as possible. In other words, do not leave a space cushion only for things you *can* see; anticipate what hazards might come up, and create space cushions for them, too.

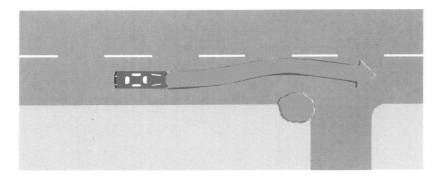

By making a slight adjustment in position, you can minimize some hazards.

COLLISION COURSE

Once you are on a collision course with another highway user, the time remaining before the crash is determined by your own and the other's speed. You may be closing on each other at any angle or from any direction. (Both of you may be contributing equally to the collision event, but determining who is at fault is of no importance at this point.) It is also possible that you may be on a collision course with a stationary object. In this case, the crash is totally a product of your own actions. Clearly, none of the responsiblity can be assigned to the object.

In either event, it is impossible for you to control the position or movement of the hazard. You can, however, control your own speed.

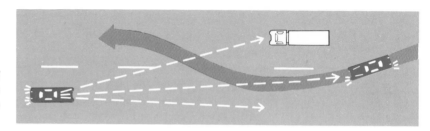

In this situation, you could "buy" time by slowing down to let the other car complete the passing maneuver.

By doing so, you can slow down the closing movement. Once again, you can exercise some control over the amount of *time* available to you.

The expert driver uses both position and speed to their best advantage, since either "buys" more time to respond. A slight adjustment of both (changing speed *and* position) is usually a better idea than a major adjustment of one or the other. For example, if a parked car pulls suddenly from the curb and into your path, a slight turn away from the vehicle and a slight reduction of speed are better than either strong braking to a stop or a sharp turn away from the vehicle. This is because abrupt and extreme maneuvers are likely to surprise other highway users. (Abrupt maneuvers may also make you lose control of your car.)

major adjustment of speed	major adjustment of position	slight adjustment of both

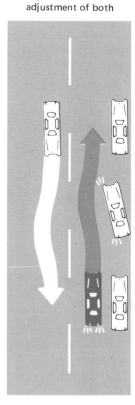

A slight adjustment of speed and position is generally a better idea than a major adjustment of one or the other.

110

MINIMIZING THROUGH CONTROL

If you have used a bicycle, you know that steering, braking, and accelerating are directly affected by the roadway surface. You have to adjust your maneuvers to whatever surface you are on. You will probably drive cars, for the most part, on dry, paved roads. As you learn to make judgments about how to control your car (by steering, braking, and accelerating) you will naturally get used to this kind of roadway surface. As a result, your judgments about speed and road position will be most dependable on dry, paved roads.

Under conditions of reduced *traction* (the friction between your vehicle's tires and the pavement surface) your judgment will be less dependable and your chances of making an error will be greater. There are many things that will contribute to reduced traction. Chief among these are underinflated tires or tires with little or no tread. Dirt, sand, gravel, wet leaves, oil, water, snow, ice, and bumps or holes in the roadway are other common causes. Under any of these circumstances, the greater your speed, the greater the risk of losing vehicle control. If these conditions are extreme, you may have difficulty maintaining speed and direction, and any abrupt change increases the likelihood that you will lose control.

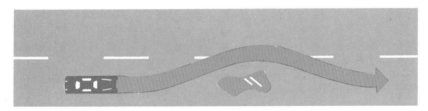

minimizing by steering

minimizing by braking

You can minimize hazards by adjusting the speed and the position of your vehicle.

If the condition affecting control covers only a small portion of the roadway, such as a patch of ice or a small pile of wet leaves, avoid it by driving around it or away from it. (This assumes, of course, that such a change in your path of travel will not cause other problems.) When the condition affecting control covers the complete roadway surface, as with rain, snow, or on a gravel road, the only alternative is to lower your speed, thus reducing the risk of losing control of the vehicle.

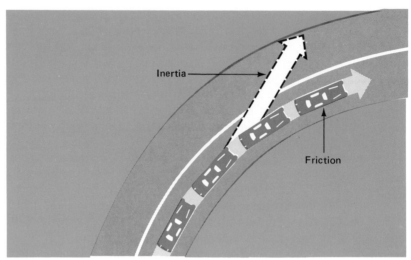

Friction acts against centrifugal force. As long as there is more friction than centrifugal force, you can make a turn.

Another factor that affects vehicle control is *centrifugal* force. An object in motion tends to move in a straight line (law of *inertia*) unless some force (centrifugal) can change its direction. You will be able to successfully complete a turn only as long as the *coefficient of friction* (the force of traction) is great enough to overcome the centrifugal force. When the centrifugal force exceeds the coefficient of friction, your car will go into a skid.

There are a limited number of ways in which you can manage these factors. As you are making a turn, you cannot change the coefficient of friction or the sharpness of the turn. You can, however, adjust your speed. In other words, one way of minimizing driving risks is by controlling the movement of your vehicle. This is called *direct minimizing,* since what you do to control your own vehicle directly reduces the risk of having an accident.

INDIRECT MINIMIZING

There are a number of ways in which you can influence the behavior of *other* highway users, and thus reduce the chances of an accident. By communicating your intentions, you can let other highway users know what you plan to do. That is, you can provide them with certain information that will help them predict what you will do. Because very few people deliberately cause accidents, the information you provide other drivers and pedestrians will help them to avoid conflicts with you. The overall result is to reduce the chances of collisions.

There are many ways in which you can communicate your intentions to other highway users. The most obvious are the use of the horn

112

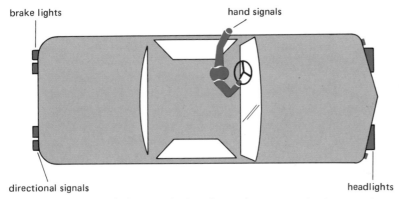

brake lights

hand signals

directional signals

headlights

You can influence the behavior of other drivers by communicating your intentions. This is one kind of indirect minimizing.

and directional signals. By using these devices, you communicate with other drivers, thus making your own intended maneuvers more predictable to them.

Obeying traffic laws is another way of making your own actions more predictable to others. The placement of your vehicle also informs others of your intentions. In addition, by doing things out of the ordinary—such as using your headlights during daylight hours—you can make your presence known to other highway users by calling attention to your vehicle. (Of course, you should not do anything that may confuse or misinform others.) These actions are not meant as a substitute for the proper selection of speed and position. They simply reduce the chance of trouble arising from the unexpected actions of others and offer protection against your own errors of judgment.

SIMPLIFYING SITUATIONS

You know that you have to give attention to those hazards that have collision potential and those that might prevent you from making a proper response. So far, we have discussed single hazards that may demand your attention. It is rather common, however, to be faced with several hazards at the same time. Such situations are called *multiple-hazard conditions*.

By positioning your car, you can sometimes help other drivers see potential hazards. In this case, the following driver might not be able to see the bicyclist early unless you adjusted your position within the lane.

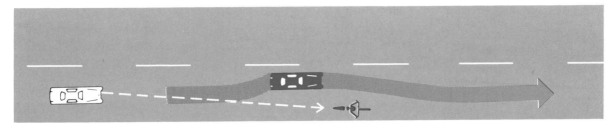

113

Some such situations are not very difficult to deal with. For example, you may be driving on a quiet residential street or country road and identify curbs or unpaved shoulders, potholes on the roadway, a few parked vehicles, and pedestrians who are well back from your intended path. Each of these items could present a hazard, but it should not be especially difficult to keep track of and to properly respond to all of them as you drive.

However, other multiple-hazard conditions may be much more difficult to deal with. In any setting, it is best to avoid having to deal with too many risks at the same time. There are several reasons for this:

1. The greater the number of high-risk items that exist at any one time, the greater the chance that some kind of difficulty will develop.

2. The greater the number of events that occur at one time, the less likely it is that there will be adequate space in which to maneuver.

3. The greater the number of events that occur at one time, the greater the stress on your decision-making abilities.

The goal of *simplifying situations* is to avoid having to cope with too many hazards at the same time. You cannot prevent hazards from arising, but you can often determine *when* you will have to deal with the hazards. If you are faced with two elements that have high-risk potential and you identify them as hazards soon enough, you can simply alter your speed. Then you can deal with each of the hazards separately, one at a time.

For example, while driving on a narrow two-lane road, you may identify a pedestrian walking on your side of the road and a truck that is approaching in the oncoming lane. By adjusting your speed, you can avoid meeting the oncoming truck and the pedestrian at the same time. If either the truck or the pedestrian did something unexpected, you would then experience less difficulty. You would have simplified the situation by separating one risk from the other.

In the same sense, you should avoid having to respond to a hazardous event when conditions could force you into a more complex situation. For example, trying to pass a bicyclist as you enter a blind curve on a narrow two-lane roadway would not be a good idea. Such an action could very well bring you into conflict with an oncoming vehicle as you moved left, over the center line, to pass the bicyclist. In effect, the bicycle represents an *active,* or moving, hazard. While the blind curve is *passive,* or not moving, it can prevent you from seeing another hazard with high collision potential.

To protect yourself, therefore, you should base decisions about where and when to do something on whether or not a serious situation *could* develop before the movement is completed. If a serious situation could develop, would you be able to manage the situation? You should realize that any time you begin a complex maneuver you are likely to be in a poor position to adjust your path of travel to avoid a

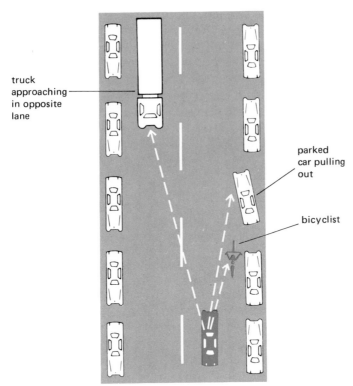

How would you separate the three potential hazards in this situation?

collision. Some rather common maneuvers that should be considered in this context are passing, lane changing, U-turns, and three-point turns. If there is any chance that the maneuver will increase the overall danger to a point where avoiding a potential collision would be difficult, you should avoid the maneuver or wait until making it would be less hazardous.

COMPROMISE

We began our discussion of decision-making with the statement of an objective—collision-free driving. Stress was directed toward perceiving those items or events that could lead to a collision (*identification*) and an analysis of how such a collision might occur (*evaluation*). This analysis included determining the *probability* that an event might become dangerous and then determining the consequences of any collision that might result. Then we discussed *minimizing* the risks associated with individual dangers. Finally, the technique of *simplifying situations* was described.

Most of our discussion has centered on the speed and position you should select in anticipation of events having high collision potential. Often, however, various kinds of information that influence the

115

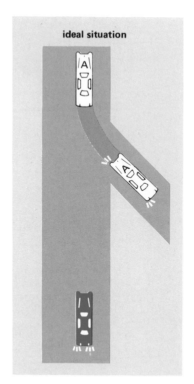

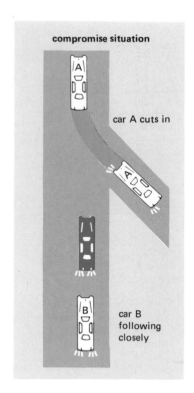

In a compromise situation, you might have to brake enough to avoid a collision with car A, but not so much that you would cause a collision with car B.

decision to minimize or simplify are in conflict. You may have several different factors influencing you at the same time. Resolving these factors into a single decision is called *compromise*.

Conflicts often occur when you are trying to maintain a sufficient time gap to the front while trying to keep trailing vehicles from closing in on your space cushion to the rear. Simply keeping up with the flow of traffic will not always resolve this conflict. By "keeping up," you may establish a safe space cushion to the rear, but you may also dangerously reduce the time gap between you and the vehicle ahead. Under such conditions, there are two points to keep in mind. First, the traffic flow rarely exceeds safe speeds by more than a few miles per hour. If you choose to drive slightly slower than the traffic flow, you will increase your forward time gap appreciably, while having a very slight effect on following traffic. (Rear-end collisions tend to occur when speed is reduced both abruptly and sharply, and not when speed is reduced gradually or slightly.) Second, your legal responsibility for whatever is in your forward path of travel is usually greater than your responsibility for what is to the rear.

You may encounter situations in which a single vehicle trails so closely that it becomes an extreme hazard. In this case, it would be best to move well to the right and to slow down gradually. This will encourage the following driver to pass. If this does not work, you may be compelled to pull off the road and allow the driver to pass.

116

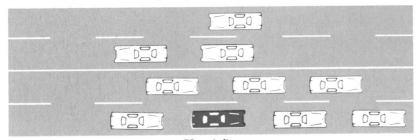

poor space management

50 mph flow

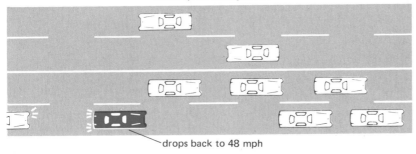

better space management

drops back to 48 mph

You can gain a better space cushion by driving slightly slower than the traffic flow.

Ordinarily, space conflicts like these should be resolved in favor of the forward path of travel. However, you should also allow space on either side of your vehicle. On your right, for example, you may have moving or stationary vehicles, pedestrians, areas of restricted vision, and curbs or unpaved shoulders. On your left, you may have elements that represent greater or lesser hazards than those on the right. You should position your vehicle laterally according to the relative dangers of these hazards. If, in your judgment, the hazards on the two sides could cause about the same difficulty, you should position yourself so that you have equal space on both sides. If the evidence indicates that the potential for trouble is greater on one side than on the other, place your car so that the greater amount of space is on the side that may give you more trouble.

So that your adjustments in position do not surprise other drivers, signal, make the adjustments early, and execute them gradually. If possible, make the adjustments *within* your lane. (Whenever you leave your own lane, you run the risk of moving toward a vehicle in your blind spot and causing an accident.) In fact, most roadway lanes are wide enough to allow you several feet of space beyond the width of your car. This means that the number of times you will need to actually leave your lane in *anticipation* of trouble is less than is generally realized.

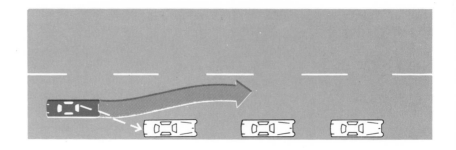

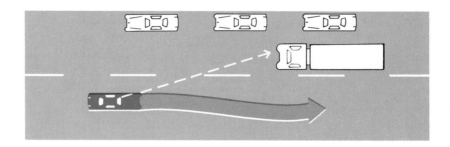

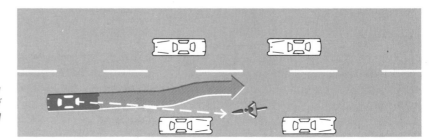

Position your vehicle so that you have the greatest amount of space possible between you and any potential hazards.

Decisions concerning choice of speed are somewhat more difficult than decisions concerning vehicle positioning. There are several more things to consider and, more importantly, the judgments and predictions involved are more difficult to make. As you may recall, your selection of speed should be influenced by your need for response time. You must also select a speed at which you can maintain control of your vehicle, during both routine maneuvers and under the stress of emergency situations. You have to ask yourself the following questions when you select a speed:

1. What speed will give you the opportunity to *gradually* adjust to meet the control requirements of ordinary stops and turns?

2. Considering the amount of space you will have available, what speed will ensure that you will have enough response time to avoid a collision if a hazardous situation begins to develop?

118

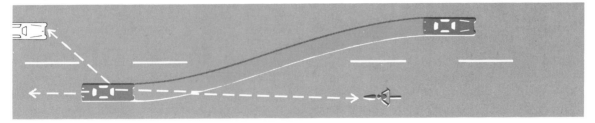

Make speed and position adjustments as early and gradually as possible.

3. What speed will allow you to maintain control in any emergency maneuver you may have to make if a collision course develops?

It is important to answer these questions accurately before selecting the best speed. Even when you understand the principles involved and have had driving experience, such decisions are difficult and errors are rather frequent. It would be easy if all you had to do was keep up with the flow of traffic and not drive faster than the speed limit. However, these should not be your only concerns. In almost any driving situation, there will be potential hazards that must also be considered.

Some situations will require very slow speeds. At other times, potential hazards may be well away from your path and traction may be good, thus safely allowing rather high speeds. A speed that is acceptable in one situation may be unacceptable in another, slightly different situation. For example, there may be enough time to respond to a pedestrian threat, even if you are traveling at 50 mph, if the pedestrian is not too close to your planned path of travel. The same pedestrian might become a much more serious hazard, however, by approaching your planned path at a sharp curve, where maintaining control might be difficult even at 20 mph. The opposite may also occur. A pedestrian very close to the road may cause you to select a low speed, even though the road you are on could otherwise be safely traveled at 50 mph. With all of these variables, two conclusions can be drawn:

1. If several hazards with collision potential occur at approximately the same point in your planned path of travel, the one that would require the quickest response is the one on which you should base your selection of speed.

2. The lowest speed needed to allow both vehicle control and adequate response time is the speed that you should select.

This chapter has presented a structure for making decisions. In broad terms, it has specified the kinds of information that a driver needs. We have also discussed how information can be gathered, categorized, and evaluated for the best choice of speed and position. With continuous practice, this process should help you achieve a high level of driving performance.

To Think About

1. Compare the importance of decision-making ability and physical ability in driving.
2. Describe some of the mistakes drivers make in processing information.
3. Discuss the technique of categorizing information. How can these techniques improve driving performance?
4. What is the major source of driving errors? Why?
5. How can a driver plan for the unexpected?
6. Describe how drivers judge the probability and consequences of collisions.
7. What factors can cause drivers to take unreasonable risks?
8. How can a driver minimize risks through adjustments of vehicle speed and position?
9. Why is it sometimes necessary to simplify situations? Give examples.
10. How should drivers compromise when making decisions about speed and position? Give examples.

To Do

1. While riding in your family's or a friend's car, try to predict the actions of other highway users. Make notes of what you see and compare your predictions with what other highway users actually do. How often were your predictions correct?
2. Photograph or sketch three areas in your community in which trees, buildings, or curves would block drivers' views. Show your sketches to five drivers and ask them how they would adjust their speed or position to compensate for the limited visibility.
3. Observe traffic in each of the three areas mentioned in question 2. How many of the drivers that you observe adjust their speed or position to compensate for the limited visibility?
4. How would you improve each of the three areas if you were able to redesign the traffic environment? Sketch the areas again, adding your improvements.

Driving Laws 5

After reading this chapter, you should be able to:

1. Describe how a person can get a driver's license and how the license can be taken away.
2. Explain the responsiblities of a driver who is involved in a serious accident.
3. Identify and explain the rules of the road.
4. Discuss the differences between fixed and flexible speed limits.
5. Identify various kinds of signs, signals, and markings.

The highway transportation system is used by many people. The mental and physical conditions of these people vary greatly. So do their reasons for using the highway system. If each individual functioned within the system according to personal desires, there would be chaos. It is easy to see that for the system to work efficiently and safely, certain rules have to be established and obeyed.

Rules and regulations do limit our behavior. There are times when all of us may find traffic laws inconvenient. This is not surprising. We would probably have this same reaction to any rules that we have to obey. In spite of this occasional feeling, we know that we must have rules to maintain order.

National Standards

With a few exceptions, making and enforcing motor vehicle and traffic laws is the responsibility of state governments. To assure some consistency in these laws, most states follow suggestions made in the *Uniform Vehicle Code*. The standards in this code have been developed by the *National Committee on Uniform Traffic Laws and Ordinances*. The *Uniform Vehicle Code* sets forth standards for rules of the road, driver licensing, vehicle registration, financial responsibility, and motor vehicle equipment. Standards for roadway signs, signals, and markings are set down in the *Manual on Uniform Traffic Control Devices for Streets and Highways*. This manual is approved as the national standard for all public highways by the United States Department of Transportation.

Administrative Laws

Each state has *administrative laws*, which regulate the registration and financial responsibility of drivers and the equipment and maintenance of motor vehicles. Besides providing revenue for the states, these laws help enforcement officials keep track of ownership, licensing, and violations.

DRIVER'S LICENSE

Freedom to travel is a right of all citizens of this country. The right to obtain a driver's license, however, is subject to certain rules and regulations made by state motor vehicle bureaus. Before you can get a driver's license, you must pass several tests. You will be tested to see that you meet certain standards of vision, hearing, and general physical condition. You will also be tested on your knowledge of the basic

Administrative laws are carried out at the state level.

If you are arrested and suspected of driving under the influence of alcohol, you must submit to a chemical test or face suspension of your driver's license.

rules of the road. Finally, you will take a driving test that measures how well you perform basic driving maneuvers. If you pass each of these tests, you qualify for an operator's license.

Once you begin to drive, you automatically accept certain responsibilities. For example, all states now have implied consent laws. These laws are in effect whenever a person operates a motor vehicle upon a highway. An implied consent law means that every driver consents to take a chemical test for the presence of alcohol if arrested for a traffic offense and the arresting officer has reasonable grounds to suspect the person driving is under the influence of alcohol. If the driver refuses to take the test, the state department of motor vehicles or the agency responsible for issuing drivers' licenses has the right to take away the individual's license to drive for a period of three to six months.

THE POINT SYSTEM

Since the right to a license requires that drivers meet certain standards, each state has rules and procedures for *revoking* (permanently withdrawing) or *suspending* (temporarily withdrawing) an operator's license. Some violations are considered to be so serious that conviction means *automatic revocation*. Driving while intoxicated, leaving the scene of a personal-injury accident, or using a motor vehicle in the act of a felony are examples of such serious offenses.

123

Most states use a *point system* to determine when to revoke or suspend a driver's license. In such a system, specific violations are assigned a certain number of points, depending on their seriousness. When a driver is found guilty of violating a law, the appropriate number of points is placed on file with the state motor vehicle bureau. Drivers who accumulate enough points in a given period of time then have their licenses suspended or revoked.

Drivers who receive more than four to five points within a set period of time (usually two or three years) may receive a warning letter. Those who receive six or seven points may be called in for an interview at the motor vehicle bureau. For drivers who accumulate eight to eleven points, a hearing might be held, and this could lead to suspension. Finally, if violations continue after a period of suspension is over, or if a driver has twelve or more points, a hearing probably will be held, and the driver's license will be revoked.

As you might expect, these rules vary from one state to another. The number of points assigned to each violation may be more or less. The number of points at which a driver is called in for a hearing may also be different. In any event, the system is designed to persuade people to drive more safely. The right to drive can be taken away from those who do not obey the law.

NATIONAL DRIVER REGISTER SERVICE

In 1960, Congress passed a law which established a special office in the U.S. Bureau of Public Roads (later part of the Department of Transportation). The purpose of this office is to maintain a data bank containing the names of drivers whose licenses have been suspended or revoked. This information is supplied to the office on a voluntary basis by most states. In turn, the motor vehicle department of any state can obtain information from this office about the driving record of a person who applies for a license. States can find out, for example, if an applicant has been denied a license in another state because of violations or for health reasons.

CERTIFICATE OF TITLE

A *certificate of title* is an official document issued by almost every state when a vehicle is purchased. It identifies the car by make, style, serial and engine numbers, and owner. Before the vehicle can be sold, the person selling the vehicle must prove ownership. This certificate is separate from the driver's license, since it is possible to own or to buy a car without having a license to drive it.

VEHICLE REGISTRATION AND LICENSE PLATES

Motor vehicle registration and the issuing of license plates is also handled by the states. An individual must own a vehicle before he or she can register it. When a vehicle is registered, a certificate of regis-

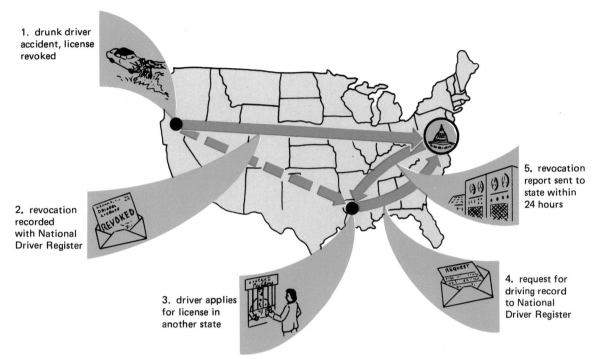

1. drunk driver accident, license revoked

2. revocation recorded with National Driver Register

3. driver applies for license in another state

4. request for driving record to National Driver Register

5. revocation report sent to state within 24 hours

States can check on driving records through the National Driver Register, which provides information about drivers whose licenses have been suspended or revoked.

License plates provide a means of identification of vehicles. Some police departments have computer systems which allow them to check almost immediately on stolen and abandoned vehicles.

125

tration is issued to the owner. This certificate identifies both the car and owner. It must be carried in the vehicle any time the vehicle is in use and can serve as immediate proof of ownership. This allows a driver to keep the title in a safe place and to avoid losing it.

At the time a vehicle is registered, license plates or tags are issued. They are important because they allow the police to easily identify a given vehicle. A number of police departments now have computer systems that allow them to immediately check on stolen or abandoned vehicles.

FINANCIAL RESPONSIBILITY

If you are ever involved in an accident that results in personal injury or death, or damage to someone else's car or property, a court could declare you to be at fault, or *liable*. You would then be required to pay the person who brought suit against you. The sum of money would be determined by a court. *Liability insurance* would provide payment of the suit up to the limit of the policy. Liability insurance pays you no money. It protects you, however, by paying the legal claims others have against you.

Most states have some form of *compulsory insurance* (insurance that drivers *must* have). In many states, drivers must present proof that they have liability insurance. Where such laws exist, drivers are required to carry a minimum amount of liability insurance before they can have a vehicle registered. Such laws are usually referred to as *financial responsibility laws*. Their purpose is to make sure that claims from accidents will be paid.

NO-FAULT INSURANCE

In essence, *no-fault insurance* is a system in which your *own* insurance company pays your losses, up to a certain amount. This eliminates the need for determining who is at fault. Some new no-fault plans pay only for losses from personal injury. (*Comprehensive* and *collision insurance* are similar to no-fault insurance because your own company pays you regardless of fault.)

RESPONSIBILITIES WHEN INVOLVED IN AN ACCIDENT

If you are in an accident, you have certain legal obligations. Failing to meet these obligations could cause you serious trouble. If you are involved in an accident, you should do the following as quickly as possible:

1. Stop immediately, as close to the scene as possible without increasing the danger of greater damage.
2. Give assistance and obtain medical aid. Call an ambulance, if needed.

126

Provide the police with the necessary information about any accident.

3. Call the police if an injury or death occurs.

4. Exchange names, addresses, and vehicle identification information with the other people involved. This is all you need to talk about. Do *not* get into discussions about who is at fault.

5. Obtain the names and addresses of witnesses.

6. Remain at the scene of the accident until your help is no longer needed.

7. Make accident reports promptly to the police and the department of motor vehicles, as required. Also inform your insurance company.

Extreme caution should be used in assisting anyone injured. Unskilled handling, particularly when there are broken bones, may increase the seriousness of the injury and may even cause death. For example, if a person with a spinal injury is moved, that person could be permanently paralyzed or die. *It may be best to avoid moving an injured person unless you are trained to do so or unless you have no choice.* (For example, if there were a fire following an accident, you might have to move the injured.) If you do not know how to move a victim properly, simply stop any bleeding as well as you can and keep the victim comfortable.

The legal consequences of a traffic accident can be serious. If you are in violation of a traffic law at the time an accident occurs, you may be penalized in several ways. Such penalty might include suspension or revocation of your license, or even a jail sentence.

There can be other serious results. You may be sued for damages arising out of others' injuries or property damage. Damages awarded by courts in personal injury or death cases may amount to hundreds of thousands of dollars. These amounts are sometimes much greater than the insurance coverage carried by either party. Some people have lost their cars, homes, and other possessions. Others have had part of their wages taken for years.

ARRIVING AT THE SCENE OF AN ACCIDENT

If you come upon an accident on the highway, you must use good judgment. If the police have already taken charge, do not stop unless you are asked. If your help is not needed, it is best to keep the area clear. You do not want to get in the way of the police, ambulances, and other emergency vehicles. If you are qualified to give assistance and your help is needed, park your car well out of the way of traffic and return to the scene of the accident.

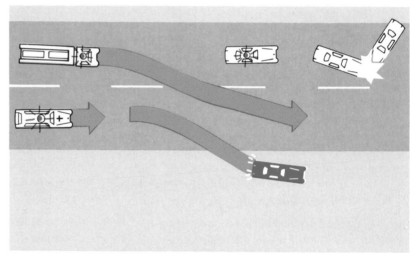

If you must stop near the scene of an accident, do not stop where you would block emergency vehicles. Stop well away from the roadway.

MOTOR VEHICLE INSPECTION

Vehicle failure can cause accidents. Tires that blow out, brakes that fail, and even windshield wipers that do not work can lead to serious accidents. Because of this, a number of states have passed vehicle inspection laws. These laws attempt to make sure that vehicles meet minimum safety standards. Some states require inspections at set intervals of time—like once a year. In other states, the inspections are performed by police spot-checking cars on the road.

Where laws require inspection at regular intervals, states may choose to check vehicles at either state inspection centers or at private garages approved by the state. These inspections usually include tests of the brakes, lights, horn, directional signals, tires, and emission-con-

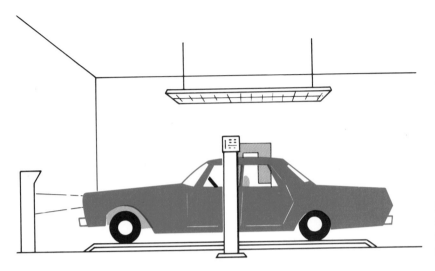

*States require periodic inspec-
tions of all motor vehicles. Some
states check vehicles at state-run
facilities.*

trol (antipollution) devices. If any of these parts are not working properly, the owner must have them repaired in a given period of time.
When the repairs are complete, the owner must present proof of the
repair before the vehicle passes inspection.

Traffic Laws

Administrative laws are concerned with the organization of the
highway transportation system and a driver's membership in that system. *Traffic laws* provide guidelines for drivers' behavior when they
use the system. For example, all drivers are expected to stop at red
lights or to turn on their headlights at night.

Traffic laws take some of the guesswork out of driving. They help
you predict how other drivers will behave. You can "reasonably" expect, for example, that drivers waiting on a cross street will not suddenly decide to drive past a red light and into your path. In the same
way, other drivers can "reasonably" expect that you will stay within
the speed limit, signal when you change lanes, or obey *stop* signs. Obviously, traffic laws are meant to encourage cooperation among
drivers.

Unfortunately, while it is true that you can "reasonably" expect
other drivers to obey the law most of the time, you cannot absolutely
depend on them. They may ignore or not know about the guidelines
for driving behavior. Human beings drive automobiles, and human
beings make mistakes. You must remain alert. Other highway users
may intentionally or unintentionally fail to follow the guidelines.

Everyone would like an accident-free highway system. To reach this
goal, however, you must do more than simply obey the law. You must
also *compensate* (make up) for the faults of other drivers.

129

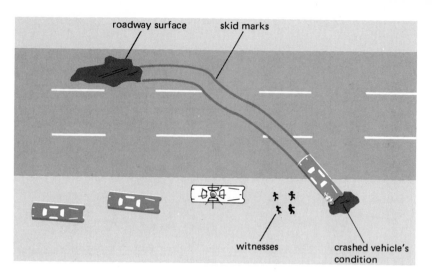

roadway surface   skid marks

witnesses

crashed vehicle's condition

When the police investigate an accident, they interview witnesses and gather evidence from the scene.

LAST CLEAR CHANCE

The police who investigate an accident draw conclusions from all available evidence. This evidence includes the final position and direction of travel of the vehicles involved. The conditions of the drivers, road, and vehicles are also considered as evidence. In addition, the police measure skid marks and ask testimony of witnesses. Since some law has usually been broken when an accident occurs, one or more of the drivers involved can expect to receive a *citation* (ticket) for a violation.

It is the responsibility of *all* drivers to contribute to the safe and efficient operation of the highway transportation system. Fault may be placed on a driver who has the *last clear chance* to avoid an accident and fails to do so. Even though the actions of another highway user may be illegal, you may be held liable for damages if you do nothing to avoid a collision.

It may seem unfair that you could be found at fault for an accident when you were driving within the law and someone else was not. However, the results of an accident can be so serious that it is to the benefit of all drivers to prevent accidents at all times.

RULES OF THE ROAD

There are several *rules of the road* taken from the *Uniform Vehicle Code* and the *Model Traffic Ordinance* that apply to all parts of the country. When obeyed by all, they lead to a safer and more orderly flow of traffic:

1. Drive to the right of the center of the road except to pass vehicles moving in the same direction.
2. Pass to the right of vehicles coming toward you.

130

3. Pass to the left of vehicles going in the same direction.

4. Allow overtaking vehicles to pass.

5. If driving slowly, keep to the right-hand lane when more than one lane is available.

6. Signal your intention to reduce speed, stop, turn, change lanes, or pass.

7. Always drive at a speed that is reasonable for existing conditions.

Directions from a traffic officer or sign, signal, or roadway marking take precedence over these rules. In all other cases, however, use these rules as a guide.

Follow directions from police or traffic officers, even when they contradict existing traffic signs or roadway markings.

RIGHT OF WAY

When the paths of highway users cross there is a conflict. Who should proceed and who should wait? In other words, who has the *right of way?*

In general, right-of-way rules require one person to *yield*—that is, let another proceed first. It is extremely important that drivers know and obey the right-of-way laws in their states and in the states in which they drive. Not knowing or disobeying these laws can lead to serious accidents. For example, in some urban areas, pedestrians in crosswalks *always* have the right of way. Drivers unaware of this would present a great hazard to themselves and pedestrians. Another, more common, right-of-way rule states that highway users must yield to emergency vehicles. The purpose of this rule is obvious: to clear the way so that ambulances, police cars, and fire trucks can get to where they have to go as quickly as possible. When you see and hear flashing lights and sirens, move as far to the right as possible to clear the way. Drivers of emergency vehicles must also drive in a reasonable manner. (Serious accidents have been caused by emergency vehicles speeding or passing through red lights.) They do, however, need your cooperation.

To help states develop right-of-way laws, the *Uniform Vehicle Code* suggests several basic rules:

1. If two vehicles are approaching or entering an uncontrolled (unmarked) intersection at the same time, the driver on the left shall yield the right-of-way to the driver on his or her right.

2. Drivers shall yield the right-of-way to pedestrians crossing legally at intersections or at marked crosswalks between intersections.

3. A driver intending to turn left shall yield the right-of-way to vehicles approaching from the opposite direction if they are so close that they present an immediate hazard.

1. emergency vehicle— sounding siren or flashing lights

2. vehicle already within intersection

3. vehicle to the right

4. pedestrians

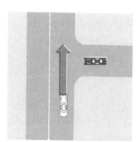
5. street traffic

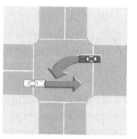
6. before turning

You must yield the right of way in all of these situations.

132

4. A vehicle coming out of a driveway or alley shall yield the right-of-way to vehicles on the street and to pedestrians on the sidewalk.

5. When moving laterally into a lane being used by other drivers, a driver must yield to any vehicle that is passing or is so close that it presents a hazard.

It is important for you to understand and obey these rules. However, *having the right of way does not relieve you of the responsibility to do all you can to avoid an accident.*

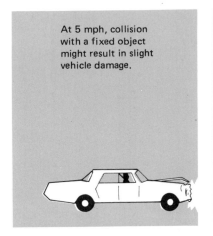

At 5 mph, collision with a fixed object might result in slight vehicle damage.

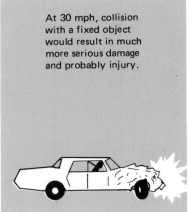

At 30 mph, collision with a fixed object would result in much more serious damage and probably injury.

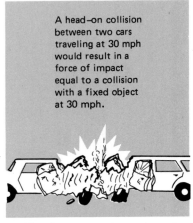

A head—on collision between two cars traveling at 30 mph would result in a force of impact equal to a collision with a fixed object at 30 mph.

The faster a car is moving when it hits something, the greater the force of impact.

SPEED CONTROL

Some experts think that excessive speed is the greatest single cause of accidents. Others disagree. In either case, there are some facts about speed that cannot be disputed:

1. The greater the speed, the less time the driver has to identify hazards and take action.

2. The greater the speed, the longer the stopping distance.

3. The greater the speed, the greater the chance of skidding or rolling over on a turn.

4. The greater the speed, the greater the danger in the event of a blowout.

5. The greater the speed, the greater the force of impact in a collision.

6. The greater the speed, the greater the personal injury and property damage in a collision.

We cannot change the forces of nature, reduce stopping distances, or eliminate curves from highways. Nor can we remove other vehicles and drivers from the roads. We can, however, select and control our own speed to suit the driving conditions we face.

Selecting and controlling speed can reduce the chances of an accident and provide more efficient traffic movement.

SPEED LIMITS

Some states have established *fixed* (absolute) speed limits to guide you in your speed selection. Other states have taken a different approach and established *flexible* limits. Unfortunately, neither type of speed limit sign can be easily adjusted to changes in roadway, traffic, or weather conditions. All speed limit signs, therefore, should be interpreted as a *maximum* limit for *ideal* conditions.

Fixed Speed Limits.   Under this type of speed limit, the maximum or "absolute" speed in miles per hour (mph) is set. Drivers are not permitted to exceed the limit under any conditions. A driver who does exceed it can be arrested and penalized. Drivers who do not exceed the speed limit may not be arrested for speeding, but they may be arrested for reckless driving if their actions warrant it. Such drivers could also be legally penalized for driving at a speed that is unreasonable or imprudent under existing conditions.

States that favor and enact fixed speed limits usually do so for two reasons:

1. The limits can be set by experts to best fit specific roadways and traffic conditions. For example, a speed limit of 25 to 30 mph in a residential area or 55 mph on the open road might be normal limits for different sections of one road.

2. Enforcement of fixed limits is easier.

Flexible Speed Limits.   Flexible speed limits, known as *prima facie* speed limits, are based on the idea that no one fixed speed limit is correct for a particular place at all times and under all conditions. However, areas under *prima facie* limits have speed limit signs just as do

134

areas with fixed limits. This speed limit represents the speed that is recommended for *ideal* conditions. A reasonable maximum speed depends on roadway type and condition, traffic, weather, light, and other factors. Drivers charged with speeding under this type of speed law can claim that their speed, even if it was over the posted limit, was not too fast for existing conditions. The court must then decide whether or not the driver is right.

Drivers can be arrested for speeding even when they are driving slower than the posted limit. In this case, an officer must convince the court that the car was being driven too fast for existing conditions. For example, a road may have been icy or the traffic may have been very heavy.

Those who favor flexible speed limits believe that there are too many different roadway, weather, light, and other conditions for fixed limits to be appropriate. They say that because weather, light, and traffic change frequently, speed limits should change with them.

THE BASIC SPEED RULE
It is not really necessary, in travel from one state to another, to know if the posted speed limit is fixed or flexible. Nearly all states incorporate into their traffic laws some version of the *basic speed rule*. This rule is stated as follows: "Always drive at a speed that is reasonable and proper for existing conditions." Regardless of the posted limit, you must select a speed that is safe. In the final analysis, the proper speed at any given time is determined more by the particular situation than by the posted limit—fixed or flexible.

DAY AND NIGHT SPEED LIMITS
Because darkness places a limitation on visibility, some states post separate speed limits for daytime and nighttime driving. Lower speeds at night give drivers more time to search for visual cues. These limits also give drivers more time to make steering corrections and to identify hazards.

States may post different speed limits for day- and nighttime driving.

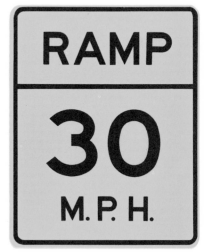

SPEED
LIMIT
50
MINIMUM
30

Minimum-speed-limit signs are usually used on high-speed roadways to ensure that all vehicles are traveling at approximately the same speed.

MINIMUM SPEED

In addition to posted maximum speed limits, minimum speed limits are posted on some heavily traveled state and local highways and all interstate roadways. One purpose of the minimum speed limit is to keep the flow of traffic moving along. Another purpose is to reduce the chance of collisions between vehicles traveling at greatly different speeds. Again, these signs are posted for ideal conditions and should be interpreted in light of the basic speed rule. When roadway, traffic, or weather conditions are poor, you can reasonably drive more slowly than the minimum limit posted.

SPEED ZONING

It is obviously impossible to set one limit for all highways within a state. A system called *speed zoning* is used to determine reasonable speed limits. On-the-spot surveys are made by traffic engineers, who determine what speed is proper for a stretch of road under normal conditions. Signs are then posted to inform drivers of the speed limit in effect in each zone. Whole sections of highway may be zoned at one speed. Lower speed limits may be applied to curves, intersections, school zones, business and residential districts, or other special areas.

EXIT
25
M.P.H.

RAMP
30
M.P.H.

Advisory speed-limit signs are often used on exit and entrance areas to advise drivers of the maximum recommended speed on a ramp.

Signs, Signals, and Roadway Markings _____

As you already know, the usefulness of any decision is based upon the quantity and quality of the information available. To assist drivers in making decisions, authorities provide drivers with many kinds of information. Much of this information is provided in the form of signs, signals, and markings. These are designed to alert drivers to any rules or laws that are in effect. They may also warn drivers of hazards ahead.

Signs, signals, and markings are important because they bring crucial information to your attention. They can help you avoid making errors. You have already been introduced to certain signs, signals, and markings in Chapters 2 and 3. Now you will read about them in greater detail.

One of the first things you should know is that traffic signs have standard shapes and colors. These shapes and colors have meanings. If you are aware of these meanings, you can begin to "read" a sign before you get close enough to actually see the words and symbols on it. Because the color and the shape of a sign give you clues about its meaning, a brief glance should be enough to let you know if the sign is of any value to you. Study the pictures of signs, signals, and markings on the following pages. Once you are familiar with them, you will be better able to sort out what information is and is not important to you as you drive.

REGULATORY SIGNS

Regulatory signs are generally rectangular in shape. (Exceptions are *stop* and *yield* signs and railroad crossbucks.) Regulatory signs either prohibit or require specific acts. If you fail to follow the directions on such signs, you are breaking the law.

Stop Sign.   This sign is always red and octagonal (eight-sided). It is found at intersections and gives right of way. A *stop* sign requires that you come to a *full* stop.

Stop signs are usually placed so that drivers can see them well in advance. By slowing down before you reach a *stop* sign, you alert cross traffic and following vehicles of your intention to stop. This action serves two purposes. First, it gives drivers behind you a chance to see your change in speed; they can then respond gradually. Second, it informs traffic on the cross street that you intend to obey the *stop* sign. This allows cross-street drivers to direct their attention to any other problems they may be facing.

Your stop should be made before any portion of your car enters the intersection (or crosswalk, if there is one). After your vehicle has come to a full stop, you may proceed when it is safe to do so. At an intersection where all streets are controlled by *stop* signs, the first vehicle at the intersection should be given the right of way. Other drivers should then take their turns in order.

Yield Sign.   The *yield* sign is triangular and usually red. (It has been recommended that all *yield* signs be red after January 1, 1975. However, yellow *yield* signs will still be acceptable.) *Yield* signs require you to give the right of way to traffic that is close enough to be a hazard.

Stop *signs are always red and octagonal. Smaller signs beneath the* stop *sign tell you if there are* stop *signs on the cross streets.*

Some older yield *signs are yellow. New standards, however, call for the red sign illustrated here.*

Railroad crossbucks are placed at railroad crossings. Sometimes, smaller signs beneath the crossbucks tell how many tracks are on the crossing. In addition, flashing red lights and mechanical gates provide drivers with further warnings.

You may find these signs on streets you are crossing or on streets into which you are merging. In either case, you must yield the right of way. Unlike the *stop* sign, the *yield* sign does not require a full stop. Simply slowing down may give you time enough to safely complete your move. You should not, however, interrupt the flow of the traffic lanes you are crossing or entering. If the traffic is heavy, come to a full stop and wait until you can make your move without interrupting the traffic flow.

Railroad Crossbuck. Railroad crossings have their own sign. It is a large, white, X-shaped sign called a *crossbuck*. This sign is placed at the crossing itself. A round railroad *warning* sign is placed several hundred feet in advance of the crossing. Frequently, a small rectangular sign just below a crossbuck will tell you of the number of tracks at the crossing.

Railroad crossings that are heavily traveled may have a pair of red lights mounted with the crossbuck. These lights flash when a train is approaching. In addition to this, a gate or barrier may drop across the traffic lane.

Railroad warning signs are yellow and circular. They are placed several hundred feet ahead of railroad crossings. In addition, pavement markings may warn drivers of the crossing.

Approach railroad crossings with extreme caution, even if the lights are not flashing and the gates are not down. (The lights and gate could be broken.) If there are no flashing lights or gates at a railroad crossing, be even more careful. Accidents at railroad crossings are extremely serious because of the size and speed of trains.

NO U TURN

NO RIGHT TURN

NO BICYCLES

KEEP RIGHT

NO PARKING BUS STOP

TOW-AWAY ZONE

DO NOT ENTER

WRONG WAY

SPEED LIMIT 50 MINIMUM 30

NIGHT 45

← ONE WAY

2° HR PARKING

8:30 AM TO 5:30 PM

CROSS ONLY AT CROSS WALKS

NO PEDESTRIAN CROSSING

TRUCKS USE RIGHT LANE

Other Regulatory Signs. There are many other kinds of regulatory signs. These include speed-limit signs, parking signs, *one-way* signs, *do-not-enter* signs, and warnings against littering, creating unnecessary noise, or making illegal driving maneuvers. You will find, if you travel from one city or state to another, that the size and color of these

Other regulatory signs may vary slightly from one state or city to another. You should therefore watch carefully for them.

unspecified danger

road
intersection

uneven
road

first aid
station

telephone

mechanical
help

International traffic signs make use of pictures and symbols instead of words.

A

B .

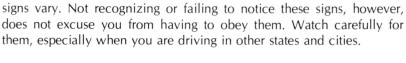

The school advance-warning sign (A) and the school-crossing sign (B) are yellow, as are other warning signs, but they have a different shape.

signs vary. Not recognizing or failing to notice these signs, however, does not excuse you from having to obey them. Watch carefully for them, especially when you are driving in other states and cities.

INTERNATIONAL TRAFFIC SIGNS

A type of sign that you may see more of in the future is the *international traffic sign,* which makes use of pictures and symbols instead of words. The advantage of these signs is obvious. If an international standard were used, you could "read" a traffic sign in any country.

WARNING SIGNS

A *warning sign* is either circular or diamond-shaped and is yellow in color. It informs you that you are approaching something on or near the roadway that requires particular attention. The words or symbols on these signs tell you what to expect. This gives you the opportunity to adjust your speed and position.

Among the dangers that these signs warn of are hills, curves, school or railroad crossings, intersections, merging traffic, and bad road surfaces.

140

Warning signs are diamond-shaped or round and yellow. Their purpose is to alert drivers to possible hazards.

Construction and *maintenance signs* usually have the same shape as warning signs, but are orange instead of yellow. They are used to warn drivers that road crews are repairing roads, adding to roads, or building new roads.

BLASTING
ZONE
1000 FT

ROAD
CONSTRUCTION
1500 FT

DETOUR

END
CONSTRUCTION

Construction and maintenance signs are orange. They warn drivers of temporary hazards created by working crews who are building or repairing roads.

INTERSTATE
55

36 WEST
Clear Lake Ave

36 EAST
Decatur

Guide signs give drivers directions and mileage.

THRU
TRAFFIC

NEXT EXIT
9 MILES

US 38   5
Greenville 40
St Louis   125

142

Route markers are used to inform drivers of what road they are on.

INFORMATION SIGNS

Guide and service signs all have symbols that can be easily recognized and understood. *Guide signs* include route markers and destination signs showing directions and mileage. In addition, such signs may identify points of interest or recreation. *Service signs* are those signs that inform you about the availability of travel and tourist services such as food, gas, and rest areas.

Some guide signs now post distances in metric measure. (There are about 1.6 kilometers in 1 mile.)

FOOD - PHONE
GAS - LODGING
HOSPITAL
CAMPING
SECOND RIGHT

Service signs inform drivers of recreation and travel facilities near the roadway.

CAMPING

TRAIL

CAMPING

HOSPITAL

BIKE ROUTE

ROCKY MOUNTAIN
← NAT'L PARK
6 MILES

TRAFFIC CONTROL SIGNALS

Commonly known as "traffic lights," traffic signals are used to control and increase the efficiency of traffic flow within the highway transportation system. As roadways become more complex and traffic volume increases, traffic signals become more important to the safety and efficiency of the system. To benefit from the information provided by these devices, drivers must be familiar with their meaning.

144

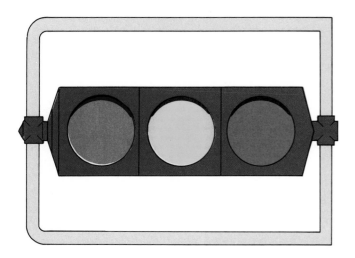

Red, Yellow, and Green Traffic Lights. The most common traffic signal is the three-lens red, yellow, and green light frequently found at intersections. These lights may be mounted on posts positioned on the corners of the intersection or suspended over the roadway.

When the *red* lens (most often located at the top) is on, drivers must stop and may not enter the intersection. There may be a line indicating where to stop, and it should be used as a reference. Otherwise, stop before entering the intersection or crosswalk.

The *yellow* lens (in the center) means that drivers should proceed with caution or stop, if they can do so. When approaching a traffic signal, you must consider the distance you need to stop. You must also

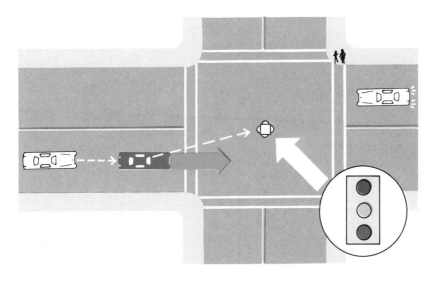

If you wait until the last second to make a "go" or "no-go" decision, you may confuse others who are behind you or waiting at the intersection.

consider the traffic in front of and behind you. Will you be able to brake to a stop without entering the intersection? If you stop, will a following driver collide with you? Will you be able to accelerate to get through the intersection? In other words, are you at the "go" (*continue*) or the "no-go" (*stop*) position? Some drivers wait until after the yellow light comes on before making a "go" or "no-go" decision. They often, then, find themselves entering the intersection on a red light, still trying to make up their minds.

When the *green* lens (usually at the bottom) is on, you may go through the intersection if it is clear. If you are waiting at or approaching an intersection when the light turns green, yield to any cross traffic or pedestrians already in the intersection.

As you approach a green light, note how long it has been on. This is particularly important if the green light has been on for some time. (Such lights are often called "stale" green lights.) There is a good chance the light will soon turn yellow.

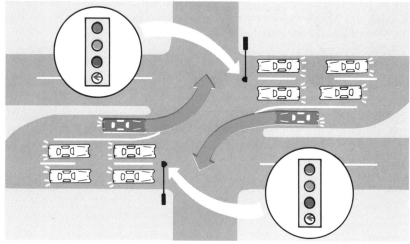

Arrows in traffic signals allow or prohibit movement only in the direction in which they point.

Red, Green, and Yellow Arrows.   In addition to red, yellow, and green lights, a traffic signal may have red, yellow, and green arrows. While the round green lens allows the driver to proceed in any direction, a green arrow permits movement only in the direction indicated. A yellow arrow means that movement in that direction is about to be prohibited. A red arrow is sometimes used in situations where there are turning lanes. A red arrow has the same meaning as a red light, except that it prohibits movement only in the direction of the arrow. (It indicates that traffic in a turning lane, for example, may not turn.)

146

Flashing Red Lights. A flashing red light has the same meaning as a *stop* sign and must be obeyed the same way. It appears at hazardous intersections where there is not enough cross-street traffic to justify a traffic light.

Flashing Yellow Lights. A flashing yellow light indicates a potential hazard and means that you should proceed with caution. You should approach one at a slower speed. Since the flashing yellow light may be used in a variety of locations—such as intersections, fire houses, or school zones—you must determine the purpose of the light before choosing a proper response.

 You must never drive in a lane under a red X signal.

  You are permitted to drive in a lane under a green arrow or green X signal.

 A steady yellow X indicates the driver should safely vacate this lane because it soon will be controlled by a red X.

 A flashing yellow X indicates the lane is to be used, with caution, for left turn movements only.

Flashing red lights have the same meaning as stop *signs. A flashing yellow light means you may proceed with caution.*

Lane-control lights can be used to reverse the flow of traffic in a lane.

Special Lane-Control Lights. There are sometimes changes in the direction of traffic flow. For example, some lanes on a multiple-lane street or highway may be used to carry traffic in one direction in the morning and in the opposite direction in the evening. The purpose might be to aid the flow of commuter traffic in and out of a city. The danger is obvious: a driver who did not know about the lane changes could cause a head-on collision. To help avoid this hazard, signal lights are sometimes suspended over the lanes affected. If the signal is a green arrow, the lane is open to traffic facing the signal. If the signal is a yellow X, traffic flow in the direction you are traveling is about to end. If the yellow X is flashing, the lane is for use of left-turning vehicles only. A red X in such a situation means that the lane is closed to those vehicles facing the signal.

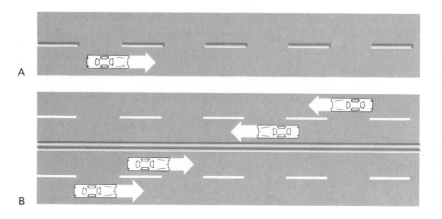

A

B

White lines separate traffic lanes moving in the same direction. Yellow lines separate traffic lanes moving in opposite directions. If you are driving on a two-lane (one in each direction) undivided highway, the lines separating traffic will be yellow (A). However, if the two lanes were both for traffic traveling in the same direction, the lane lines will be white (B).

A new warning sign that differs from the traditional diamond shape is the no-passing-zone sign, which is pennant-shaped.

PAVEMENT MARKINGS

Markings on the pavement are used either alone or along with signs and signals. They are generally used in places where it might be difficult for a driver to see signs or signals.

Lane and Center Line Markings. The most common roadway markings are lane lines and center lines. These lines may be either yellow or white. A *yellow line* separates or divides traffic traveling in *opposite directions*. A *white line* separates or divides traffic going in the *same direction*.

If a line is *solid* (unbroken), you must remain in the lane, regardless of whether the line is white or yellow. Drivers cannot legally cross a solid line, even in a passing maneuver. If the line is broken, you may cross it either to pass another car or to turn.

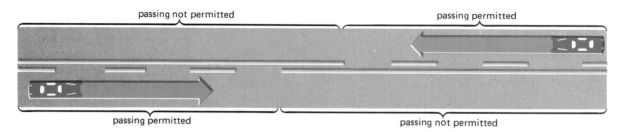

If the solid line is on your side of the center of the roadway, you may not pass.

No-Passing Zone. On two-way roads you will find that the center of the road is generally marked with a broken yellow line. However, as you approach the crest of a hill or a curve you may find a solid line along one side of the broken yellow center line. If the solid line is on your side of the road, you are either approaching a potentially hazardous situation or your field of vision is limited. In any case, you may not legally pass. Vehicles traveling with the broken line on their side, however, may pass with caution. If there is a double solid line, passing is prohibited for traffic in both directions.

Special Pavement Markings. You may find regulations painted directly on the roadway surface. Examples of such regulations are "left turn only," "right turn only," or "thru traffic." These words may be accompanied by painted arrows, signs, or signals. The letters RR painted on the roadway surface are frequently used along with other signs and signals to warn drivers of a railroad crossing.

Heavy white lines are used with *stop* signs or traffic lights to indicate where vehicles should stop. They are also used to mark pedestrian crosswalks.

Diagonal lines, commonly known as "zebra" lines, are frequently used to mark fixed obstructions, like traffic islands and lane barriers; occasionally, they are also used to mark no-parking zones. You should not drive or park in any area marked with diagonal lines.

It should be obvious that signs, signals, and markings can provide you with a great deal of information about the roadway environment. With a brief glance you can gather information about many roadway hazards and possible points of conflict with other roadway users.

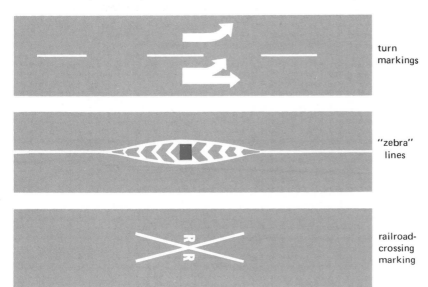

turn markings

"zebra" lines

railroad-crossing marking

Pavement markings are another source of information.

149

To Think About

1. What is the purpose of having national standards for motor-vehicle and traffic laws?
2. Is it important for all vehicles to be registered? Why or why not?
3. If you are involved in an accident, should you discuss with the other driver which of you is at fault? Why or why not?
4. What steps would you take if you arrived at the scene of a serious accident?
5. Explain what is meant by *last clear chance*.
6. Describe three situations in which there would be right-of-way conflicts. How should each of the conflicts be resolved?
7. What are the differences between fixed and flexible speed limits? Can you be stopped for speeding in an area that has flexible speed limits? Why or why not?
8. Identify the shapes and colors of *stop* and *yield* signs.
9. Who has the right of way at an intersection where all of the streets are controlled by *stop* signs?
10. What are some of the advantages of international traffic signs? Do these signs have any disadvantages?

To Do

1. Find out from your state's motor vehicle bureau what tests a person must pass to get a driver's license. Do you think the tests adequately measure driving performance and knowledge? How would you change the tests if you were able?
2. For what reasons can licenses be suspended or revoked in your state? Survey judges, police, drivers, and nondrivers and write down their opinions about suspension and revocation laws. Do you agree or disagree with their opinions? Should the laws be changed? How?
3. Station yourself at an intersection that is controlled by a *stop* sign. How many drivers make a *full* stop at the sign? How many only slow down? Report your findings to your class.
4. Observe traffic at an intersection controlled by a traffic light. How many drivers go through the intersection when the light is yellow? How often do waiting drivers "jump" the light by entering the intersection before the light turns from red to green? Report your findings to your class.

Highway Conditions 6

After reading this chapter, you should be able to:

1. Discuss why collisions do not necessarily involve more than one highway user.
2. Define *traction* and explain why it is important for vehicle control.
3. Describe two kinds of limited visibility and explain how each is hazardous.

A highway is made up of the roadway and those areas *adjacent* (near) to it on either side. Whether you are driving in the city or the country, you must pay attention not only to the roadway but to the areas on both sides of it. Vehicles, pedestrians, or animals that may be some distance off the road could cause difficulty. Objects near the road or the condition of the shoulder may limit where you can steer if you are forced to leave the roadway. Other things, either on or off the roadway, could limit your field of vision.

It should be obvious, then, that collision-free driving requires that you extend your area of attention beyond your intended path of travel. You have to identify and interpret other elements that could block your path if you were forced to leave the roadway or to make some other emergency maneuver.

Collisions

The term *collision* is easily understood when it refers to striking another vehicle, a pedestrian, or an animal. However, when the term is applied to striking certain objects, particularly those that

151

are part of the roadway itself, it is difficult to determine what should and what should not be identified as a collision.

There is little question that hitting a utility pole is a collision. However, can striking a bump in the road be called a collision? Does the answer depend on the size of the bump? Does it depend on the speed with which contact is made? The answer to each of these questions is *yes!*

COLLISION ELEMENTS

Your selection of speed and road position should depend, in part, on the possible consequences of any action you take. Striking anything that could have serious consequences should be called a collision. In other words, you should search for any object on or near the roadway that could cause personal injury, damage to the vehicle, or loss of control.

ON-ROAD HAZARDS

Even if we do not count vehicles and other highway users, the number of potential collision items on any roadway is almost infinite. The importance of these items varies, depending on the collision potential of each and on the context in which each appears. In one situation, a hole in the road may be so deep and wide that you would choose to avoid it. In a more complex situation, where there might be less space and time for maneuvering, you might prefer to strike the same hole because otherwise you would risk hitting a pedestrian or another vehicle.

Examples of items that are often found on the roadway and that deserve attention are bumps, boards, bottles, boxes, and cans. Other objects that are found less often, but are not unusual, are obstructions associated with road construction and repair, tree branches, and parts of vehicles, such as broken mufflers or old tires. Attempting to list everything that could be included is

Even if you do not count other vehicles and highway users, the number of potential hazards on any roadway is almost unlimited. Search for items that could cause personal injury, vehicle damage, or loss of control.

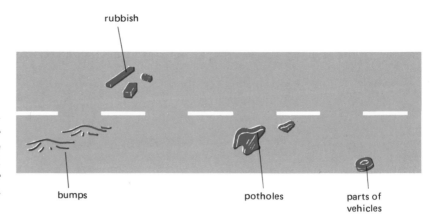

rubbish

bumps

potholes

parts of vehicles

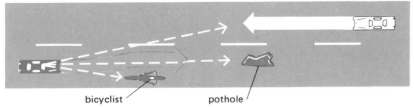

bicyclist   pothole

To avoid on-road hazards or to reduce damage, you will sometimes have to adjust your speed and path of travel. However, do not change your path if you will endanger yourself or other highway users.

pointless. Rather, you must improve your visual efficiency by searching for things with collision potential and evaluating them in terms of their probable consequences.

You can use a space cushion or your vehicle's position to minimize the risk if there is enough space available. However, what would you do if there were not enough space for you to adjust your position? What would be the consequences of collision? How confident are you that you can avoid colliding with the object? Remember, we are referring to stationary objects, which cannot move toward you.

Frequently it is possible to simply straddle objects on the road. This usually results in little or no change in your path. There may, however, be obstructions that extend over much or all of the roadway. These obstructions may be so slight that they would have only minor consequences. Yet, they may be potentially severe. In either case, you may have to drive over them at a slower speed so that the consequences are reduced to an acceptable level. If the hazard is too great, you may be forced to turn around and take another route.

Sometimes you may be able to straddle hazards on the road. For example, you may be able to safely drive over a deep pothole that is not very wide.

OFF-ROAD HAZARDS

Stationary objects off the roadway are generally less hazardous than those that are on the road. This is true simply because of their position. However, they cannot be ignored. For example, something on the road could force you to use the off-road area as an escape route that you might need to avoid a collision. Failure to search ahead and to observe off-road conditions could lead to a serious accident. By attempting to avoid a moderate hazard on the road, you might steer off the road and move toward a much more serious hazard.

It is also possible for your car to drift off the road because of inattention or loss of control. Scanning off-road conditions provides important information about shoulder conditions and off-road objects that may be more hazardous than what you are trying to avoid on the roadway. Objects close to the roadway

Some roadways are not well designed. The off-road areas in this illustration are very hazardous. Could you plan an escape route if you were driving on this highway?

If oncoming drivers feel threatened by off-road hazards, they may move closer to the center of the road. In such cases, you should slow down and adjust your position.

(within 9 to 10 feet) pose a threat to some drivers. Very large objects, such as light poles, bridges, signs, or trees, are especially threatening to some drivers. In reacting to these apparent threats, some drivers tend to move laterally away from the object. Such a reaction could lead other drivers into a collision course.

Scanning ahead and planning safe escape routes will reduce the hazards of suddenly leaving the road. In addition, if you have

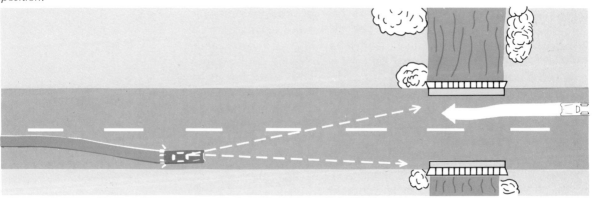

correctly perceived and evaluated the off-road areas, you will increase your chances for smooth recovery if you are forced to steer onto the shoulder.

Most of the items that cause hazards on the road (such as holes, bumps, or litter) also appear in off-road areas. In addition, utility poles, sign posts, fire hydrants, trees, bushes, fences, ditches, and embankments are typical off-road hazards. Again, these items simply serve as examples of objects with collision potential. There are too many potential off-road hazards to list here.

You may some time be faced with choosing between an on-road and an off-road collision. If a collision is unavoidable, remember that off-road areas often present objects with less serious consequences. This is especially true if the on-road hazard involves another vehicle or a pedestrian. For example, it would be better to collide with some off-road shrubbery than to collide with an oncoming car or a bicyclist who suddenly entered your path. However, if leaving the roadway will result in a collision with a massive fixed object, you may have to make a different decision.

Some roads have hardly any shoulders at all. On a highway like this, you would have to drive slowly and even more alertly.

155

Vehicle control depends on the friction between the small area in which your vehicle's tires and the roadway surface are in contact.

Traction

To drive safely you must maintain control of your vehicle during both routine and emergency driving situations. You must make every effort not to cause a collision because of loss of control. You should not be involved in a collision simply because you did not anticipate how difficult it would be to control your vehicle.

Vehicle control ultimately depends on the *friction,* or resistance to slipping, between your tires and the surface upon which you are driving. The greater the friction, the less the chances that the tires will skid on a given surface. Once a skid begins, your ability to control the speed and direction of your vehicle is greatly reduced. Smooth, effective recovery of control can generally be accomplished only after training and experience.

The friction of an object on a surface is referred to as *traction.* One of the purposes of the design and construction of a tire is to provide maximum traction. The effectiveness of the tires, however, is influenced by the roadway surface. There are several problems related to traction that you must be aware of if you are to drive safely:

1. The amount of traction is not constant. It varies with tire construction, tread depth, and the type of surface on which you are driving. In addition, traction is reduced if there are loose or slick substances on the surface of the roadway.

2. It is difficult to judge traction accurately. We can usually make our most dependable judgments of traction on dry, paved surfaces. This is because we are used to driving on this kind of surface. As traction varies, our judgment is less reliable because we are forced to think about it in such indefinite terms as "good," "fair," or "poor."

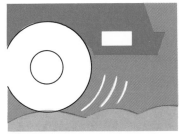

bumps and holes

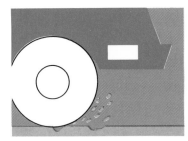

loose dirt or gravel

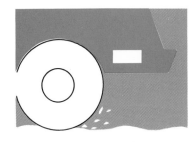

water, snow, or ice

worn tires

curves

road contours

oversteering

overbraking

overaccelerating

Traction can be influenced by many factors.

3. Acceleration, cornering, and deceleration seriously affect traction and must therefore be controlled. In other words, judging how much traction is available is most difficult just when decisions about traction are most critical. When you are accelerating, decelerating, or driving on a curve, you put stress on your tires and strain against the traction available.

Driving straight ahead on a level, dry, clean, hard, paved surface is the ideal condition for maintaining traction. The chances of losing control on this kind of roadway are at a minimum. Any change from this ideal standard, however, requires a driver to make decisions that will compensate for reduced traction.

How much traction is available in a situation like this? How would you compensate for reduced traction in this case?

REDUCED TRACTION

There is a good chance that you will sometimes have to drive on unpaved surfaces. Variations in traction will occur, not only from surface to surface, but also from one area to another on the same surface. For example, if you are driving in a rural area, your route may take you from a paved road onto an unpaved gravel road. This change in roadway surface would suddenly reduce traction, and you would have to adjust your speed. In addition, once you were on the gravel road, you would have to scan for areas of the gravel surface that were particularly bumpy or uneven, because such conditions would reduce traction even more.

Judging the exact amount of traction on a surface is difficult, but there is a way in which you can test the traction available. First, check to see that there is ample space and that there are no other highway users around. At a low speed (15 to 20 mph), quickly press the brake pedal down to lock the brakes, hold it for an instant, and then release the brake pedal. Your car's response should provide some indication of the skid conditions without placing you in an unmanageable situation.

Highway conditions that cause reduced traction generally fall into one of two categories: First, the type and condition of the driving surface, and second, the substances on the surface. For all practical purposes, there is little variation in the amount of traction available on hard-surfaced concrete or asphalt roadways. However, if the driving surface is tar and gravel, sand, or gravel, or if the pavement is worn and broken, the variations in traction can be great. For example, a well-maintained, dry, hard, dirt road can provide fairly good traction. If, however, the surface area is a

158

The traction available on a shoulder area like this may be even less than the traction available on the roadway surface.

mixture of loose dirt and small stones, gravel, or is wet, loss of control is much more likely.

SEARCHING FOR AN ALTERNATE PATH OF TRAVEL

As previously stated, you should continually scan the area near the surface of the roadway for pedestrians, vehicles, and other objects. It is just as important, however, to analyze the off-road area to determine its condition. In case it is necessary to leave the road, or if you should leave the road unintentionally, you will want some idea of how your vehicle will respond to the off-road surface.

Are the shoulders and the areas beyond the shoulder level, firm, and clear? Would you be able to brake and steer if you were forced to leave the roadway? Drivers often fail to analyze the off-road surface. This is probably due to the fact that they are seldom forced to drive on it. If you find yourself on the shoulder and do not have adequate knowledge of its characteristics, you may well be involved in an accident because you will not know how to respond.

FACTORS AFFECTING TRACTION

Traction on paved roads can be significantly affected if there is anything on the surface that reduces the contact between tires and the roadway. The most common cause of reduced contact is adverse weather conditions.

You will frequently have to drive on wet roads. Most drivers tend to overestimate the amount of control they have when roadways are covered with water. As a result, the number of ac-

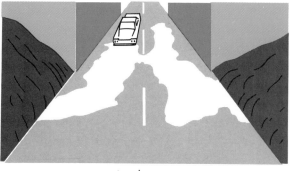

at underpasses

at the foot of hills

near cliffs

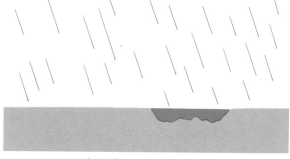

where the surface is damaged

Look out for areas where water may accumulate during and after heavy rains.

cidents tends to increase sharply whenever it rains. In general, then, wet surfaces provide less traction than dry surfaces. In addition, there are two special conditions about which you should be aware :

1. Roads are especially slippery for 10 to 15 minutes just after it begins to rain. This is due to the combination of water, dirt, rubber, dust, and oil that accumulates on the road, creating a very slick mixture. (This mixture may, after a while, be splashed or washed away.)

2. Excessive accumulation of water on the road (caused by very heavy rains or poor drainage) can also be especially dangerous. Large amounts of water, combined with worn or underinflated tires and high speeds, can cause your car to *hydroplane*. (A car that hydroplanes actually rides on top of a film of water that develops between the tires and the roadway surface. Thus, all direct contact between the pavement and the tires is lost.)

Snow and ice on the road are also very dangerous. Drivers tend to forget that snow and ice get even more slick as they melt. (Ice that is wet, for example, is more slippery than ice that is dry.) Any increase or decrease in speed or any change in direction may well

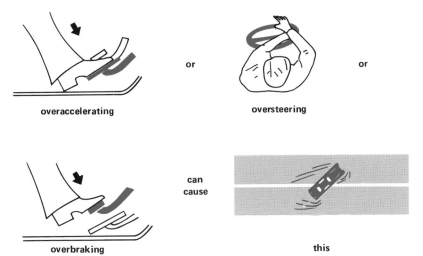

overaccelerating   or   oversteering   or

overbraking   can cause   this

You can reduce the chances of losing traction by not abruptly steering, braking, or accelerating.

result in a skid. The more abruptly you make any of these changes, the more likely you are to skid.

Several other factors on the roadway surface also reduce traction. Oil from vehicles and sand or gravel can cause severe problems. In the autumn, fallen wet leaves are an additional common hazard. Metal surfaces, such as those on some bridges or those in construction areas, can cause problems, especially when they are wet. The same holds true for wooden planks on bridges and around construction sites.

In addition, any irregularity in the roadway surface, such as bumps, holes, or rough surfaces, can cause your car to bounce, thereby reducing traction. Even if your suspension system is in good repair, the bouncing reduces the tires' contact with the road, thus reducing your ability to control speed and direction.

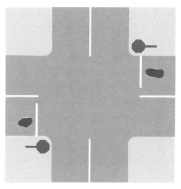

Oil and other fluids may accumulate on the roadway surface at intersections where vehicles often brake to a stop.

MOMENTUM AND CENTRIFUGAL FORCE

The law of *inertia* can be stated as follows: "Any object in motion tends to remain in motion in a straight line." You already know that as the speed of a vehicle increases, it becomes increasingly more difficult to decelerate and stop. The tendency for an object to remain in motion *in a straight line* causes problems when you are making a turn. This "straight-line" force causes your car to move to the outside of a turn. If your traction is sufficient to overcome centrifugal force, you can make the turn successfully. If it is not, your car will slide to the outside of the turn or continue in a straight line.

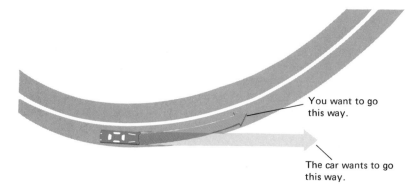

You want to go this way.

The car wants to go this way.

Objects in motion tend to stay in motion in a straight line. As you make a turn, your vehicle will pull toward its straight-ahead path.

There are three factors that determine the amount of centrifugal force in a turn:

1. The sharpness of the turn
2. The speed of the vehicle
3. The size of the vehicle

While you can do very little to change the sharpness of the turn or the size of the vehicle, you can select a speed that will keep the force of inertia low enough so that your car will not go into a skid when you make a turn.

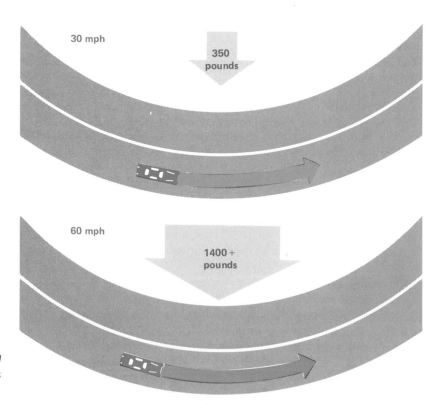

30 mph

350 pounds

60 mph

1400+ pounds

As your speed increases, so will the centrifugal force that pulls your car out of the turn.

On a banked curve, the contour of the road helps a car hold its path by tilting it toward the inside of the curve.

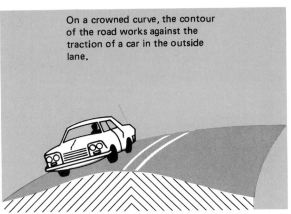

On a crowned curve, the contour of the road works against the traction of a car in the outside lane.

The slope of the roadway surface will also influence the amount of traction available.

The *contour*, or slope, of a road surface will also influence the effect of centrifugal force. A well-designed and well-constructed road is built so that the surface is *banked*, or sloped up toward the outside of a turn. This means that as you make a turn, your car is tilted toward the inside. The angle of this tilt, or slope, works to diminish the effects of centrifugal force.

Some roads are *crowned*. This means that they are somewhat higher in the center than toward the edges. Such roads will aid you in right-hand turns because they are then tilted toward the center. However, left turns can be dangerous because the slope is toward the edge of the roadway.

GRAVITATIONAL EFFECTS OF HILLS

When you are driving on an uphill grade, you will find that your vehicle has less acceleration capability. This may be a disadvantage, especially if you need an increase in speed to avoid a hazard. In contrast, however, an uphill grade decreases the distance required to make an emergency stop. The opposite is true when

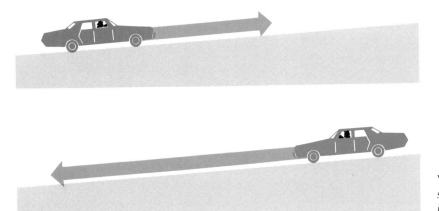

Your vehicle will accelerate more slowly on upgrades. The opposite is true on downgrades.

you are driving on a downhill grade. It becomes easier to accelerate if an increase in speed is needed, but stopping distances increase.

In either case, adjust your speed and position to compensate for the effects of gravity. For example, on a downhill grade you may want to increase the space cushion between your car and the vehicles ahead and behind. On an uphill grade, you would not want to pass another vehicle, even if the passing lane were clear, unless you were sure that your car could provide the extra power needed to accelerate on the grade.

Visibility

One of the most frequently heard excuses for having an accident is "I didn't even see the car!" Assuming the driver has good eyesight, this statement may imply either that the driver had poor visual search habits or that the driver's field of vision was somehow obstructed. With practice, you should make few errors in your visual search. The restrictions on your field of vision, however, are more difficult to manage because you cannot always control them.

If you are behind a large vehicle your view will be blocked (A). You can compensate for this by creating a greater space cushion between you and the large vehicle ahead (B).

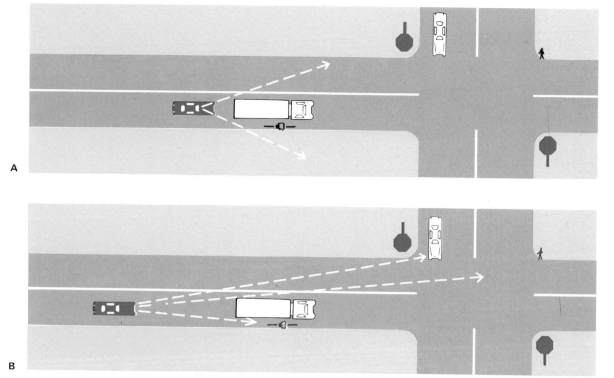

A

B

164

An example of limited visibility is that which is created by darkness. There are many other factors that cause similar problems. Some of them are obvious, others are more subtle. The problem of dealing with limited visibility is twofold. First, visual obstructions can prevent you from identifying objects with collision potential that are in or near your intended path of travel. Second, when you do not have direct visual contact with a potential danger, it will be nearly impossible for you to make accurate judgments and evaluations.

Limited visibility may be caused by either atmospheric or environmental conditions. Either type of condition can completely prevent you from seeing an object or can permit you so little visual contact that you can detect only partial or distorted evidence upon which to base your judgments. These restrictions can be either stationary or moving. (A large sign is an example of a stationary visual obstruction. A large truck ahead of you on the road is an example of a moving visual obstruction.) Your vision may be limited for only a brief period of time (as occurs when you approach the crest of a hill) or for an extended period of time (such as when you are driving in fog).

ATMOSPHERIC CONDITIONS

Restrictions placed on your vision by atmospheric conditions tend to be stationary, and they generally remain a factor for some period of time.

Nighttime or Darkness. Visual conditions at night are always poor. Even a full moon does not provide sufficient light. Headlights, when properly cleaned and adjusted, help. It is a mistake,

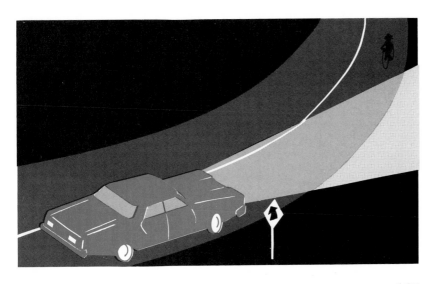

Remember that headlights do not completely illuminate the road ahead. This is especially true on curves.

however, to think that the amount of light they give, even when they are on high beam, is enough to give you very good visual efficiency. Furthermore, even if properly adjusted, they direct beams of light only straight ahead. They offer little help in lighting off-road areas, and they do not, of course, light the road very far ahead as you are making a turn.

The source of the light provided by your headlights is near ground level instead of overhead, as it is in the daytime. This means that objects illuminated by headlights cast completely different shadows from those illuminated by sunlight. The combination of distorted shadows and dim illumination can easily result in mistakes in identifying and interpreting cues and can lead to errors of judgment.

Your vision is especially reduced when you operate with your headlights on low beam. However, you must use low beams when meeting or following other vehicles at night because low beams reduce the level of glare for other drivers. When meeting oncoming vehicles, do not stare at their headlights. If you do, the glare will temporarily reduce your ability to see into the dimly lit areas ahead and near the roadway.

If a vehicle approaches you with high-beam headlights on, the greater glare will further reduce your visibility. You can usually encourage the other driver to switch to low beams by flashing your own high beams on and off quickly. If this fails to work, do not try to "get even" by switching on your high beams. This serves only to decrease the visibility of both of you and will increase the chances of a collision.

Fog and Smog. The density of fog or smog determines how much vision is limited. It can be so slight that it has only a moderate effect on your view through your projected path of travel. It can, however, be so dense that it is difficult to see even the front of your car's hood. Spotty fog is especially hazardous because its density can change abruptly. You may be driving with little or no problem and, before you can react, the fog can become extremely heavy. Your visual lead could, in an instant, be cut in half or

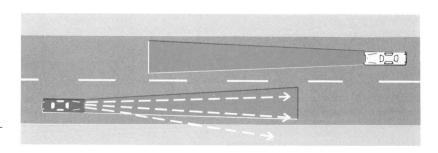

At night, avoid staring at the headlights of oncoming cars.

Large vehicles that pass you on rainy highways can splash water up onto your windshield, reducing visibility even more.

completely eliminated. Though changes can occur without warning, you can prepare for fog and its potential hazards by adjusting your speed and position.

If you are driving in fog at night, use low-beam headlights. They will give you better visibility than high beams because the particles of water in the fog will reflect the high-beam light back into your eyes. The resulting glare makes it more difficult to see. Low-beam headlights will not reflect back at your eyes as much and will give others sufficient warning of where you are.

It is best to assume that when conditions are bad and you are not continuously gathering information from a 12-second visual lead, you are in a hazardous situation. In situations of reduced visibility, drivers sometimes think they are safe if they can stop within the distance they can see. Although this may allow them to avoid collisions with stationary objects, it may not give them time enough to successfully avoid collisions caused by the closing movements of other highway users.

Snow and Rain. As you know, snow and rain can seriously reduce traction. They can also cause serious visibility problems. A hard rainfall can limit vision so much that you may be forced to pull off the road and wait for the rain to let up. If you do pull off the road under such conditions, it is essential that you turn on your four-way warning lights.

Snowfall can present even more serious visibility problems. Snow may stick to the windshield and other windows, blocking all areas except those that are cleared by the windshield wipers. During a heavy wet snow, the wipers may not be able to keep the windshield clear. Even more hazardous, both in terms of traction and visibility, is a rapid change in temperature, which may cause wet snow, freezing rain, fog, or sleet.

Rain can abruptly reduce your visual lead. How would you respond if you drove into this situation and your wipers did not work?

As with fog or other conditions that reduce visibility, the problem is the need to have a visual lead that will give you the opportunity to cope with potentially dangerous events.

Sun Glare. When you are driving toward a sunrise or a sunset, you may have to cope with very intense glare. (The glare will be especially intense and difficult to deal with if your car's windshield is dirty or scratched.) Sun visors or sunglasses can reduce the effect of the glare. However, it is also necessary to reduce

Glare from the sun can make it difficult for drivers to see the road ahead.

your speed so that you will have time to respond to any hazards or cues (such as another vehicle's brake lights) that may be hidden or partly obscured by the glare.

ENVIRONMENTAL CONDITIONS

There are many times when your vision is limited by objects that are commonly found within the highway environment. Like atmospheric factors that limit vision, environmental factors may partially or totally hide from you something with collision potential. Unlike atmospheric factors, environmental factors usually tend to hide hazards for short periods of time. In addition, this type of condition may vary with the type of highway on which you are driving.

Hill Crests.   As you approach the top of a hill, your vision will be temporarily limited. The *grade* (uphill or downhill slope) of the hill at its crest will determine how limited your vision is. The problem of objects moving or stopped in your path over the top of the hill demands careful consideration. More critical is the possibility of a vehicle, pedestrian, or animal, just out of sight, moving toward you on a collision course. As you approach the crest of a hill, you should be aware of the need to select a speed and position that would enable you to respond to any hazard that may arise.

Objects Adjacent to the Road.   Objects of almost any size not only have collision potential, but may also hide from view other objects of importance. An object need only be large enough to hide a small child or animal to deserve your careful attention. At a given angle, a tree trunk or utility pole is large enough to hide an adult pedestrian. Sign boards, walls, or buildings near the roadway present the same type of problem. They may hide from view anything from the smallest animal to large approaching vehicles.

Environmental factors, such as hill-crests, can hide potential hazards from view.

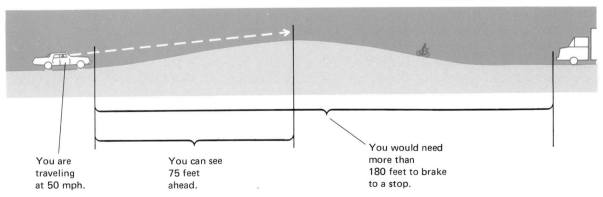

You are traveling at 50 mph.

You can see 75 feet ahead.

You would need more than 180 feet to brake to a stop.

Bushes and Shrubbery. The same limited-vision problem is created by bushes, shrubbery, and any other dense growth beside the roadway. These types of visual obstructions often receive too little attention, since they are usually away from drivers' intended paths. However, depending on their size, they can also obscure hazards that could drastically influence your choice of speed and position.

Blind Turns. The phrase *blind turn* refers to those turns in which drivers have less of a visual lead than their normal projected path of travel. Some conditions that would classify a turn as blind are bushes, buildings, walls, or similar objects on the inside of a turn. In addition, if the roadway is graded from the side of a hill, the terrain beside the road can limit vision. This is a problem that is quite common in hilly or mountainous areas, but it may appear almost anywhere.

Other Vehicles. Almost all other vehicles cause a problem of limited vision in addition to the problem of their own collision potential. The larger the vehicle, the greater the area of limited visibility. At certain angles, they can hide objects that are as large as or larger than they are.

Stationary vehicles (parked in off-road areas or on the street) can easily prevent you from seeing someone who is about to open a door and step out. They can also hide other vehicles or pedestrians who may be about to move into your path.

Moving vehicles generally cause fewer visual problems than parked vehicles because the area of the highway that they are obstructing at any given instant will be visible a second or so later. One important exception to this is a vehicle driving in front of you in your lane. Because this vehicle causes a continual blockage of your path of travel, it is a constant visual problem. Once again, its size is the biggest factor in determining how much of a

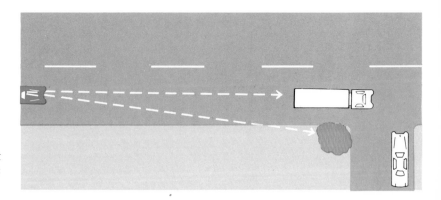

Collision-free driving requires that you anticipate collision hazards where your vision is blocked.

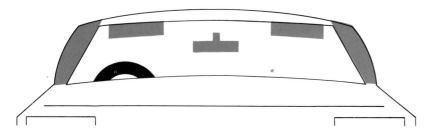

Objects within the vehicle can block vision.

hazard it is. Buses, trucks, vans, and improperly loaded station wagons or passenger cars are particularly serious problems. Cars do not usually cause as much difficulty because they are smaller and their windows provide somewhat more visibility. (You can actually look through the vehicle itself.)

Visual Obstructions Inside a Vehicle. As you sit in the driver's seat, you will find your view is blocked, to some extent, by passengers, the rear-view mirror, door posts, and the other posts that support the roof. Though the amount of blockage is not necessarily great, at certain angles and in certain positions other vehicles may be entirely hidden from your view. Vision from within the vehicle can be further obstructed when boxes or packages are piled on the seats or if clothing is hung on a rod in the back seat. If the trunk is loaded in such a manner that the trunk lid must be raised, vision to the rear may be totally obstructed.

It is not possible to achieve collision-free driving if you respond only to those highway events with which you make direct visual contact. It is necessary to give consideration to roadway conditions and to the possibility that visual obstructions may hide potential hazards from you. You can manage such situations only if you have anticipated them and adjust your speed and position.

To Think About

1. Name five hazards that are the result of roadway conditions. (Do not include hazards that involve other highway users.) How would you respond to each?
2. Name five off-road hazards that have collision potential. Are the five hazards equally serious? List them in the order of their seriousness.
3. Describe a situation in which you would choose to be involved in an off-road collision so that you could avoid an on-road collision. Explain the possible consequences.
4. What evidence would you use to determine how firm a shoulder area is? How would you estimate the traction available on the same shoulder area?
5. Why does the number of accidents generally increase whenever it rains?
6. Why are roadway surfaces especially slick just after a rain begins?

7. Why do bumps and potholes reduce traction? Describe three situations in which drivers would respond in different ways to bumps and potholes.
8. What is *centrifugal force?* What factors increase the amount of centrifugal force in a turn?
9. Describe three situations in which visibility would be limited by atmospheric conditions.
10. Describe three situations in which visibility would be limited by environmental conditions.

To Do

1. While driving with a family member or with a friend, think about possible off-road escape routes you would take if your path were suddenly blocked. Then ask the driver if he or she agrees with the possible escape routes you have chosen.
2. Observe traffic at night. Do drivers cooperate with each other by adjusting their vehicles' headlights to low beams when they are meeting, following, and passing other vehicles? How many drivers cooperate and how many do not? Report your findings to your class.
3. Find out from local traffic authorities whether the number of accidents increases significantly when weather conditions decrease visibility and traction. What weather conditions are particularly hazardous in your part of the country?
4. Select a section of a local roadway that seems to provide especially limited visibility. How could the roadway be improved?

Vehicle Performance 7

After reading this chapter, you should be able to:

1. Describe signs of failure or wear in three different vehicle systems.
2. Explain the importance of frequent vehicle checks and maintenance.
3. Describe how drivers can judge the performance capabilities of other vehicles on the roadway.
4. Discuss how your vehicle's performance capability should affect your driving decisions.

It is easy to overlook the fact that maneuvers you make must fall not only within the limits of your own driving skills, but also within the performance capability of the vehicle you are driving. It does not take a great deal of experience to learn to control a motor vehicle under normal driving conditions. However, in reacting to an emergency situation, an inexperienced driver is likely to make errors in judgment.

The purpose of this chapter is to help you to become familiar with your vehicle. You do not have to become an automobile mechanic, but you should have some knowledge of how a car operates. You must be aware of the importance of keeping your vehicle in good operating condition and know what kind of performance you can expect from it.

Automobile Systems

The automobile is made up of several major systems. These are the power train, the fuel system, the electrical system, the exhaust system, the lubricating and cooling system, and the suspension and steering system. To understand how an automobile

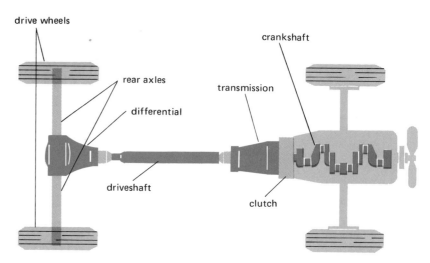

drive wheels

crankshaft

rear axles

transmission

differential

driveshaft

clutch

The power train delivers power from the engine to the drive wheels.

operates, you need to have some knowledge of these systems and how they affect vehicle performance.

THE POWER TRAIN

The purpose of the power train is to deliver power from the engine to the drive wheels. (On most cars, only two of the four wheels are actually turned by the motor. These two wheels, most often the rear two, are called the *drive wheels*.) Once power is generated in the engine, it is transmitted in the form of *rotary* (circular) motion to the clutch and transmission, which together allow the driver to select the gear ratio desired. The transmission is connected by the driveshaft to the differential, which is located in the drive-wheel-axle housing. The differential serves two purposes:

1. It changes the direction of rotation of the driveshaft by 90 degrees to turn the drive-wheel axles.

2. It allows each of the drive wheels to turn at a different rate of speed, such as when the car is turning a corner.

Internal Combustion Engine. The power to move a motor vehicle is generated in the engine by the controlled explosion of an air-fuel mixture within a combustion chamber or cylinder. The amount of power generated depends on the following:

1. The number and the size of the cylinders
2. The quality and quantity of the air-fuel mixture
3. How much the mixture is compressed
4. How the spark, which ignites the mixture and causes it to explode, is timed

174

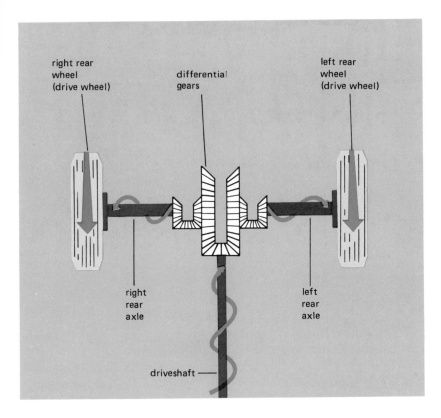

right rear wheel (drive wheel)

differential gears

left rear wheel (drive wheel)

right rear axle

left rear axle

driveshaft

The differential transmits power from the driveshaft to each of the drive-wheel axles. It also allows each of the drive wheels to turn at a different rate of speed.

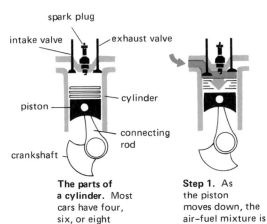

spark plug

intake valve

exhaust valve

piston

cylinder

connecting rod

crankshaft

The parts of a cylinder. Most cars have four, six, or eight cylinders. The piston in each cylinder is attached to a part of the crankshaft.

Step 1. As the piston moves down, the air–fuel mixture is drawn into the cylinder through the intake valve.

Step 2. The piston moves up and compresses the air–fuel mixture. (The intake and exhaust valves are both closed.)

Step 3. A spark explodes the compressed fuel–air mixture. This pushes down the piston, which turns the crankshaft.

Step 4. The piston moves up and forces the burned gases out through the exhaust valve. The cycle begins again.

The most common type of internal combustion engine is the four-stroke piston engine. In a four-step cycle, the controlled explosion of an air-fuel mixture pushes the pistons up and down. The pistons, in turn, move the crankshaft.

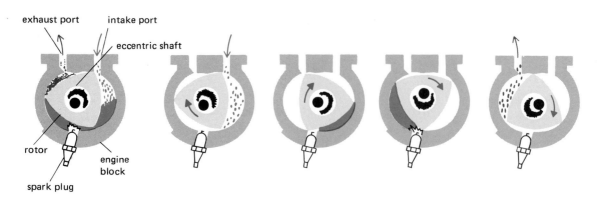

exhaust port   intake port

eccentric shaft

rotor

engine
block

spark plug

The parts of a rotary motor.
In one complete turn of the rotor, all four steps take place.

Step 1. As the rotor turns, the air–fuel mixture is drawn into the engine block.

Step 2. The air–fuel mixture is compressed as the rotor turns.

Step 3. A spark from the spark plug ignites the compressed fuel-air mixture.

Step 4. The burned gases are forced out and the cycle begins again.

The Wankel (or rotary) engine, which is less common than the four-stroke piston engine, produces continuous circular motion. This motion is applied to an eccentric shaft that connects the engine to the rest of the power train.

To produce power, an air-fuel mixture is drawn into the cylinders or combustion chambers, where it is compressed to approximately one-tenth of its original volume. A spark then ignites the mixture and it explodes. The power generated by the explosion is used to rotate a driveshaft in a piston-driven engine or an eccentric shaft in a rotary engine. The unburned gas remaining in the combustion chamber after the explosion is cleared from the cylinders by way of the exhaust system.

THE FUEL SYSTEM

The fuel system consists of a fuel-storage tank, a fuel pump, a carburetor, and an intake manifold. The fuel pump moves the fuel from the fuel tank to the carburetor, where the fuel is mixed with air as it is drawn into the intake manifold. From the intake manifold the air-fuel mixture is drawn through the intake valves and enters the combustion chamber, where it is compressed and ignited. The critical functions of the fuel system, then, are delivery of the fuel from the tank to the carburetor, mixing the fuel and air in the proper ratio, and delivering the mixture to the combustion chamber.

THE ELECTRICAL SYSTEM

The electrical system consists of an energy source (a 6- or 12-volt battery), an alternator (or generator, in older cars), a voltage regulator, and insulated wires that carry the electricity to various accessories. The battery provides the initial power to start the engine or to operate accessory equipment, such as the lights or

176

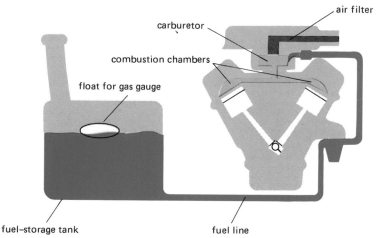

The purpose of the fuel system is to store fuel and deliver the correct air-fuel mixture to the engine.

radio, for a short period of time when the engine is not running. Once the engine is started, the alternator provides electrical current to keep the engine running, to recharge the battery, or to operate the accessories. The function of the voltage regulator is to control the amount of power generated and the rate at which the battery is recharged.

The ignition system consists of an ignition switch, a starter motor, an ignition coil, breaker points, a condenser, a distributor, a set of ignition wires, and spark plugs. (An electronic ignition system does not have breaker points. Instead, a magnetic

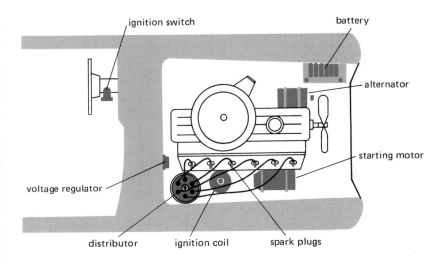

The electrical system supplies the energy to start the car and distributes the electrical charges to each of the cylinders.

pickup device in the distributor and an electronic amplifying device start and stop the flow of current.)

Depending on its size, the battery supplies electric current at 6 or 12 volts to the system. However, more than 30,000 volts are needed to ignite the air-fuel mixture in the combustion chamber. The increase in voltage and the precise control of the spark is achieved either through the use of an ignition coil (a transformer), breaker points, a condenser, and a distributor (a rotating switch) or through the use of an electronic ignition system and a distributor. The electric current is carried from the distributor to each of the individual spark plugs by insulated wires. The critical function of the ignition system is to increase the voltage from 6 or 12 volts to 30,000 volts and to then deliver the electrical charge to the proper spark plug at precisely the right time.

THE EXHAUST SYSTEM

The purpose of the exhaust system is twofold. First, it carries off hot, unburned gases—carbon monoxide, nitrates, and lead oxides—left over from the explosion of the air-fuel mixture within the combustion chamber. Second, it *baffles* (reduces the noise of) the explosion within the engine. The exhaust manifold serves as a collector for the unburned gases as they are expelled from the combustion chamber. The exhaust pipe carries the gases to the muffler, which serves as a noise baffle. The tail pipe carries the gases to the rear of the car for elimination into the air.

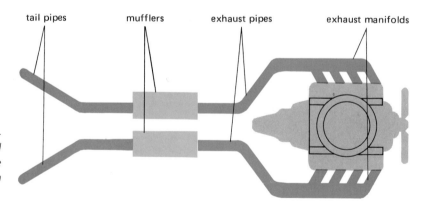

tail pipes   mufflers   exhaust pipes   exhaust manifolds

The exhaust system carries off un-burned gases from the engine and reduces engine noise. It should be checked often for holes and worn fittings.

Exhaust Emission-Control System. Unburned fuel and other harmful gases produced by combustion collect in the engine crankcase. If left in the crankcase, these gases would cause serious engine damage. Previously, these gases were simply vented into the air through a "breather pipe." Beginning in 1963, all cars produced in this country were required to have a positive crank-

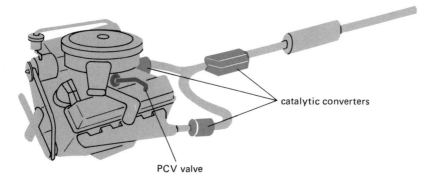

catalytic converters

PCV valve

The exhaust emission-control system. The positive crankcase ventilation (PCV) system draws vapors from the crankcase back into the combustion chamber for reburning. A newer development, catalytic converters, are designed to reduce the amount of harmful gases in the exhaust.

case ventilation system, or PCV. This device is designed to recycle the gaseous vapors in the crankcase back through the combustion chamber for reburning. Many newer vehicles are equipped with catalytic converters, which further reduce the amount of harmful gases in the exhaust. Other devices either recirculate exhaust gases or control evaporation of gasoline vapors from the fuel tank and carburetor.

Proper adjustment of an engine's timing and its carburetor, as well as the use of air-injection pumps and high-temperature thermostats, will result in more complete combustion.

LUBRICATING AND COOLING SYSTEM

Since the operation of an internal combustion engine involves the rapid, continuous movement of many metal parts, one against the other, a great deal of friction is generated. This friction generates heat. This heat, added to the heat generated by the explosion of the air-fuel mixture, produces engine temperatures greater than 4000 degrees Fahrenheit. If not cooled in some manner, the engine would soon melt or weld itself into a solid unit. To take care of this problem, the engine is equipped with lubricating and cooling systems.

The Lubricating System. The lubricating system reduces heat by coating the engine's parts with oil. The primary job of the motor oil is to reduce friction and wear between moving parts. Secondary functions of the motor oil are to cool hot spots within the engine, to help seal the joint between the piston rings and cylinder wall, to absorb bearing shock, to clean internal engine surfaces, and to prevent rust and corrosion from collecting on the engine's internal parts.

The motor oil needed to lubricate the engine is stored in the oil pan, which is attached to the bottom of the engine. An oil pump, powered by the engine, pumps oil from the oil pan to moving

179

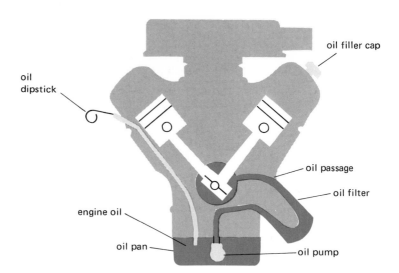

oil filler cap

oil dipstick

oil passage

oil filter

engine oil

oil pan

oil pump

The purpose of the lubricating system is to deliver oil to the engine. Oil is pumped directly to some parts of the engine and splashed onto other parts.

parts in the upper portion of the engine. Other areas are lubricated by the splashing action of the engine parts.

The Cooling System. The purpose of the cooling system is to get rid of the heat generated by combustion. In cars equipped with air-cooled engines, this is accomplished by forcing a large volume of air over metal cooling vanes that surround the cylinders.

The more common, but more complex, system used is the so-called water-cooled engine. (Actually, engines are rarely cooled by water alone. Rather, a special coolant that withstands wider variations in temperature is used. This coolant boils at a higher temperature and freezes at a lower temperature than does water.)

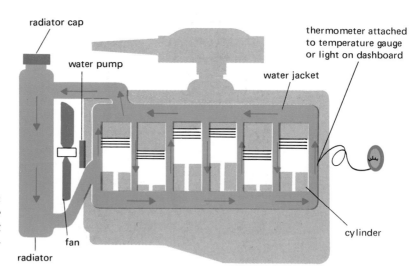

radiator cap

water pump

thermometer attached to temperature gauge or light on dashboard

water jacket

cylinder

fan

radiator

The cooling system circulates a coolant around the engine. The coolant draws off the excess heat that builds up around the cylinders.

The cooling system includes a water jacket within the walls that surrounds each of the cylinders. A radiator, through which the liquid passes to be cooled, has a pressure-sensitive radiator cap, which maintains a high enough pressure within the radiator so that the coolant will not boil. Hoses connect the engine to the radiator, and a pump forces the liquid through the system. A thermostat acts as a gate to control the flow of liquid and to maintain the best operating temperature. A belt-driven fan forces air through the radiator grid to more effectively cool the liquid.

Failure of the cooling system will cause the engine to overheat. (In the case of very cold weather and not enough antifreeze, the system can fail because the coolant will freeze.) Information about engine temperature is provided by the temperature gauge. A temperature warning light or a gauge reading *hot* requires immediate attention. Extensive damage can occur if you fail to stop an engine that is overheated.

SUSPENSION AND STEERING SYSTEM

You already know that you change the direction of the front wheels by turning the steering wheel. You may not know, however, that a change in the direction of travel depends on contact between the tires and the roadway surface. For a vehicle to respond properly to a driver's steering, all wheels must maintain contact with the roadway. Excessive bouncing is one thing that reduces this contact. While a good suspension system means a smoother ride, its primary function is to reduce the effects of bumps so that maximum contact between the tires and the roadway will be maintained.

Springs and Shock Absorbers. Springs and shock absorbers connect the car's frame to its wheels. Springs are designed to "soft-

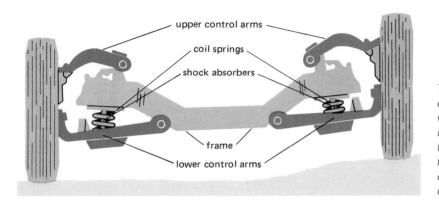

upper control arms
coil springs
shock absorbers
frame
lower control arms

The suspension system is made up of springs and shock absorbers which connect the car's frame to its wheels. The purpose of the system is to "cushion" the car's frame and to maintain as much contact as possible between the car's tires and the roadway.

181

en'' the jarring effect of bumps. However, if only springs were used, the car could continue bouncing up and down after it passed over a bump. This bouncing would, in turn, reduce the traction available for control.

To control the bouncing, shock absorbers are mounted between the frame and axle near each wheel. As the term implies, shock absorbers "cushion" the car's frame and thus reduce bouncing. They not only assist in smoothing out the ride, but allow the tires to maintain contact with the roadway. The result is better steering and braking control.

Steering Control. The steering system allows a driver to guide a vehicle by turning the front wheels left or right. The steering wheel, which the driver turns, is linked by a steering shaft and a series of movable metal rods to the front wheels.

The wheels of a vehicle must be held in an upright position. They must also be able to move up and down while they are turned in various directions. Steel plates called *control arms* hold the front wheels upright. Upper and lower control arms are hinged with ball joints to allow the wheels to move up and down over bumps when the vehicle is moving.

The purpose of the steering system is to control the direction of the front wheels. A system of gears and rods transmits movement from the steering wheel to the front wheels. If you notice any change in the "feel" of your car's steering, have it checked.

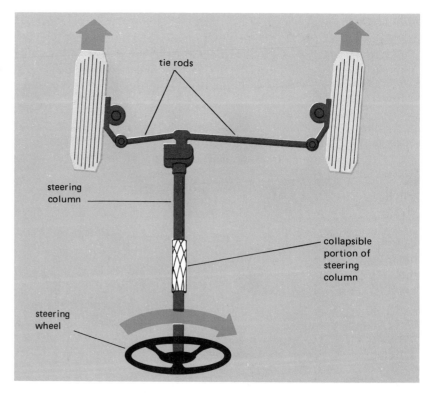

tie rods

steering
column

collapsible
portion of
steering
column

steering
wheel

A failure in any part of the steering and suspension system will have a pronounced effect upon your ability to control your vehicle. The reason, again, is that any loss of contact between the tires and the roadway will result in a loss of braking and steering control.

BRAKE SYSTEMS

Passenger vehicles are equipped with two brake systems. One is the hydraulic brake system and the other is the mechanically operated parking brake. The purpose of the hydraulic brake system is to stop a vehicle that is moving. The parking brake is designed to hold the vehicle in position after the vehicle has been stopped.

The Hydraulic Brake System. The hydraulic system is made up of the brake pedal, a master brake cylinder, brake-fluid lines, wheel cylinders, brake shoes and linings, and wheel drums. (Some cars may have brake discs and brake pads instead of brake linings, brake shoes, and wheel drums.)

The operation of the brake system is rather simple. When you press down on the brake pedal, a piston in the master brake cylinder moves forward, forcing brake fluid into the brake-fluid lines. Because a fluid cannot be compressed, this additional fluid creates pressure in the fluid lines, and this forces pistons in the wheel cylinders outward against the brake shoes. This action forces the brake lining against the wheel drum or the brake pads against the wheel discs. The friction that is developed slows the car. When you remove pressure from the brake pedal, strong springs attached to the brake shoes or pads release the pressure against the wheel drum or discs. At the same time, the pistons in the wheel cylinders force the brake fluid back through the fluid lines and into the master brake cylinder.

Some cars have what are called *power brakes*. The addition of such a power assist to the brake system simply reduces the amount of force that you must exert on the brake pedal. Power brakes have no effect on stopping distance.

Parking Brake. The parking-brake system is made up of a foot or hand-operated pedal or lever which is attached to a metal cable that in turn is attached to the rear brakes. A simple ratchet system is provided to hold and release the parking brake.

The primary purpose of the parking brake is to hold the vehicle in a given position once it is stopped. Only under extreme conditions, such as if the hydraulic brake system fails, should you attempt to stop a vehicle by using the parking brake.

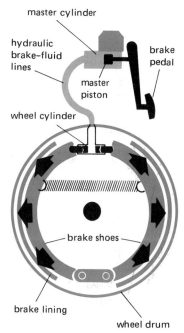

In the most common type of hydraulic brake system, pressing down on the brake pedal forces the brake shoes and brake lining out against the wheel drum. This causes friction, which slows the turning of the wheel.

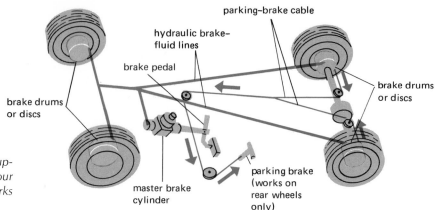

parking–brake cable

hydraulic brake–
fluid lines

brake pedal

brake drums
or discs

brake drums
or discs

master brake
cylinder

parking brake
(works on
rear wheels
only)

The hydraulic brake system supplies stopping power to all four wheels. The parking brake works only on the rear wheels.

Vehicle Maintenance

Even if you are driving a car that is operating perfectly, it will not function at peak performance forever. Normal wear of the engine, tires, brakes, and other parts must be expected. To drive safely and economically, you have to maintain your car in the best possible condition. Regular servicing and maintenance checks will improve both vehicle performance and fuel economy.

As you drive, you will become more familiar with your car. If you sense some change in the way it responds—in the way it steers, brakes, or accelerates—something needs attention. While you need not be a mechanic to notice many of these changes, you should try to become familiar with your car—inside, outside, and under the hood. Remember, any change in its performance could indicate possible trouble.

MAKING YOUR OWN INSPECTION

There are many checks that you can make on your car. The best source of information concerning maintenance is your *owner's manual.* This booklet is included when you buy a new car. If you buy a used car and such a booklet is not included, you should get one from an automobile dealer or the company that built the car. The manual will contain a specific program of inspection, care, and servicing that the company considers essential for proper operation.

Outside the Vehicle. For routine purposes, the following list of outside visual checks can be made on all vehicles:

1. Check the ground under the car for signs of leaking oil or radiator fluid. Make this check after the vehicle has been parked for an hour or so.

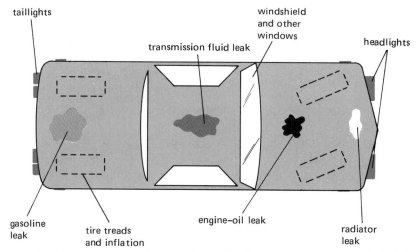

taillights

windshield and other windows

transmission fluid leak

headlights

gasoline leak

tire treads and inflation

engine–oil leak

radiator leak

You should make these routine outside checks of your car to make sure that it is in proper working order and has not been damaged.

2. Check for damage to any glass area (windows, windshield, or mirrors) and burned out or broken headlights, brake and signal lights, or side warning lights.

3. Check tire inflation and look for damage or unusual tire wear.

4. Check for damage to the car body and trim.

Under the Hood. The following outside checks should be made often, and especially whenever you are about to take a long trip:

1. Check the amount of fluid in the radiator, battery, and windshield-washer fluid tank. (Make sure the fluid in the radiator is cool before removing the radiator cap. Many people are scalded by superheated liquids boiling out when the cap is removed.) The engine-oil and power-steering and master-brake-cylinder reservoirs should also be checked.

2. Check the fan belts and the belts in the power steering, power brakes, and air conditioner. They may be worn or need adjustment.

3. Check all hoses and hose connections.

4. Check for loose or disconnected wires.

5. Check the transmission fluid level. This test must be made with the engine running and the selector lever in the *P (park)* position. You will have to start the engine and allow it to run for a few moments to allow the transmission fluid to warm up.

A good habit to develop is to have the attendant at a service station check under the hood each time you get gasoline. These rou-

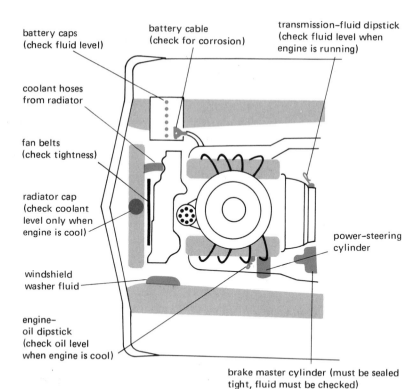

battery caps
(check fluid level)

battery cable
(check for corrosion)

transmission–fluid dipstick
(check fluid level when
engine is running)

coolant hoses
from radiator

fan belts
(check tightness)

radiator cap
(check coolant
level only when
engine is cool)

power–steering
cylinder

windshield
washer fluid

engine-
oil dipstick
(check oil level
when engine is cool)

brake master cylinder (must be sealed
tight, fluid must be checked)

You or an attendant at a service station should make these underhood checks each time you get gasoline.

tine inspections should include checks of the battery, the engine-oil level, and windshield-washer fluid tanks. By making these checks, you can prevent many problems and catch small problems before they become serious.

VEHICLE SYSTEMS MAINTENANCE

All automobile manufacturers provide maintenance schedules and standards that should be observed for safe and efficient vehicle operation. Some kinds of service (such as oil changes and grease jobs) are standard to all vehicles, but recommended service schedules vary from one make and model to another.

You have been introduced to the basic operating systems and their functions. It is just as important that you become aware of the type of maintenance needed to achieve top performance. It is best not to wait for something to go wrong before you have your car serviced. Regular servicing will extend the life of your car and, in the long run, will reduce the cost of operation.

The company or person you select to maintain or repair your car, whether it is the dealer from whom you bought the car or a service station, is critical. This is particularly true if your knowledge of vehicle servicing is limited. (An increasing number of areas in the country are requiring that both garages and mechanics meet certain standards before they can be licensed to do auto repair.) If you do not already know of a reliable mechanic or service station, take time to get advice from family or friends.

Before you commit yourself to a major repair job, you may want to let several different mechanics or service stations do minor repairs. This will allow you to compare the quality of their work. It is best, for your own protection, to get a written estimate of the cost of your repairs in advance. Make it clear to the mechanics that you want to be contacted, *before* the work is done, if the actual cost of repairs will be more than the estimate.

THE INTERNAL COMBUSTION ENGINE
The "heart" of the power train is the engine, and it is the engine and its various subsystems that require the most frequent adjustment and maintenance. Generally, a car driven 12,000 miles per year should receive an engine tune-up one to three times, depending upon the type of use and environmental conditions. (For specific information, see your owner's manual.)

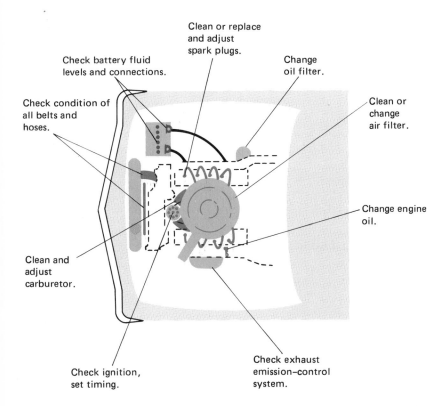

Clean or replace and adjust spark plugs.

Check battery fluid levels and connections.

Change oil filter.

Check condition of all belts and hoses.

Clean or change air filter.

Change engine oil.

Clean and adjust carburetor.

Check ignition, set timing.

Check exhaust emission–control system.

Each time you have your car engine tuned, you should have the mechanic check these items.

187

An engine tune-up involves changing the engine oil and oil filter, checking the carburetor adjustment, and cleaning or changing the air filter. In addition, the alternator, ignition wires, and timing and voltage must be checked. The various drive belts and hoses must be checked for wear. Also, the fluid levels in the battery and radiator must be looked at. The battery terminals may need cleaning, and various of the emission-control devices may have to be adjusted or replaced.

While performing a tune-up, a mechanic may recommend replacement parts (such as spark plugs) or new fluids (such as coolant or transmission fluid) to put your car back in proper running order. Any replacement parts that you may use must meet the car manufacturer's specifications. What many people forget, however, is that replacement fluids must also meet the manufacturer's specifications. Again, check your owner's manual for details.

If the engine was running unevenly before a tune-up and this condition continues afterward, an engine compression check will probably be necessary. A compression test may identify more serious problems, such as burned and improperly seated intake or exhaust valves, worn piston rings, or damaged cylinder walls. Problems like these cannot be corrected with a tune-up. They would require, instead, a complete overhaul of the engine.

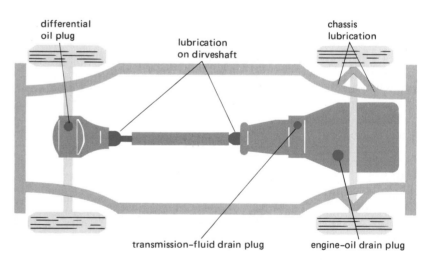

Lubrication and maintenance of the power train other than the engine is often overlooked.

OTHER PARTS OF THE POWER TRAIN

The maintenance schedule for other parts of the power train is somewhat less demanding than the maintenance schedule for the engine. However, all parts of the power train require servicing.

The fluid level in either an automatic or a manual transmission should be checked. In addition, the fluid level in the rear-axle housing should be inspected. Fluid should be added, if necessary, whenever the engine is tuned, or every 6,000 miles. Furthermore, the fluid in an automatic transmission should be completely changed every 24,000 miles, or as specified in the owner's manual.

Universal joints are used to connect the driveshaft to the transmission and differential. If these units are not sealed, they should be greased every 6,000 to 8,000 miles. If the units are sealed, they should be checked for signs of leakage or damage. They may then have to be replaced.

SUSPENSION AND STEERING SYSTEMS

Sudden failure of the suspension or steering systems is quite rare. Problems usually develop gradually. However, it is important that you have these systems checked and serviced at least every six months. Some manufacturers recommend lubrication of tie-rod fittings and ball joints at 4,000 to 6,000 miles or at intervals of 4 to 6 months. Other manufacturers indicate a maintenance interval of 25,000 to 36,000 miles. Regardless of the schedule, check the condition of the various parts of both the steering and suspension systems while your car is up on a hoist for servicing. Shock absorbers should be checked for signs of fluid leakage and the condition of the fasteners. If any part shows signs of excessive wear or looseness, the shock absorber should be replaced.

The condition of the tires can tell you something about the condition of the steering and suspension systems. Greater tread wear on either side of one or both front tires usually indicates the need for front-end alignment, new shock absorbers, or both. Flat spots in the tire tread indicate that the tires need to be balanced.

You should also remain alert for other evidence of suspension and steering system problems. As you drive, you may notice that

free play in the steering wheel

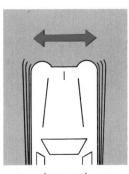

front–end wobble

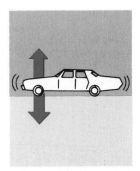

excessive bouncing

Be alert for signs of wear in the steering and suspension systems.

there is free play in the steering wheel. That is, you may find that the steering wheel can be turned quite a bit before the front wheels actually change direction. Two or more inches of free play in the steering wheel of a manual steering system indicates a problem. Any free play with power steering is serious and should be checked immediately. Other evidence of trouble includes front-end *shimmy,* or wobbling, and a tendency for your car to pull to the right or to the left as you drive. Any of these conditions may mean that the front end needs to be realigned or that the wheels need to be rebalanced.

Shock absorbers deteriorate gradually. If you notice that your car bounces more than once after going over a small bump or that it sways or leans on a turn, you have evidence that the shocks are wearing. You can check your shock absorbers by pushing down hard on the trunk or hood several times, bouncing the car frame. If the car bounces more than once after you stop, the shocks should be replaced.

Selecting Shock Absorbers. When considering the purchase of a new car or when replacing shock absorbers, you should ask several questions. What type of driving will you be doing? What size load will you be carrying? Will you be pulling a trailer or carrying loads on top of your car? Heavy-duty suspension systems are available for special use. Most heavy-duty systems will result in a somewhat harder ride under normal conditions but will improve vehicle handling when the car is loaded. Some special shock absorbers, designed for use on the rear wheels, can be adjusted. By inflating them with air, you can adjust their stiffness to accommodate the added weight of a trailer or other load.

WHEEL BEARINGS

It is recommended that the wheels be pulled off every 20,000 to 30,000 miles. At this time, the front-wheel bearings should be repacked with grease and the grease seals should be replaced. The rear-wheel grease seals should be also inspected for leakage. Leaking grease seals present two major problems. The first is that leaks may result in inadequate lubrication of the wheel bearings. The second is the possibility that grease will leak into the wheel drums and onto the brake linings. Either of these conditions will have extremely hazardous results.

THE BRAKING SYSTEM

When you press down on the brake pedal, you should feel resistance that is firm, and your vehicle should come to a smooth, straight stop. The first indication of brake trouble may occur when you are driving. You may find that you need to press down

190

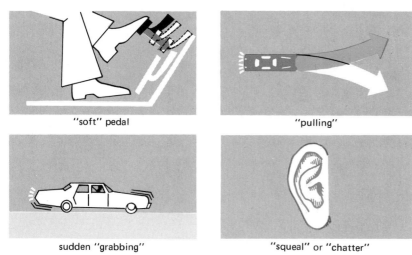

"soft" pedal

"pulling"

sudden "grabbing"

"squeal" or "chatter"

If there are any signs of wear in the brake system, have it checked immediately.

the brake pedal further than usual before the brakes begin to hold. In addition, your car may pull to the right or to the left, or the brakes may suddenly "grab" as you press the pedal down with light pressure. If the pedal feels soft or if the brakes grab, squeal, or pull unevenly, the brake system should be inspected immediately.

Brake-system maintenance schedules will vary considerably. These variations result from both the conditions under which the vehicle is operated and the way the individual operator drives. The level of fluid in the master-brake-cylinder reservoir should be checked every time the engine is tuned. In cars equipped with disc brakes, the fluid level may go down slightly as the pads wear down. Any noticeable or continued loss of fluid, however, should alert you to the need to inspect the total system for leaks.

The brake linings should generally be checked at 15,000 and 25,000 miles and every 5,000 miles thereafter. It is critical that the brake linings be changed before they wear through to solid metal. Continuing to use brakes on which the linings have worn thin could be very costly: the wheel discs or drums might be damaged and have to be replaced. In addition, driving with worn linings is an extremely dangerous practice.

TIRES

If the tires do not provide sufficient traction to execute the desired maneuver, *you are in difficulty.* The general construction of the tires, their tread depth, and their inflation are all important to vehicle control.

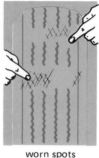

| tire depth | worn spots | cuts | bulges |

Check the condition of your tires often.

Inspecting Your Tires. Frequent inspection of your tires is essential. Improper inflation and cuts or blisters on the side wall or tread mean trouble. The same is true of nails, glass, or metal stuck anywhere in the tire.

Tread depth can prove to be critical in certain situations. The minimum legal tread depth, $\frac{2}{32}$ inch, is indicated on newer tires by a tread-wear indicator bar that is built into the tire. However, while $\frac{2}{32}$ inch of tread may be adequate on a smooth, dry surface, it may be dangerous on a wet surface.

Tire Inflation. Most manufacturers recommend a range of tire pressures. Pressure should never be allowed to fall below the suggested minimum. In fact, vehicle control generally improves slightly when tires are inflated up toward the pressure recommended for long-distance high-speed driving. This higher pressure may sacrifice some of the smooth ride that a softer tire provides, but it will give additional traction. Furthermore, tire side walls will flex more when they are underinflated. This increases the internal friction of tire fabrics and thus increases the chances of tire failure.

Hydroplaning. A wet surface reduces traction and increases the chances of losing control. As tread depth and tire inflation decrease and water depth increases, this problem can become

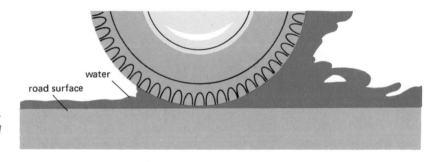

water

road surface

When a car hydroplanes, it actually loses contact with the road and rides on a thin film of water.

192

very serious. In a heavy rain, your tires can lose contact with the roadway surface and actually ride on top of a film of water. This is known as *hydroplaning*. When this occurs, a vehicle's direction and speed are no longer under the driver's control. (On a straight section of roadway, the driver may be unaware that this condition exists.)

The precise point at which a car will begin to hydroplane is difficult to identify because it is influenced by the speed of the car, the amount of water on the road surface, the depth of the tire tread, and the tire inflation. You should be alert to the problem any time that water is standing on the pavement or when rain is falling hard enough to cause the raindrops to bubble as they hit the roadway.

Tire Rotation. Because tires do not usually wear down at the same rate, they need to be rotated. (That is, their positions should be switched from front to rear and left to right.) Tires should, in most cases, be rotated every 4,000 to 6,000 miles. When rotating tires, however, you should keep two things in mind:

1. Tire rotation plans differ, depending on the type of tire construction. Be sure to check your owner's manual for the proper plan.
2. If uneven tread wear occurs on the front tires, tire rotation should not be used as a substitute for front-end alignment or new shock absorbers.

You can drive in the tracks of a car ahead to reduce the chances of hydroplaning.

THE EXHAUST SYSTEM

The life expectancy of the exhaust system, like the brake system, depends on the conditions under which the vehicle is driven. Stop-and-go, short-trip driving is much harder on the system than long trips. On long trips, heat and evaporation get rid of the acid waters that tend to collect on and corrode the metal.

The exhaust system should be inspected, from the exhaust manifold to the tail pipe, every time the car is serviced. Points that require special attention are the connections at either end of the muffler, the muffler itself, and the tail pipe. Two points of the

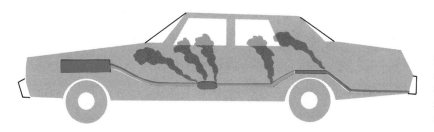

Leaks in the exhaust system or a rusted-off tail pipe are extremely dangerous. They can leak poisonous gases into the passenger compartment.

tail pipe that require careful inspection are the last several inches of pipe that carry the exhaust gases out from beneath the vehicle and the section of pipe that bends up over the rear axle.

To drive a vehicle with an exhaust leak anywhere in the system or with a tail pipe from which the last several inches have rusted off is extremely hazardous. Such leaks will allow exhaust gases, including carbon monoxide, to be trapped beneath the vehicle, even when the vehicle is moving. If there are any holes in the floor or wheel wells, these gases can be drawn up into the passenger compartment. Since carbon monoxide has no odor, color, or taste and is dangerous in even small quantities, the driver or passengers may be in serious trouble without being aware of it. It is critical, therefore, that the exhaust system be repaired at the first sign of wear.

VEHICLE LIGHTING SYSTEM

The vehicle lighting system is frequently overlooked in a program of routine maintenance. While checks may be made for burned-out brake lights, signal indicators, or headlights when the vehicle is serviced, there are other checks that must also be made. Probably the most critical of these is a check of the headlights. They must be wiped clean, because even a fine film of dust will reduce the amount of light available to you when you are driving. Dirt and debris splashed up onto the headlights during a rain or snow storm can reduce lighting to a truly dangerous level.

Another important check to make is headlight alignment. Headlight alignment simply means directing both the high- and low-beam headlights so that they provide maximum illumination. Few people are aware that striking a hole in the road or running

Clean, properly adjusted headlights are critical to safe driving.

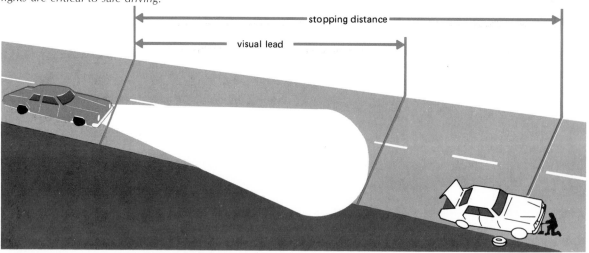

into a curb can knock the headlights out of alignment. Your first indication of poor alignment may be the actions of other drivers at night. If you are driving with your headlights on low beams and oncoming drivers often flash their headlights, high to low, your headlights may be poorly aligned. The same is true if drivers ahead often reach up to adjust their rear-view mirrors as you draw closer. Further, if your high-beam headlights do not seem to light up the roadway far enough ahead, they may need alignment.

Vehicle Performance and Decision-Making

Having studied the basic systems of the automobile and their maintenance, you may well be asking, "How does this affect my decision-making when I am driving?" Remember, collision-free driving means the proper management of time and the proper control of your vehicle. You influence these factors with your selection of speed and road position. You should now realize that the performance characteristics of motor vehicles vary according to the vehicle's original design and the extent to which it is maintained in good working condition. You must learn to make decisions that are based upon the performance capability of your own car and those of all other vehicles around you on the highway.

ASSESSING VEHICLE PERFORMANCE

To better enable you to judge time and space requirements when selecting speeds and roadway positions, you need to gain an understanding of three basic vehicle-performance characteristics:

1. Acceleration and speed
2. Directional control and cornering
3. Braking and deceleration

Understanding these variables will help you to better estimate the response you can expect from your own car and the limits of other vehicles on the highway. The most important question to ask before making any driving decision is: "Will the maneuver I want to make be within the performance capabilities of my vehicle?"

Before making any driving decision, you must ask yourself this basic question in one of many forms: "Will there be enough time to pass safely now? Is there enough distance between me and the overtaking vehicle for me to merge, change lanes, or pull from the curb before the vehicle is too close? Will I be able to stop if that child runs into my path? Would I be able to steer away quickly enough if the door of that parked car suddenly opened?"

195

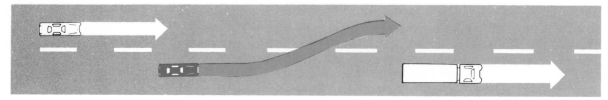

When you make a driving decision, you must estimate the performance capabilities of other vehicles. Would you be able to pass this truck on a hill without risking a rear-end collision with the other car?

In the final analysis, no decision can be considered correct unless the maneuver you choose to make is one that your vehicle is capable of performing.

ACCELERATION

You must consider the ability of your own and other vehicles to accelerate from one speed to another and to maintain a given speed if you are to be able to choose the best possible roadway position.

Acceleration is an increase in speed, either from a stopped position or from one speed to a higher speed. The time it takes to accelerate from one speed to another is called the *rate of acceleration*. In any given vehicle, acceleration, or pickup, depends upon the engine power, the transmission and differential gear ratios, and the traction between the drive wheels and the roadway surface.

Because you will have to estimate the acceleration capabilities of the vehicles around you on a highway, you should know some-

Because they cannot accelerate quickly, large vehicles may have difficulty merging with traffic. If you are following a large truck on an entrance ramp, increase your space cushion ahead.

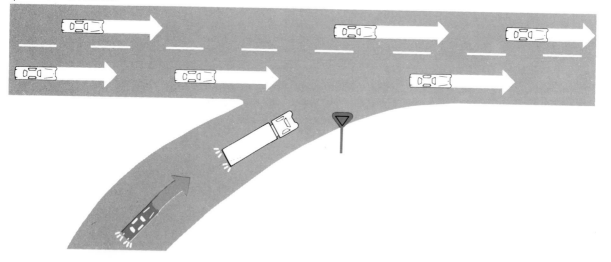

thing about how, in general, different kinds of vehicles accelerate. For example, many subcompact cars do not maintain speed well and have limited acceleration capability because of their size and because their engines are not very powerful. However, a number of small specialty cars are designed with powerful engines, and their acceleration capability may be very great.

On the other hand, larger vehicles, especially large eight-cylinder cars, generally have good acceleration capabilities and speed-holding characteristics. This is not to say, however, that all large vehicles accelerate and hold speed well. For example, tractor-trailer rigs and intercity buses are equipped with huge engines capable of maintaining a relatively high rate of speed once in motion, particularly on straight, level roadways. However, when loaded, they tend to accelerate very slowly. If you did not know this, you might fail to keep an adequate space cushion and you could become involved in a rear-end collision. Generally, it is best to accelerate gradually, but you may have to accelerate rapidly to complete maneuvers like pulling from a curb, merging, crossing intersections, and turning at intersections. Due to the high possibility of error or loss of control, you should try to avoid situations that demand extreme acceleration. Beginning drivers are particularly prone to make errors related to the need for rapid increases in speed. As a result, it is critical that you become aware of general acceleration characteristics of different kinds of vehicles.

Acceleration Rate Changes. A fact about acceleration that many drivers are unaware of is that acceleration capability varies with speed. *As the speed of the vehicle increases, the acceleration capability of the vehicle decreases.* This simply means that it will take more time, for example, to accelerate from 50 to 60 mph than it will to accelerate from 20 to 30 mph.

Another factor that influences the rate of acceleration is the gear ratio of the transmission and the differential. A lower drive-train gear ratio provides more power and, therefore, a higher rate of acceleration. In contrast, vehicles with high drive-train gear ratios have less power. For example, the power and acceleration rate of a vehicle equipped with a manual transmission can be increased at 25 mph by shifting from *third* or *fourth* gear to a lower gear. In a vehicle equipped with an automatic transmission, this extra power is provided by what is often called a *passing gear*. Suddenly depressing the accelerator to the floor will cause a downshift to a lower gear and give the vehicle a more rapid rate of acceleration. However, because of the errors in judgment that all drivers make, you should not make a maneuver that would require maximum use of your vehicle's acceleration capability.

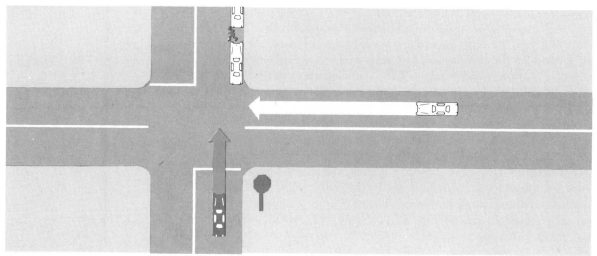

In this situation, if you accelerated as quickly as possible you might get across the street without colliding with the car approaching from the right. However, would you have time to brake for the pedestrian?

SPEED

The speed a vehicle is traveling is stated in miles per hour (mph). However, since it is seldom possible to drive at a constant speed, we tend to state speeds in terms of averages. In other words, if it takes 1 hour to go 30 miles, the average speed is 30 mph, even though the actual speeds may have varied from 0 to 55 mph.

Monitoring Your Speed. Since it is very difficult—particularly for new drivers—to estimate speed, a speedometer is important. Your speedometer tells you, within a few miles per hour, how fast you are actually traveling. However, such things as tire size, tire inflation, and the amount of tire tread can cause errors in the speedometer reading of up to 5 percent. With experience, you will probably find that you are more aware of speed changes without checking the speedometer. For example, as speed varies, you will notice differences in the car's vibration or in the level of the sound from the tires, wind, or engine.

It is more difficult to estimate your speed following a large change in speed. If you are driving at 20 mph for a long period of time and suddenly accelerate to 45 mph, you will temporarily feel as if you are moving much faster. On the other hand, if you have been traveling at a high rate of speed on an expressway and suddenly reduce your speed to exit or to manage a potentially difficult situation, you are likely to make the error of slowing down less than you really should. This problem may occur simply because you have become accustomed to the higher speed. Of the two errors, the latter is the more dangerous. In either case,

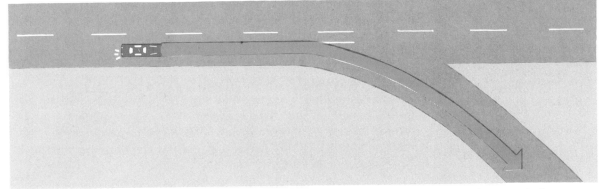

As you slow to exit from an expressway, check your speedometer to make sure that you have reduced your speed enough.

however, the only way that you can compensate for such an error is to refer to your speedometer.

The speed of your vehicle is most directly controlled by the amount of gasoline supplied to the engine. However, gravity also affects a vehicle's speed. When you are driving downhill, your speed will tend to increase. Therefore, to maintain a safe speed on a downgrade, you will sometimes need to release the accelerator and apply light or moderate brake pressure. Otherwise, you may accelerate to an unmanageable speed before you realize it.

OTHER VEHICLES

The increasing number of specialty cars on the road will make the task of evaluating other vehicles more difficult. Many of these specialty cars are designed and built to meet high performance standards: they tend to have quick acceleration and improved cornering capability. You can expect the drivers of specialty vehicles to take advantage of these high performance standards.

Motorcycles are also appearing on roads and highways in increasing numbers. Like automobiles, motorcycles depend on their engine size and gear ratios to accelerate and maintain speed. Statistics indicate that motorcycles are, in terms of their numbers on the road, involved in more than their share of accidents and fatalities. The same statistics, however, indicate that over two-thirds of these accidents are the result of improper actions by other highway users.

Many of these accidents appear to be due to failure of drivers of cars or other vehicles to see a cyclist. In other cases, drivers mistake motorcycles for bicycles and make serious errors in estimating acceleration, speed, handling, or stopping ability.

In general, underpowered vehicles have difficulty maintaining speed when they are going up long hills. If you identify an underpowered vehicle ahead in your lane, be prepared to start a lateral move early. Some drivers come up behind slow-moving vehicles so fast that they are forced to brake hard or steer quickly into other lanes to avoid a rear-end collision.

DIRECTIONAL CONTROL AND CORNERING ABILITY

As soon as you put your car into motion, you must be able to control its direction. Specifically, you must be able to maintain it on a desired course—either straight ahead or in turns. How well you will be able to maintain steering control depends on the directional control and cornering stability of your vehicle.

Directional Control. The ability of your vehicle to hold a straight line when it is not influenced by outside forces is called *directional control*. If your car has good directional control, it should continue moving in a certain direction once you point it in that direction. Factors such as the contour of the road, traction, or wind may require that you make steering corrections. However, a vehicle with good directional control does not lose its course because of a lack of stability in the vehicle itself.

When you are driving straight ahead, the rear wheels should track in line behind the front wheels for maximum control. If you observe a vehicle in the traffic around you that is not tracking this way (for example, a vehicle with a bent frame or a vehicle that is sagging to one side), you should be especially alert. Due to improper tracking, the vehicle's directional control will be less precise, and the room it would need to maneuver in an emergency will be more than ordinary.

Cornering Ability. The ability of a vehicle to be steered around a turn without loss of precise control is called *cornering ability*. A vehicle should remain relatively level as it makes a turn. Any vehicle that tends to roll or sway excessively may well lose control.

Some vehicles tend to over- and understeer on turns. This refers to the tendency of a vehicle to move away from the path of

A vehicle's directional control can be influenced by many factors.

suspension

road contour

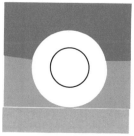

traction

wind

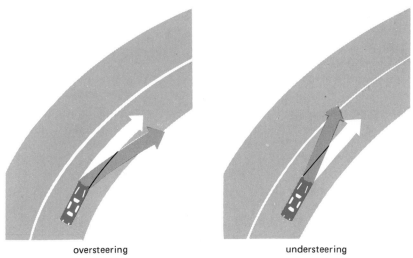

oversteering   understeering

A vehicle which has good cornering ability holds turns well; it does not oversteer or understeer.

travel projected by the driver. *Oversteering* is best described as a tendency for the front end to move toward the inside of the path projected by the driver while the rear end tends to slide out. *Understeering* is just the opposite: the front end tends to plow straight ahead rather than follow the intended path. For most drivers, oversteering is the more dangerous, since it requires turning the steering wheel in a direction opposite to the desired path of travel. In contrast, unless it is severe or is compounded by excessive speed, understeering can be corrected simply by reducing speed and providing more steering input in the desired direction.

Even when they are properly maintained, the steering systems of different vehicles do not respond the same way. Some vehicles simply require more steering input than others.

The most obvious differences in steering response are between vehicles with power steering and those without it. In full-size passenger vehicles equipped with large engines, air conditioners, and other options, power steering is essential for many drivers. Without such assistance, it is practically impossible for some drivers to turn a corner. When properly maintained, power steering requires much less effort. In addition, it provides quicker vehicle response. Furthermore, it reduces the possibility of the steering wheel being jerked from the operator's hands if one of the front wheels strikes an obstacle.

There are certain factors that drivers should be alert to when they change from nonpower steering to power steering. One is

201

the partial loss of feedback from the roadway. Experienced drivers are alert to information about the roadway surface that is transmitted to their hands on the steering wheel. With power steering, much of this feedback is lost. A second factor is the possible failure of the power-assist unit. The most frequent cause of such failure is a stalled engine. It is important to remember that if the power unit fails, you will still be able to steer, but it will require much more effort. At slow speeds such a failure can be particularly difficult because the effort required to turn the steering wheel will greatly increase.

Factors Influencing Directional Control and Cornering. The suspension, steering system, and tires play an important role in the maintenance of directional control and cornering. Defects in any of these systems will cause a decrease in your ability to control the vehicle. Even under good roadway conditions, soft or unbalanced tires, worn or improper shock absorbers, or poor front-end alignment will affect vehicle handling. Furthermore, a vehicle that is overloaded or loaded improperly with either passengers or packages will suffer a decrease in handling response. All these factors should be considered every time you drive.

Another factor influencing directional control is the way a vehicle is loaded. The higher and heavier a load, the less stable a vehicle will be.

You must, of course, pay attention to the directional control and cornering ability of the vehicles around you on the highway. Keep the following in mind:

1. Vehicles that appear to sag on one side or to the front or rear may have either worn shock absorbers or broken springs.

2. If a vehicle is overloaded, its back end will be lower than normal. An overloaded trunk will make directional control difficult and will increase the influence of centrifugal force. This increases the chances of rear-end spin-outs on sharp curves or turns.

3. Watch for cars with luggage in carriers on the roof. Both the position of the luggage rack and the size of the load are important. Heavy loads, particularly when placed to the rear of the vehicle, will influence directional control. In addition, top-loaded vehicles—like vans or cars with luggage racks—have a high center of gravity and are especially affected by winds.

4. Wheel shimmy, wobble, and bounce are indicators of tire, steering, or suspension systems defects. Any such defects decrease vehicle handling.

5. Cars with raised, or "raked," rear ends, will usually have poor cornering characteristics. Another hazard connected with such vehicles is the fact that their fuel tanks are often exposed. This increases the chances of fire in case of a rear-end collision.

6. Vehicles pulling other vehicles or trailers will almost always lose some directional control, cornering ability, and acceleration.

7. Motorcycles require special attention. Obviously, they can be driven through spaces that are too narrow for ordinary cars. It is also obvious that they are highly maneuverable when properly controlled at slow speeds. However, at highway speeds, traction and centrifugal force have a marked effect on the motorcycle operator's ability to respond quickly and safely. Unless motorcyclists are highly skilled, they require at least as much space as cars to make lateral maneuvers. In other words, do not crowd them simply because they are smaller than most vehicles.

BRAKING AND DECELERATION

Many factors, such as the condition of the roadway, your vehicle, your speed, and your vehicle's performance ability, work in combination to determine stopping time and distance. As a driver, you must attempt to adjust to or modify these factors to avoid accidents. To make the necessary adjustments, you need some understanding of the factors involved.

Few drivers are fully aware of the implications of perception time, reaction time, and braking time—or the total stopping distance or time. Consequently, they make errors in their decisions. To stop a vehicle a driver must do three things:

1. Perceive a need to stop
2. Physically react by releasing the gas pedal and by moving to the brake pedal
3. Depress the brake pedal and brake the vehicle to a stop

perception time—
you see a hazard

reaction time—
you release accelerator
and apply the brake

braking distance—
you apply controlled
pressure

The total time elapsed before you can brake to a full stop is made up of the time needed to perceive, react, and brake.

Each of these actions takes time. While it is nearly impossible to remember a long list of numbers, the following table provides a reference for judging the distances and times required for a complete stop.

Speed	Perception-time distance	Reaction-time distance	Braking-time distance	Total stopping-time distance
30 mph	? ft	¾ sec or 33 ft	45 ft	78+ ft
40 mph	? ft	¾ sec or 44 ft	80 ft	124+ ft
60 mph	? ft	¾ sec or 66 ft	190 ft	256+ ft

This table demonstrates two important things:

1. Braking distance increases at a rate equal to the *square* of the difference in speed. (For example, if the speed of a vehicle is doubled, its braking distance is four times as great.)

2. The time required to stop increases from approximately 2 seconds at 30 mph to over 3 seconds at 60 mph. Even this amount of time, however, offers little room for error, since the time you may need to identify a crisis is an unknown factor.

These factors demonstrate the need for determining in advance an immediate planned path of travel at least 4 seconds ahead in case it becomes necessary to make an emergency stop.

Deceleration, or a reduction in speed, is most directly achieved either by removing pressure from the gas pedal or by applying pressure to the brake pedal. This reduction in speed is the result of friction. However, a certain amount of deceleration also occurs as a result of the retarding force of engine compression, friction generated in the drive train, friction between the tires and roadway surface, and air resistance.

Braking to a Stop. Controlled stopping depends on the friction generated between the brake linings and wheel drums, or wheel discs and pads, when pressure is applied to the brake pedal. This friction slows the rotation of the wheels and tires, which in turn creates friction between the tires and roadway surface.

Assuming the brake system is functioning properly, there are a number of factors that influence the distance required to bring a vehicle to a stop after the brakes have been applied. Among these factors are the area of the braking surface (drum and brake lining); the vehicle's size, weight, height, and load; the tire's size, tread, and inflation; and the roadway surface.

Once the wheels begin to turn more slowly, the rate at which speed is reduced is governed by the coefficient of friction between the tires and the roadway. Regardless of the friction that can be generated between the brake linings and wheel drums, the maximum usable braking force cannot exceed the amount of available friction between the tires and the roadway. Maximum braking force is obtained just before the tires start to slide on the roadway surface. At this point, the friction generated by the brakes and the friction between the tires and the roadway are nearly equal. Further pressure on the brake pedal would lock the wheels, but does not increase the usable braking force. In fact, the heat resulting from friction between the tires and the roadway surface may melt the rubber and actually lengthen the stopping distance slightly.

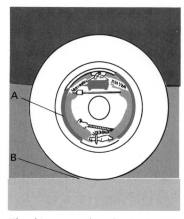

The friction within the brake (A) must not exceed the friction between the tire and the road (B). Otherwise, the wheel will lock.

Brake Usage. Extended hard braking builds up heat so that braking efficiency may be reduced. Repeated hard brakings or a long continuous brake application can in fact produce a condition called *brake fade,* in which the brake linings get so hot that they lose this ability to stop the wheels from turning. If enough overheating occurs, total brake failure can result. If permanent damage has not occurred as a result of the overheating, the brakes will usually regain their normal level of performance after a brief period of cooling.

To avoid such a condition, braking should start well in advance of a stop. The amount of pressure applied should be just enough to bring your car to a smooth steady stop. A properly timed pumping action of the brake pedal (with pressure adjusted to the roadway surface) provides the best vehicle control. This type of speed reduction also causes the least disturbance in a stream of traffic and alerts drivers around you of your intention to stop. It also requires less braking force, thus providing you with reserve braking power if needed.

Wet Brake Linings. Wet brake linings usually result from one of two conditions. The first condition may occur when condensation collects on the brake drums. (This is most common when your car is parked outside overnight, in humid weather, or when there is a moderate drop in temperature.) Drivers most often notice this problem just after leaving a parking space, when they brake to a stop. The most common symptom is brakes that pull to the left or to the right. A simple solution or safeguard against this problem is to rest your left foot gently on the brake pedal for a moment or so as soon as you start moving. This action generates heat, which drys the wheel drums.

The second, more serious, problem is that created when you are forced to drive through very heavy rain or water that is so deep that the brake drums are under water. When water over the road is several inches deep, it is critical that you drive very slowly to avoid "drowning" the engine. Your slow rate of speed, however, almost assures flooding of the brake drums. Under such circumstances it is essential that you try your brakes as soon as you have driven out of the flooded area. If the brake drums are flooded, the brakes will not stop your car. If this occurs, apply moderate pressure to the brake pedal with your left foot. At the same time, apply light pressure to the gas pedal so that you continue moving slowly. The pressure of the brake lining against the drum will again generate heat and evaporate the water. Continue this process until the brakes work normally when pressure is applied.

Braking Characteristics of Other Vehicles. When determining your speed and position in traffic, it is a good idea to observe vehicles around you to identify whatever might affect their braking capability. Anything that suggests a defective suspension system will have a bad influence on a vehicle's ability to make a rapid, controlled stop. When you are driving on snow-covered or wet roads, or when you are stopped at a traffic sign or signal, you can check the tire tread and inflation of the vehicles around you. Both low tread depth and tire pressure will increase stopping distances. This is especially true if there is moisture or debris (such as sand or gravel) on the road.

Vehicles that are overloaded or improperly loaded will require increased time and distance to stop. In addition, they will have more difficulty holding to a straight line while stopping. Large vehicles (such as tractor-trailer rigs, buses, mobile homes, vans, and camper units) usually require greater stopping distance, and so they, too, have less stability when they are brought to a quick stop. This problem is particularly noticeable if such vehicles are forced to brake on long or steep downgrades.

Motorcycles again deserve special attention. The braking characteristics of motorcycles are relatively good at lower speeds.

However, at highway speeds they may present problems. The distance needed to stop a motorcycle at highway speeds is at least as great as, and frequently greater than, the distance needed to stop an automobile. Stopping from highway speeds is further complicated by the chance that the motorcyclist may lose control in a high-speed braking situation.

In addition to evaluating the braking capabilities of vehicles around you, you should also be alert to defective brake lights. While your selection of speed or position should always be based on the assumption of being challenged, a sudden reduction of speed on the part of another vehicle—without the warning provided by brake lights—could place you in a situation that you could not handle safely.

To Think About

1. Discuss the importance of a complete program of vehicle maintenance.
2. How is the up-and-down motion of the pistons changed to the rotary motion of the driveshaft?
3. How is the rotary motion of the driveshaft transmitted to the drive-wheel transmitted to the drive-wheel axle?
4. What are the major differences between a piston engine and a rotary engine?
5. What are some of the characteristics and effects of carbon monoxide?
6. Name two important functions of the exhaust system.
7. What is the purpose of engine oil?
8. Is passenger comfort the only function of the springs and shock absorbers?
9. What are the differences between the hydraulic brake system and the parking brake? If the hydraulic brake system failed, how would you use the parking brake to stop your vehicle?
10. Describe the outside and under-the-hood checks you should make before you drive.
11. What are some signs of trouble in the suspension and steering systems?
12. What are some signs of trouble in the braking system?
13. Why is proper tire inflation critical?
14. Describe what you would look for when you checked your vehicle's tires.
15. Why is it important to judge the performance capabilities of other vehicles on the roadway?
16. What factors affect a vehicle's directional control and cornering ability?
17. What factors affect a vehicle's braking ability?
18. Explain why the total stopping-time distance is the sum of the perception-time, reaction-time, and braking-time distances.

To Do

1. Make an under-the-hood check of your family's or school's car. Identify as many of the parts of the engine as you can.
2. Visit a local service station or diagnostic center and report on the way it operates. Ask the owner what kinds of maintenance car owners most often neglect. Report to your class.

3. Make a list of the kinds of mechanical defects you would recognize after reading this chapter. What defects are most dangerous and which would result in the most costly problems if neglected?
4. Study the owner's manual of your school's or your family's car. Has your school or family followed the suggestions made in the manual? Report to your class.
5. Interview several experienced drivers. In what kinds of situations do they adjust their speed and position according to the performance capabilities of other vehicles? Report to your class.

Other Highway Users 8

After reading this chapter, you should be able to:

1. Name and describe three types of nonmotorized highway users.
2. Discuss why young children and the elderly are most often involved in pedestrian accidents.
3. Define the term *ground search*.
4. Explain why the number of bicycle accidents has increased dramatically in the last few years.

Nonmotorized highway users include the many pedestrians, bicyclists, and animals with whom you must interact as a driver. Some of these highway users (such as bicyclists) may be on a roadway on purpose. Others (such as children at play) may move onto the roadway without intending to do so. They are often not aware of or prepared for the vehicles with which they share the roadway.

Drivers must be licensed to operate motor vehicles on roads and highways. This provides at least some control over who can and cannot drive. There are few controls, however, for nonmotorized users of the highway. Almost all people of all ages are pedestrians. Anyone big enough to operate a bicycle may do so almost anywhere. Both wild animals and pets roam about at will. While there are some laws designed to control or guide the behavior of most nonmotorized highway users, the application and enforcement are spotty at best.

Pedestrian Accidents

In the United States, there are about 11,000 pedestrian fatalities annually. In other words, pedestrian deaths account for approximately 20 percent of all traffic fatalities. An additional 120,000 pedestrians suffer nonfatal injuries each year. Nearly 85 percent of the pedestrian accidents and 67 percent of the fatalities occur in urban areas. (In cities with a population over 200,000 persons, 33 to 50 percent of all traffic fatalities are pedestrians.)

While most pedestrian accidents occur in urban areas, rural pedestrian accidents are more often serious. This is because vehicle speeds in rural areas are generally higher. The probability of a fatality in an urban pedestrian accident is 1 in 20; in rural areas the probability is 1 in 5.

WHO IS INVOLVED?

Age and alcohol are two major factors in pedestrian accidents. The greatest number of pedestrian accidents involve persons between 4 and 7 years and between 64 and 68 years of age. Pedestrian fatalities follow a similar trend: The highest number of fatalities involve children between 4 and 5 years of age, while over age 65 the number steadily increases. It is important to note that among the adult population, 20 to 25 percent of all pedestrians killed had been drinking.

Young, active children, who have not yet developed traffic skills, are often involved in pedestrian accidents.

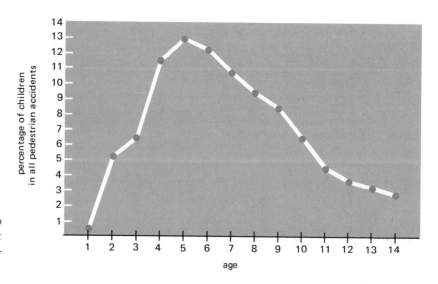

WHERE DO PEDESTRIAN ACCIDENTS OCCUR?

Suburban residential settings create special pedestrian traffic problems. Because there is usually not much vehicle traffic and because intersections are often far apart, many people cross suburban streets in the middle of the block. Meter readers, postal employees, or delivery personnel, all concentrating on their jobs, are apt to step into your path if you are driving in such an area. Other people may step into the street while mowing their lawns or sweeping their sidewalks. They tend to be less alert to vehicles than they should be.

210

The behavior of children is an even more serious problem. Everyone who drives an automobile has heard the following warning: "Be prepared, because behind every ball that bounces into the street there is a child." This is sensible advice, but drivers should be alert to the possibility of children running into the street well before they see a bouncing ball.

You already know that certain highway conditions and locations increase the chances of accidents between vehicles. (For example, rain, a blind curve, or an uncontrolled intersection may each contribute to the likelihood of accidents.) The same holds true for pedestrian accidents. Crowded city streets, suburban residential areas, cars parked on either side of a roadway, and anything that limits visibility will add to the chances of pedestrian mishaps.

CUES OF CONFLICT

Visual cues should always directly influence your selection of speed and position. What should you look for? How are the cues of possible conflicts with other vehicles different from the cues that signal possible conflicts with pedestrians?

You should be alert for young children walking or running, riding tricycles or wagons, playing a game like tag, or simply throwing a ball to one another on the sidewalk or in any area near the roadway. You should not, however, limit your attention to the children you can see. Watch for children across the street who may run to join the group already playing. In addition, as you drive near construction sites or disabled vehicles, look out for children. They may be attracted to such areas.

Play areas near a street should alert drivers to the possibility that children may be in the area.

211

Pets near a roadway present a hazard. They are difficult to see and often dart out into the roadway. However, their presence may also mean that there are children in the immediate area. In addition, bus stops, school zones, playground areas, and crossing guards and safety patrols should alert you to the possibility that children may be playing nearby.

GROUND SEARCH

You already know the importance of a 12-second visual lead when driving. Driving in a residential area, however, should trigger another type of scanning, called a *ground search*.

Young children, because of their size, are particularly difficult to see. Since they may play behind parked vehicles, it is essential for you to search for any movement, or even shadows, under and around vehicles parked on or near the street.

What does this sign alert a driver to? What precautions should a driver take when approaching an intersection like this?

DART-OUT BEHAVIOR

Childhood pedestrian fatalities peak between the ages of 4 and 5 years. One of the major reasons for the higher number of fatalities in this age group is that these children often dart out into the street without giving any thought to traffic on the street. Drivers, on the other hand, are often not aware of the cues that should make them especially alert for children.

As might be expected, this type of accident occurs most frequently in residential areas, where parked cars often seriously cut down visibility and limit escape routes. When driving in such areas, your only defenses will be a strict control of speed and an extra alertness for cues that will help you anticipate dart-out behavior.

212

Groups of children playing near a street may not be aware of traffic hazards.

BEHAVIOR OF YOUNGSTERS

Elementary school children often fail to behave predictably. As a driver, you must look out for situations in which children may unwittingly run into your path of travel. Once away from adult guards or school patrols, children often run, either alone or in groups. Horseplay, pushing, and shoving are other routine activities that deserve special attention. Children who are at play are much more likely to forget about traffic and to run into a road without looking.

Children often dart out into a street without giving any thought to possible traffic hazards.

LACK OF SIDEWALKS

The problem of pedestrians in residential areas is aggravated when there are no sidewalks. The absence of sidewalks increases the likelihood of persons of all ages walking on the roadway itself. It also tends to encourage children to use the street as a playground.

213

Homes with driveways that slope steeply to the street present a special hazard. Children may roll down the driveways on bicycles, tricycles, wagons, or other toys.

This problem may be even more complex if homes are built on lots with driveways that slope down to the street. Where this condition exists, children may coast down the driveway into the street on bicycles, tricycles, wagons, or other toys.

BUSINESS-DISTRICT ACCIDENTS

In residential areas, most accidents occur in the middle of the block. In contrast, most pedestrian mishaps in business districts occur at intersections. Drivers frequently fail to stay alert for pedestrians when approaching intersections in business districts. Instead, they give most of their attention to vehicle crowding or to traffic signals.

Drivers can increase the number of hazards to pedestrians in business districts.

A. driving too fast for conditions
B. failing to yield to pedestrians in a mid-block crosswalk
C. driving while under the influence of alcohol
D. obstructing view by parking too close to crosswalk
E. failing to stop before crossing sidewalk
F. passing stopped vehicle which blocks view of pedestrian
G. failing to yield right-of-way to pedestrian in crosswalk

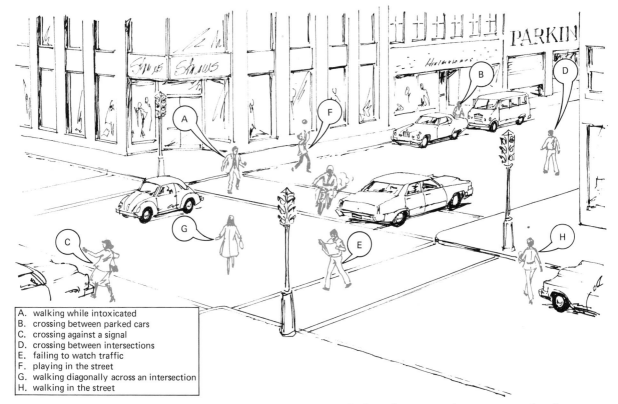

A. walking while intoxicated
B. crossing between parked cars
C. crossing against a signal
D. crossing between intersections
E. failing to watch traffic
F. playing in the street
G. walking diagonally across an intersection
H. walking in the street

On the other hand, few pedestrians appear to give much thought to crossing a street at an intersection. In fact, a pedestrian crossing at an intersection can control the probability of being struck by a motor vehicle. As with other traffic activities, critical factors appear to be the pedestrian's own vision, perceptions, decision-making ability, and physical condition.

The greatest number of pedestrians are struck by a vehicle just as they step into the street. The car is most often in the lane closest to the sidewalk and is usually driving straight through the intersection. The apparent explanation for the high number of accidents in this situation is that the driver, having projected a safe path of travel through the intersection, is unable to respond fast enough when a pedestrian suddenly steps into the street. This situation is often complicated by the maze of posts, signs, vehicles, and other pedestrians at the curb. Adding to this problem is the failure of pedestrians to accurately judge the speed of traffic and, as a result, the time needed to cross the street.

Pedestrians, like drivers, must learn to accurately judge gaps in traffic. For example, the typical young adult can cross a two-lane street in a residential area in approximately 4 to 6 seconds. A child needs about 7 seconds. On the other hand, an elderly person, even without severe physical impairments, may need anywhere from 7 to 10 seconds to cross the same street.

Pedestrians can, by their own actions, endanger themselves.

215

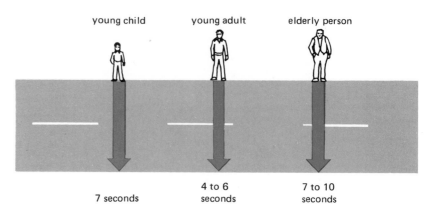

young child

young adult

elderly person

7 seconds

4 to 6
seconds

7 to 10
seconds

Like drivers, pedestrians must be able to judge gaps in traffic and to know their own abilities. Depending on their age and physical condition, pedestrians may need as much as 10 seconds to cross a two-lane street.

With this information, you as a motor-vehicle operator should be in a position to better assist pedestrians. You should be able to estimate the amount of time a pedestrian will need to cross a street. You should also be able to adjust your speed so pedestrians will have enough time to cross before you arrive at a point of conflict.

BEHAVIOR OF THE ELDERLY

The fact that elderly persons generally take longer to cross streets presents special problems. Occasionally they simply do not check for traffic, or they make mistakes in judgment. If the intersection is controlled by a pedestrian traffic light, they may wait too long to start across after the light reads *walk*. As a result, they cannot complete the crossing by the time the light changes again. In some cases they may simply require more time to cross than the *walk* signal allows.

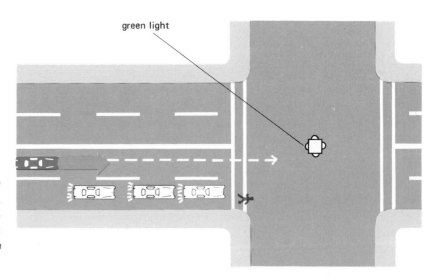

green light

In this situation, the traffic signal is green and the lane ahead appears to be clear. However, the driver's view of the crosswalk is partly blocked. How would you handle this situation?

216

As a precaution, you should be especially careful any time that you approach a red light that suddenly turns green. This is particularly true where there is more than one lane of traffic going in your direction. One lane may be stopped while your lane is clear, and you may be tempted, because you have a green light, to drive on. What you may not know, and may not be able to see, is that the other cars could be stopped so that one or more pedestrians can get across the street. Under such conditions the clear lane may, in fact, be a trap. Pedestrians hidden from your view by the stopped vehicles may step into your path just as you accelerate to go through the intersection. You would really not have anywhere to steer to and not enough time to stop.

BLIND PEDESTRIANS
Drivers sometimes fail to give special consideration to the blind. Most blind people can be identified because they carry white canes or have seeing-eye dogs that lead them. Most blind people, however, have learned to cope with their disability very well and may not, from a distance, appear to be having any difficulty. For this reason, drivers may not recognize that they, as pedestrians, have a serious handicap. In some cases, drivers may, through ignorance, fail to yield the right of way to blind people. This is, of course, against the law.

INFANT STROLLERS OR CARRIAGES
People pushing strollers or carriages may, in attempting to cross intersections, have difficulty getting down off the curb. Under such a condition, they may fail to control the carriage properly. As a result, the carriage could roll into the path of moving traffic.

Your best defense against conflicts like these is to position your car on the roadway so that your vehicle is visible to the pedestrians and you have the best possible field of vision. Adjust your speed and lateral position in such a manner that you can better manage time and space. If there is a question of whether or not a pedestrian can see you or will notice you, lightly tap the horn to gain the pedestrian's attention. This can help you avoid many potentially hazardous situations. If the pedestrians that you are responding to give any evidence of lack of attention or unpredictable behavior, slow down and move laterally away from them as far as traffic permits.

Cues to blind pedestrians include seeing-eye dogs and white canes.

Bicycles and Other Vehicles

Since 1971, the number of bicycles sold annually in the United States has exceeded the number of motor vehicles sold. With this dramatic increase in the number of bicycles has come an increase in the number of injuries and fatalities. In fact, the number of bicycling fatalities has risen from 820 in 1970 to 1,150 in 1973.

LEGAL CONTROLS

Some of these injuries and fatalities are the result of a lack of legal controls. Bicyclists are in some cases regulated by the same laws that apply to the operation of motor vehicles. However, many laws that control motor-vehicle operators do not apply to bicyclists. The most obvious example is that bicyclists, unlike motor-vehicle operators, do not have to have operator's licenses before they can ride on the streets or highways. A driver's license at least indicates that a person has reached a certain age and has demonstrated certain abilities. This simple difference would explain, in part, why it is among the young, beginning bicyclists (5 to 14 years of age) that the greatest number of injuries and fatalities have traditionally occurred.

Another problem is that bicyclists may operate among pedestrians in one situation and among motor vehicles in another. In many areas, for example, there is confusion about the restrictions on where bicycles can be operated—on the sidewalks or on the streets. The present laws vary from city to city and even within cities according to the age of the rider and the location of bicycle paths.

Bicyclists operate as pedestrians in some situations and as drivers in others.

Another restriction requires a bicyclist to ride in the extreme right-hand lane of a street (except during rush-hour traffic, when the right lane is reserved for buses). Some other laws are more specific, requiring bicyclists to ride as close as practical to the right-hand edge of the roadway. However, what does "as close as practical" mean? Within 18 inches, 3 to 4 feet, or just somewhere in the right-hand lane? In short, laws relating to the use of bicycles are not clear and consistent nationwide. To make the problem worse, many laws that do exist are not strictly enforced. As a driver or a bicyclist, you have to compensate for this by being especially careful.

218

WHO OPERATES BICYCLES?

For many years bicycles were thought of only as recreational vehicles or as toys for children. The shortage of fuel, the concern with the environment, and many physical fitness campaigns have added to the number of people who use bicycles as their basic form of transportation. This has greatly increased the number of bicycles operated in heavy commuter traffic, even on streets and highways where high speeds are permitted and under all types of weather conditions and hours of day and night. Partly as a result of this change, and the increased difficulty in seeing a bicyclist under even the best conditions, the number of injuries and fatalities occuring among the 15-to-24-year age group has risen sharply since 1970.

DRIVER RESPONSES

When you are driving in a stream of traffic, your ability to see bicyclists will frequently be limited by a number of factors. One of these factors is your own level of alertness to bicyclists. Equally important is a bicycle's small and light frame. (Bicycles are not large, solid objects like cars and trucks.) An increasing number of bicyclists are making use of flags, lights, and reflectors that increase their visibility. However, many others do not use such devices. It is essential, therefore, that you build into your visual search plan a special alertness for bicyclists and those factors that could influence their paths of travel.

CUES TO DANGER

There are a number of cues that should alert you to hazards which are peculiar to bicycles. The style of a bicycle and the equipment on it provide some information. A small child's bicycle should alert you to

Look for cues of young, un-skilled, or unsafe bicyclists as you drive.

In a situation like this, make sure that your turn does not cut off the bicyclist.

the possibility of erratic behavior. (Training wheels on a bicycle, for example, are evidence of a real lack of ability to control the bicycle's movement.) Racing bicycles (which today are often used for more than racing) can also create hazards. Because such bicycles have low-slung handlebars, their operators do not ride in an upright position. This may make it more difficult for you to see them, just as it may make it more difficult for them to search the roadway around themselves. Operators of racing bicycles are more likely to be skilled and experienced, but their bicycles are not really equipped for crowded traffic conditions.

In any case, it is your responsibility as a driver to look out for hazards that might require bicyclists to stop quickly or to change their path of travel.

SCANNING THE ROADWAY AROUND BICYCLISTS

It is extremely important that you, as the driver of an automobile, scan the roadway to determine whether or not anything ahead will require an adjustment on the part of the bicyclist and, as a result, an adjustment in your own speed or position.

How would you react if you were following this bicyclist in a car?

Some roadway conditions that are not hazardous to motor vehicles are hazardous to bicycles. Drivers have to make adjustments when bicyclists steer around the hazards.

Bicyclists, like motorcyclists, are more limited in their ability to steer and stop than is popularly believed. In other words, you must allow a bicyclist a good deal of room and time to respond. For example, such things as railroad crossings, small stones, gravel on the roadway (which would not mean very much to you as the operator of an automobile) require major adjustments on the part of bicyclists. The bars that cover storm drains are another serious hazard to bicyclists. These are usually placed next to the curb and have steel gratings or openings that run parallel to the roadway. While this is of little or no importance to you as the driver of a car, a bicyclist forced to ride over such a grating is very apt to find the front wheel of the bicycle lodged between the bars. This could stop the bicycle in its tracks and throw the bicyclist onto the pavement. Bicyclists who see such obstacles will usually steer around them. This means that they must move further from the curb and toward or into the lane of traffic.

OTHER SPECIAL VEHICLES

There are increasing numbers of other vehicles that present problems similar to the major problem created by bicycles: the lack of laws controlling who can operate them and where. Among these are both three- and four-wheeled vehicles. The three-wheeler resembles an oversized tricycle and is used by an increasing number of physically handicapped and elderly persons as a basic means of transportation. The four-wheeler is similar to a child's pedal car but is large enough to seat two adults side by side. While these vehicles are more visible than bicycles, due to their size and design, the rate of speed at which they travel is generally less than that of a bicycle. As a result, the danger which they present is caused by the difference between their speed and that of motor vehicles.

In certain parts of the country, snowmobiles represent a special problem. While snowmobiles are motorized, they create many of the same problems as nonmotorized vehicles. Such vehicles are, in fact, generally prohibited from using state highways. (Local communities

Special vehicles like snowmobiles can present hazards because their operators may be unlicensed and unskilled. In addition, they are often difficult to see.

sometimes designate selected roadways for their use.) Like bicycles, such vehicles are difficult to see because they sit very close to the ground. In addition, they may be driven over light, fluffy snow and create a cloud of snow that makes them even more difficult to see.

The handling and stopping characteristics of snowmobiles on snow-packed roads are not good. Another feature of these vehicles that makes them somewhat more dangerous is their ability to travel, with other vehicular traffic, at high rates of speed for long periods of time. Since the operators of such units are frequently young children, it is especially critical that you provide ample time and space to adjust to any maneuver that they may make.

Animals

The final group of nonmotorized highway users is animals, including wild animals, farm animals, and pets. The number of conflicts between motor vehicles and animals, wild or tame, varies widely, depending on location.

SMALL ANIMALS

Pets represent a special problem because of their size and quick movement. They frequently dart out into the roadway. In many cases, drivers fail to see an animal in time. Then, in attempting to avoid the animal, the driver may swerve into a fixed object or suddenly apply the brakes and be struck from behind. The best defense against such accidents is the same type of ground search recommended for driving in residential areas.

Take special precautions at cattle crossings. Do not do anything that may frighten the animals.

LARGE ANIMALS

If you see *cattle-crossing* or *open-range* signs or see farm animals (such as cows, horses, sheep, or pigs) near the road, take special precautions. The behavior of such animals is almost totally unpredictable, and the result of a collision at even moderate speed is usually severe. Even if such animals are being attended to or herded along, it is best to slow down well in advance. Be prepared to stop and to allow them as much room as possible. Once you have adjusted your speed and position, pass by the animals at a relatively low speed.

Animal-drawn carts or wagons and horses ridden on or near the road also deserve special attention. Such animals may shy or bolt from any sudden noise. Your best safeguard, again, is to adjust your speed so that you will be better prepared to respond and move laterally as far away from the animal as possible. If you feel that the horn should be used to alert the rider, tap the horn lightly. (Any loud noise may frighten the animal.)

WILD ANIMALS

Nearly everyone is aware of the number of rabbits, pheasants, raccoons, and other small game killed each year by automobiles. Few people, however, realize how many deer, antelope, and other large animals are killed. Nor do they realize how much vehicle damage, injury, and death is caused by collisions between vehicles and large wild animals.

In some areas, particularly in mountainous and forested regions, the problem is a major one. State highway and game conservation groups in such areas continue to put up *deer-crossing* signs and to issue warnings to the driving public, but with limited success. In part, the problem arises as a result of the infrequent appearance of these large animals in any one person's experience. In addition, a large percentage of these accidents occur after dark, when, due to limited illumination, drivers cannot see objects to the side of the road.

223

There are not many preventive measures you can take to avoid such accidents. However, you can reduce your speed when driving in an area where deer or other wild animals may be crossing. You can also force your visual search beyond the area illuminated by your headlights and look for any evidence of movement or the reflections off the eyes of deer and other wild animals.

To Think About

1. What are some of the things a driver should watch for when approaching pedestrians in urban areas?
2. Why do rural pedestrian accidents, more often than urban pedestrian accidents, result in fatalities?
3. How is a ground search different from an ordinary visual search? In what kinds of driving situations is a ground search most important?
4. You know that children do not always behave predictably. How would you compensate for this fact when driving?
5. Why is it dangerous to drive through an intersection, even if the traffic light is green, when another lane of traffic going in your direction is still stopped?
6. Why are the elderly often involved in pedestrian accidents? What can drivers do to compensate for some of the common handicaps of the elderly?
7. What are some of the cues that alert drivers to blind pedestrians? Why are these cues often difficult to spot?
8. What is the major difference between the laws relating to bicyclists and the laws relating to motor-vehicle operators? What problems does this difference create?
9. Name three roadway conditions that are not extremely hazardous to motor-vehicle operators but that create extreme hazards for bicyclists. As a driver, how can you compensate for these hazards?
10. Why are snowmobiles often difficult to see?
11. Discuss the bumper-sticker slogan "I brake for animals."
12. What are some of the hazards created by pets? If you were driving and saw a dog running near the roadway, what else would you look for?

To Do

1. Ask your local police department to supply statistics of pedestrian accidents in your area. Are there any streets or intersections that have especially high numbers of such accidents? What age groups are most often involved? How often is alcohol a factor? Do weather conditions and the time of day seem to be important factors? Report your findings to your class.
2. Observe pedestrian and driver behavior at an intersection near your home. How many pedestrians check traffic in all directions before crossing? How many drivers adjust their speed and position in response to possible pedestrian hazards? Report to your class.
3. Survey your area for safeguards that help drivers and other highway users safely share the roadways. Are school-crossing guards or safety patrols on duty at the right places and right times? Are bicycle paths well marked and well maintained? Discuss with your class how these safeguards could be improved.
4. Interview a local police officer or traffic official and discuss these questions: Are laws relating to bicyclists and pedestrians consistent throughout your state? Are these laws, if they exist, enforced strictly? Do you and the officer or official think that the laws are adequate and properly enforced?

System Failures 9

After reading this chapter, you should be able to:

1. Describe four predriving procedures that will help you cope with emergency situations.
2. Define an *evasive action* and give three examples.
3. Describe two situations in which your vehicle might begin to skid.
4. Name four types of vehicle failure and describe ways to compensate for each.

When the highway transportation system is operating effectively, the movement of people and goods is accomplished in a safe and efficient manner. However, breakdowns in the system may occur at any time. An error on the part of a highway user, the mechanical breakdown of a vehicle, or a failure of the highway itself can disrupt the efficiency of the system.

When normal operations are interrupted, in even a small portion of the system, the safety of all users in that general area is reduced. Such failures will require immediate adjustments on the part of all drivers concerned, if they are to avoid or reduce the possible consequences of accidents or lost time.

It is important to remember that you do not have to learn *new* skills to respond to emergency situations. Rather, you will have to develop the basic driving skills you already have.

Preparing for Emergencies

Proper predriving procedures will help you respond to emergencies or, if you are involved in an accident, will protect you and your pas-

driver error

vehicle failure

breakdowns of the roadway

System failure can be caused by drivers' errors, vehicle failure, or breakdowns in the roadway itself.

sengers. The importance of predriving procedures will become clearer as you learn more about the requirements for safe driving. The basic predriving procedures are:

1. *Adjust the seat.* A properly adjusted seat will make you more comfortable as you drive. Even more importantly, it will help you control your vehicle.

2. *Fasten and adjust the seat belt and shoulder belt.* These devices keep you behind the wheel so that you can better control your car prior to or after a crash. They also help to prevent or reduce injuries in the event of a crash.

3. *Adjust both mirrors.* Proper adjustment of the rear-view and side-view mirrors provides additional visual coverage and will keep you better informed of what is going on around your car.

4. *Adjust the head restraint.* When properly adjusted, this device will prevent head and neck injuries in case of a collision, particularly if you are struck from the rear.

5. *Lock all doors.* Locked doors will help keep you and your passengers inside the car in the event of a collision.

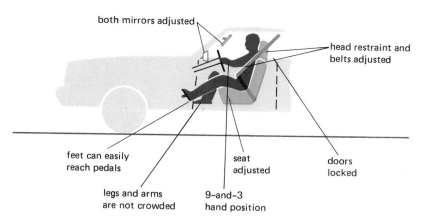

both mirrors adjusted

head restraint and belts adjusted

feet can easily reach pedals

seat adjusted

doors locked

legs and arms are not crowded

9-and-3 hand position

For maximum vehicle control, make these checks and adjustments each time before you drive.

Evasive Actions

To avoid collisions, you may have to make sudden and extreme changes in your vehicle's speed or direction. This is called taking *evasive action*. These actions include abruptly moving your vehicle left or right, controlled braking, or abrupt acceleration.

LATERAL EVASIVE

Swerving sharply to the right or left to avoid colliding with an object in your intended path is called a *lateral* evasive action. This move is best accomplished if it is begun with your hands at the 9-and-3 position on the steering wheel and with the driver's seat properly adjusted. From this position, you should be able to steer firmly and accurately. You should also be able to turn the steering wheel 180 degrees in either direction without having to remove either of your hands from the 9-and-3 position. Lateral evasive maneuvers require quick and accurate steering. To avoid a possible collision, you may have to turn the steering wheel left or right as much as 160 to 180 degrees. You would then immediately turn the steering wheel 320 to 360 degrees in the opposite direction and then back again to keep moving parallel to your original path of travel.

Because they are small and very responsive, sports cars and high-performance vehicles require less steering adjustment than large passenger cars. All vehicles, however, require smooth, precise steering. Without firm and accurate steering, sudden lateral moves may place you on a collision course with oncoming vehicles or with objects off the road.

As you drive, you should continuously scan the roadway and off-road areas ahead to identify possible escape routes. It is important to do this even if no immediate hazards are apparent. If any situation forces you into a lateral evasive maneuver, you will most likely have to complete the maneuver quickly. In other words, you will not have time to search for and evaluate various escape routes.

To make a quick evasive maneuver to the right, you have to steer right, then left, and then right again to recover a straight path.

As you approach the crest of a hill, you will not know what is on the other side. You can, however, search the shoulder for an escape route.

For example, imagine that you are driving at 55 mph on a two-lane road. As you reach the top of a hill, you see a vehicle with a flat tire stopped in your lane, 2 to 3 seconds ahead. Because it is too late to avoid a collision by braking to a stop, you must make a lateral move. But which way, right or left? Are there any off-road obstacles? If there are obstacles, how far are they from the road and what would be the consequences of colliding with any of them? Are there oncoming or following vehicles? What is the condition of the road surface and the off-road areas?

Clearly, you would not be able to answer or even ask all these questions in the time available. You would be able to make the best decision only if you had gathered the correct information and made certain assumptions before you reached the top of the hill. For example, you should already know something about the shoulder conditions on either side of the road. (It would be fair to assume that, generally, the size and condition of the shoulder areas would not be drastically different on the far side of a hill.) If you had made this observation before reaching the top of the hill, you would not be forced to begin your search from scratch.

If you were confronted with oncoming traffic, you would have to apply controlled brake pressure and steer off the road to the right. Your decision, however, would be much more complex if you found that both lateral escape routes were blocked. For example, on the right shoulder, there may be shrubbery within 3 or 4 feet of the roadway. Under these circumstances, you would have to choose the alternative that had less severe consequences. Which path would cause less personal injury and property damage?

Your evasive move would still be to the right, even though the shrubbery may hide hazardous objects. A move to the left is almost certain to have extreme consequences. If you tried to get to the left shoulder, you could cause a head-on collision. And even if you did make it to the left shoulder, you might cause one of the oncoming drivers to panic and steer off the road or into some other vehicle.

OFF-ROAD RECOVERY

There will be times when you either partially or completely leave the roadway. You may leave the road intentionally, to avoid a collision or some other hazard, or you may do it unintentionally. In either case, returning to the roadway from a shoulder can be extremely dangerous if you try to perform the maneuver improperly. Problems in trying to return to a roadway usually occur for two reasons:

1. Steering will become difficult if there is a difference between the level of the roadway and the shoulder. The tires may drag against the edge of the road, reducing directional control. Steering may also be difficult if the off-road area is not maintained and the shoulder consists

228

of loose sand, mud, or grass, or if the shoulder is uneven or bumpy.

2. The traction necessary to control and slow the car is reduced. If the shoulder area and the roadway have different kinds of surfaces, your vehicle's traction will suddenly change.

Controlling Off-Road Recovery. Drivers, without slowing or properly positioning their vehicles, often attempt to ease back up onto the roadway in places where the surface of the pavement is several inches higher than the surface of the shoulder. If the side of one tire gets caught on the edge of the pavement, the rubber in the tire will *distort* (stretch out of shape). In such cases, the bottom of the tire continues to point straight ahead while the front wheels are pointing toward the roadway. When the "caught" tire finally snaps up onto the roadway, the steering angle may be so great that the vehicle will suddenly shoot across the roadway onto the far shoulder or into oncoming traffic.

Suppose that you are driving on a two-lane, two-way road that has a smooth and firm shoulder which is 3 or 4 inches below the surface of the pavement. An oncoming vehicle crosses the center line and forces you to move right so that your right wheels leave the roadway. Once the oncoming vehicle has passed, what should you do? If the shoulder continues fairly smooth and free of obstructions, you could return to the road by doing the following:

1. Hold the steering wheel firmly, with your hands at the 9-and-3 position.
2. Check for traffic ahead and to the rear.
3. Reduce your speed approximately 20 to 25 mph by letting up on the accelerator and braking gently.
4. Steer to the right until both wheels are about 1 to 2 feet off the roadway and parallel to it.
5. Select a spot where the shoulder and roadway are nearly level.
6. Check traffic again and signal.

If you are forced to leave the road, follow these steps to recover roadway position.

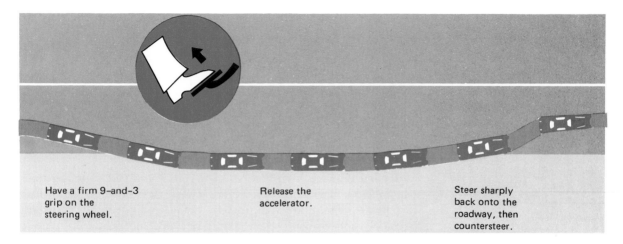

Have a firm 9–and–3 grip on the steering wheel.

Release the accelerator.

Steer sharply back onto the roadway, then countersteer.

7. Steer quickly to the left about a quarter of a turn of the steering wheel. As the right front wheel touches the edge of the pavement, countersteer about 160 to 180 degrees to the right to avoid entering the oncoming lane. Then straighten the steering wheel and proceed.

The procedure for recovery is the same if you are forced to leave the roadway so that all four wheels are on the shoulder.

Emergency Off-Road Recovery. You may at some time drift off the roadway or steer to the shoulder to avoid a collision and suddenly find yourself on a collision course with some object on the shoulder. If time permits, you should perform as many of the safety checks for a routine off-road recovery as you can.

Some object in your immediate path—such as a bridge abutment, a large tree, or a pedestrian—may force you to return to the roadway immediately. If you have both hands firmly on the steering wheel, you will be able to recover, even if there is no time to slow or if there is a difference of several inches in height between the roadway and shoulder surfaces.

Under these circumstances, it is critical that you move the vehicle far enough to the right so that both the front and rear wheels that are off the road are free of the pavement edge. Then, do the following:

1. With your foot off the accelerator and brake, turn the steering wheel quickly and sharply to the left, about 120 to 130 degrees.

2. As the right front wheel strikes the edge of the road, steer smoothly back to the right about 240 to 260 degrees and then immediately back to straight steering.

Since you are traveling at highway speed, the quickness and smoothness of steering must be precise if you are to keep your car within a single lane.

In either a controlled or an emergency off-road recovery, the critical factor is the quick, smooth steer back onto the roadway followed by a quick, smooth countersteer to control your lane position. The purpose of the sharp steering is to allow the leading edge of the front tire to climb up onto the edge of the pavement so that it keeps its proper shape and maintains contact with the pavement surface.

BRAKING EVASIVE

In some emergency situations, lateral evasive action may not be possible. Braking may be the only way to avoid an accident or at least to reduce the consequences.

Controlled Braking. You already know that you should adjust your speed and position so that you could, if necessary, come to a complete stop before striking anything in your path. If you evaluate situations accurately and adjust to them ahead of time, you should be able to bring your car to a stop quickly and completely under control.

| Jab the brake, pushing the car's weight forward. | Release the brake. The car will rock back. | Jab the brake again. | Release the brake again. | Apply steady braking once speed is reduced enough. |

To stop quickly, you can jab the brakes and slow down without making the wheels lock.

A controlled stop or controlled braking is accomplished by applying pressure to the brake pedal without making the wheels *lock* (stop turning). Quick, steady pressure or quick, firm jabs on the brake pedal are the best ways of controlling braking. (Actually, each quick jab may lock the wheels for an instant, but not long enough to cause loss of control.) Under the stress of trying to stop quickly, drivers often overreact and lock the wheels. If this happens to you, release the brake immediately and quickly reapply slightly less pressure.

The purpose of controlled braking is to achieve the shortest possible stopping distance without losing directional control. Slamming on the brakes and locking the wheels may, in fact, increase stopping distances and result in a complete loss of directional control.

ACCELERATION EVASIVE

The control device that is least frequently used in emergency situations is the accelerator. This is because most of the dangerous events that you must respond to will be in front of you. However, the accelerator can sometimes be used effectively to avoid hazards at intersections and in merging situations. For example, you may be near an intersection or blind alley and suddenly see a vehicle moving toward you. Accelerating may be your only means of escape. Braking would probably bring you to a stop directly in the path of the threatening vehicle. A lateral maneuver may be impossible or useless. In that case, a quick burst of speed may remove you from a collision path. Obviously, this response would be useful only if you had a clear path ahead.

Skid Control _____

Skidding can occur at almost any time. The pavement surface or the condition of your tires may be so bad that you begin to skid. Your forward momentum may be so great that you lose traction and skid while trying to stop. Centrifugal force may exceed the amount of available traction, thus causing a skid.

Skidding means loss of vehicle control. Alert drivers try to avoid those situations and actions that cause skids. If your car does go into a skid, you are not always helpless. There are responses, given enough time and space, that can help you regain control. However, the best

Avoid using your brakes if your car goes into a skid.

course is to avoid actions that could lead to a skid. Among the most common causes of skidding are:

1. Any quick adjustment of speed or direction
2. Any adjustment of speed or position made under conditions of poor traction

It is critical that once you start to skid, you *stay off the brake pedal*. It is possible to accelerate out of some skids, but traffic conditions and the widths of most highway lanes make it dangerous and impractical. The best response is to stay off the brake and accelerator.

If you do begin to skid, it is also critical that you steer correctly. The important thing to remember is to *steer in the direction in which the rear end of your vehicle is skidding*. Most likely, you will naturally tend to steer in the proper direction when your car begins to skid. Further trouble usually arises because cars tend to skid back and forth ("fishtailing"). To moderate a skid, a driver has to countersteer. As the skid begins to reverse direction, immediately countersteer. As you develop a sense of feel and timing you will be able to countersteer, as needed, until the skid is moderated and you have the car back under full control.

Skids fall into four groups: braking skids, power skids, cornering skids, and blowout skids. Responding to each kind of skid is not difficult, but you must stay calm.

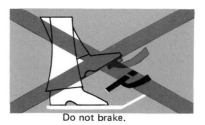

Do not brake.

Do not accelerate.

Steer in the direction of the rear-end skid.

If you begin to skid, always steer in the direction in which the rear of your car is skidding and be ready to countersteer.

BRAKING SKIDS

A *braking skid* occurs when your brakes are applied so hard that one or more wheels lock. If brakes are properly adjusted, all the wheels will lock at the same time. Regardless of the number of wheels that lock, however, steering control will be lost.

If all four wheels lock, or if only the front wheels lock, your car will skid straight ahead unless it is influenced by some other force (such as a slope in the roadway). If only the rear wheels lock, a loss of traction will make them move forward faster than the front wheels. Your vehicle may then go into a 180-degree spin. (In other words, you may end up skidding backwards on the pavement.)

Response to Braking Skids.   Release the brakes so that the wheels can turn. When the wheels start to run, steering control will return. If braking is still necessary, use less pressure so that the wheels will not lock again.

Examples of Braking Skids.   You may go into a braking skid if you are forced to abruptly decrease speed in an emergency. Such a skid can also be expected when you brake on roads that are wet or are covered with sand, gravel, wet leaves, ice, or snow.

POWER SKIDS

If you suddenly press hard on the accelerator, you may experience a *power skid.* Since in most cars power is delivered only to the drive wheels, sudden acceleration may cause the rear wheels to lose traction. Though the cause of the skid is different, a power skid is much like a braking skid. If the drive wheels are in front, the resulting skid will cause a loss of steering control and the car will plow straight ahead. If the drive wheels are in the rear, the back end will skid to the side, begin to overtake the front end, and perhaps spin the car around.

Response to a Power Skid.   To correct a power skid, simply ease up on the accelerator until the wheels stop spinning. Make steering corrections as necessary.

Examples of Power Skids.   Quick acceleration on a slippery surface will usually result in a power skid. Even on dry surfaces, sudden hard pressure on the accelerator can cause a power skid.

CORNERING SKID

If you make a turn and the centrifugal force is greater than the available traction, your car will go into a *cornering skid.* Regardless of which way you turn the steering wheel, your car will continue straight ahead, away from your intended path of travel around the turn.

Response to a Cornering Skid.   If your car begins to skid when cornering, ease up on the accelerator and steer in the direction of the skid. This will realign your front and rear wheels and return vehicle control.

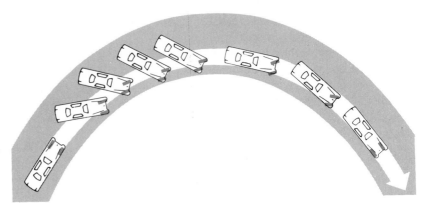

In a cornering skid, the rear end of your car may begin to "spin out." In this case, you should gradually release the accelerator and steer left until you regain control.

Examples of Cornering Skids.   A cornering skid may occur any time you attempt to make a turn, even at normal driving speed and on dry pavement. If traction is significantly reduced by poor tire or road-surface conditions, or if your speed is even a little too fast, you may begin to skid.

BLOWOUT SKIDS

Any time that there is sudden decrease in a tire's air pressure, your car can be thrown into a skid. Even if a skid does not occur, there is frequently a dramatic change in the handling characteristics of your vehicle.

If a front tire blows out, there will be a strong pull toward the side of the blowout. If a rear tire blows, the car will tend to sway from side to side ("fishtail") or pull toward the side of the blowout. Either type of blowout is especially likely to cause a skid if it occurs on a turn.

Response to a Blowout.   If a tire blows, the most important thing to do is to stay off the brake pedal and to maintain directional control. Correct any change in direction and avoid abrupt changes in speed. After you have reestablished your path of travel, gradually reduce your speed and pull to the curb or off the road.

Your response to a blowout skid should be basically the same as your response to other skids. That is, stay off the brake and continue steering until you have the car under control. Remember, however, that steering just after a blowout may be especially difficult. A firm and steady grip on the steering wheel is therefore essential. Without control of your vehicle, you are defenseless. There are several points that will help you prevent skids and recover from them:

1. If you know what kinds of conditions cause skids, you will be better prepared for them and will be less likely to panic.
2. The sooner you respond to a skid, the easier it is to correct.
3. Skids tend to be exaggerated by abrupt changes in speed, either through acceleration or braking.

4. A firm grip of the steering wheel during a skid reduces the chance of further loss of control.

5. Steering corrections must be made quickly and firmly, but not so abruptly that you cause another skid in the opposite direction.

Vehicle Failure

Regardless of how well you maintain your car, there is a chance that it may break down suddenly and without warning. Such breakdowns range from those that are merely inconvenient to those that are extremely dangerous. How critical a situation becomes depends upon the kind of breakdown, when and where it occurs, and how well you cope with it.

The danger of any vehicle failure obviously increases when you are moving. Remember that all such vehicle failures require the same basic response: you must control the vehicle's speed and direction and move it out of the stream of traffic. Once you are stopped safely off the roadway, you can deal with the problem without causing new dangers.

BRAKE FAILURE

Cars now manufactured in this country are equipped with a *dual-service brake system*. This means that there are separate systems for front and rear wheels. As a result, total brake failure rarely occurs. If partial or total failure does occur, however, there are several things that you should try to do:

1. Shift your car to a lower gear. This by itself will not stop you, but it will provide a "drag" force from the slowing of the engine and power train. This will help to slow your speed.

2. Pump the brake pedal rapidly. This action may build up some pressure in the brake lines and provide some braking force.

3. While holding the release button open, rapidly apply and release your parking brake. Remember, however, that the parking brake works

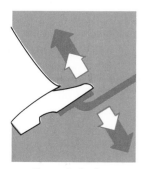

Pump the brakes.

Shift to *low*.

Pump the parking brake.

If your car's brakes fail, take these steps. Be sure not to put steady pressure on the parking brake.

only on the rear wheels. Steady pressure on the parking brake may result in uncontrollable skidding.

If these actions do not slow your car and gradually bring it to a stop, sound your horn to alert other highway users. If you can, rub your car against the curb to slow it. Otherwise, search for open areas like fields, yards, or parking lots. Also look for uphill roads or lanes that will slow you down and take you away from other highway users.

If a collision is unavoidable, try to select the one with the least serious consequences. Try to steer into large bushes or small objects, or steer to the side of the road so that you rub against a fence, a guard rail, a roadside embankment, or even parked cars. Any of these choices is better than a head-on collision or a collision with a pedestrian or large fixed object.

STEERING FAILURE

Fortunately, total steering failure is as rare as complete brake failure. Steering failure most often occurs when vehicles equipped with power steering stall. When the engine stalls, the power-assist unit in the steering system does not work.

A stalled engine, a broken drive belt to the power-steering pump, or a defective pump make steering difficult, but they do not completely eliminate steering control. More effort is required to turn the steering wheel. If this type of failure occurs, *keep steering* and get your car safely off the road and stopped.

A far more serious problem is the breakdown of an upper or lower control arm or ball joint. If this type of failure occurs, one front wheel will simply collapse. As with a skid, *keep steering and stay off the brake pedal.* Even moderate brake pressure may cause the car to pull abruptly to one side. If you cannot safely coast to a stop, take the same steps you would take in case of brake failure: shift to a lower gear and use the parking brake. (However, if you use the parking brake, remember that the brake release must be held open.)

ENGINE FAILURE

Engine failure is the most common kind of vehicle breakdown. There are several factors that may cause engine failure: a broken timing gear, running out of gas, electrical system malfunction, or a cold engine that stalls for any one of a number of reasons.

As soon as you sense that the engine is failing, begin to steer off the road. If the engine stops completely before you are able to leave the road, try to coast to a safe area. It may help to shift to *neutral,* since the car will coast further in *neutral* than it will if it is left in gear. In *neutral,* you can also try to restart the engine, since the problem may be a minor one, such as a temporarily stuck choke.

236

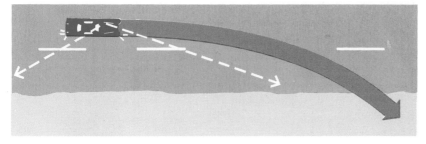

If the engine fails, signal and try to coast to a safe place.

Power steering or power brakes will not function normally when the engine is off. You will therefore experience some difficulty steering and braking. However, with some extra effort you should still be able to manage the situation.

Whether you are able to leave the road or not, be sure to turn on your emergency flashers to warn other highway users. If you carry flares in your car, set them up some distance behind your car. This will provide advance warning of trouble to other drivers. (At night, a flashlight can also be used as a warning device.)

STICKING ACCELERATOR PEDAL

The accelerator pedal may get stuck either part way open or completely jammed to the floor. If, and only if, you have a clear road ahead, attempt to release the accelerator pedal by slipping the tip of your shoe under it and pulling it up. Under no circumstances should you try to release the accelerator by bending over and using your hands. In such a position, you are totally unable to function as a driver.

If the accelerator is suddenly jammed in a wide-open position, which may occur as a result of a broken engine mount, you have a major problem. Leave the car in gear and turn off the engine. Turning off the engine will increase the effort needed to turn the steering wheel, but leaving the car in gear will prevent you from turning the key so far that you lock the steering column. If you have power-assist brakes, do not pump them. Rather, apply steady, moderate pressure and steer to the curb after signaling. Without the engine to operate the power-brake unit, pumping the brake will exhaust its reserve power very quickly. If you are slowing too rapidly and you need to coast further, shift to *neutral*.

HOOD FLY-UP

Clear, unobstructed vision is vital to safe driving. The danger of having the hood fly up directly in front of you should be obvious.

Your best defense against such an occurrence is to check the hood often. Make sure it is locked after you or anyone else checks the engine. You can also check the hood as you are driving. If the hood and fenders do not line up properly or if the hood appears to vibrate, there may be a problem.

If the hood does fly up, you should try, as well as possible, to get a view of the road ahead. Try looking out the side windows or bending forward to see through the space under the hood. If there is no alternative, brake to a stop in your lane. There is, of course, a chance of being struck from behind. However, a following driver will most likely have clear forward vision; you will have practically none.

FIRE

Even in collisions, motor vehicles rarely catch on fire. However, if your car does catch fire, or if you see or smell smoke, pull off the road immediately, turn off the engine, and get all passengers out of and away from the car.

If the fire is small and confined to the passenger compartment, you might try to put it out with a fire extinguisher. (A 1-pound dry chemical extinguisher can be carried conveniently in the glove compartment or trunk.) Otherwise you might try water, sand, dirt, or even snow. However, if you cannot put out the fire very quickly, get away from the vehicle before the fire spreads and causes an explosion.

If you do not have a fire extinguisher, you can try to smother an engine fire with dirt, using a hubcap as a shovel. Do not, however, take chances.

If the fire is under the hood, in the body of the car, or in the trunk, there is a good chance of a gasoline explosion. If you have a fire extinguisher, use it. However, *do not take chances*. If there is any question of an explosion, clear all passengers away from the area of the car and call for a fire-fighting unit.

FLAT TIRE

There will undoubtedly come a time when you walk out to your car and find that you have a flat tire. There will be other times when air leaks slowly from a tire. In the latter case, you will notice it through a gradual change in the response of the car as you try to steer. As in the case of a blowout, you will feel the car begin to pull toward the right or left (in the direction of the soft tire) if it is a front tire that is leaking. If a rear tire is leaking, you may feel a "fishtailing" effect. If this should occur, apply enough extra effort to maintain control and steer the car well off the roadway.

In either case, you will have to change the tire. If you are not careful, this can be a hazardous job. For the sake of safety, take the following steps:

1. Make sure the car is parked on a level surface before attempting to change the tire.
2. With the engine off, set the parking brake and place the selector lever in *park*. (In a manual-transmission car, put the shifting lever in *reverse*.)
3. Get all passengers out of the car.
4. Use a piece of wood (a 2×4, 8 to 10 inches long) or a rock to block the wheel diagonally across from the tire that is flat.

If you hear a steady thumping as you drive, your car may have a bulging tire that is about to blow out. Check it immediately.

Most cars have a list of steps to follow for changing a tire. The list can usually be found in the owner's manual or on the inside wall of the trunk near the jack. In general, however, follow these steps:

1. Remove the jack, jack handle, and spare tire from the trunk. Place the spare tire on the ground near the flat tire.
2. Remove the wheel cover and loosen (but do not remove) the lug nuts.
3. Place the jack in position and jack up the car until the flat tire clears the ground.
4. Check the wheel block to see that it is still in place. (Never go under the car or so near to it that you would be injured if the jack failed or if the car fell off the jack.)
5. Remove the lug nuts and place them in the wheel cover so they will not get lost.
6. Remove the flat tire.
7. Install the spare tire and replace the lug nuts.
8. Tighten the lug nuts, first by hand and then with the lug wrench.
9. Remove the jack and let the car down to the ground. Use the lug wrench to make sure that the nuts are tight. Then replace the wheel cover.
10. Place the tire, jack, and wheel block back in the trunk or storage area.

Once you have changed a tire, make sure that you have the flat tire repaired or replaced so that there is a spare available if the situation should arise again.

If you are changing a tire, block the wheels to make sure that the car will not roll away from the jack.

DEAD BATTERY

If you turn the ignition switch to *start* and the starter motor does not respond, you probably have a dead battery. (In cars with an ignition interlock system, the motor may not start because you or one of the front-seat passengers has not fastened a seat belt.)

If the problem is a dead battery, you can usually get your car started by using the electrical supply of another car. This process is called *jump starting*. It is relatively easy to do if you have jumper cables, which you should carry in your car. Follow these simple steps:

1. Position the vehicles so that the jumper cables will reach from the good battery of one car to the dead battery of the stalled car.

2. Turn off the ignition and electrical acessories in both cars.

3. Shift both cars to *neutral* or *park* and set the parking brake.

4. Make sure both batteries are the same voltage (either 6 or 12 volts). Check the fluid level in both batteries and make sure that all cell caps are in place. Do not attempt to jump start a battery that is frozen, because it may explode. Cover both batteries with a heavy cloth to protect against the possibility of splashing boiling battery fluid.

5. Attach one end of the first jumper cable to the positive (*p* or +) post of the good battery. Attach the opposite end of the first jumper cable to the positive post of the dead battery.

6. Attach one end of the second jumper cable to the negative (*n* or −) post of the good battery. Attach the other end of the cable to the engine block or frame of the car with the dead battery. When connecting the cable to the engine block or frame, connect it as far away from the battery as possible to protect against splashing in the event of an explosion.

7. Start the engine of the car with the good battery and press the accelerator pedal so that the engine is at a high idle.

8. Switch on the ignition of the car with the dead battery and start the engine.

9. Remove the jumper cables one at a time, negative connections first.

If this procedure does not start your car, you will probably have to call for road service.

WET ENGINE

Even if you drive through puddles at a reasonable speed, it is possible to splash enough water on the engine to make it stall. There are two reasons why the engine may stall:

1. Water may short out the electrical system.

2. Water may be drawn into the engine combustion chamber through the air cleaner and carburetor.

If your car stalls under conditions like these, steer to the side of the road, turn off the ignition, raise your hood, and check for water around

You can dry wet distributor caps, the coil, and the plugs with a rag.

the spark plugs. If the plugs are wet, dry the porcelain part of the plug with a cloth. (Be careful not to burn yourself on the hot engine.) If the car still will not start, you will have to wait until it dries. If it is not raining, you may speed up this process by leaving the hood up.

OVERHEATED ENGINE

There are several factors that can cause overheating. Driving in slow-moving traffic during hot weather, climbing long, steep upgrades, a loose or broken fan belt, a broken water pump, insufficient coolant in the cooling system, a stuck or broken thermostat, or a clogged radiator can all cause overheating.

If you are caught in a traffic jam and your engine begins to heat up, shift to neutral and race the engine. This will increase the flow of coolant around the engine.

Another common problem is insufficient antifreeze, either for winter driving or for operating an air conditioner. This problem can usually be identified by ice or frost that forms on the radiator. When the engine overheats, the fluid in the system boils and runs out of the overflow valve in the radiator.

Removing the radiator cap, even when the radiator is at a normal operating temperature, can be extremely dangerous. When the cap is removed, the pressure is abruptly reduced and fluid may boil, splashing out and scalding you. Your best safeguard is to wait for the engine to cool. For your own protection, cover the cap and top of the radiator with a cloth (such as a folded towel) when you remove the cap.

While waiting for the engine to cool, see if you can spot any problems. Check for a broken hose or a loose hose connection that you can tighten. If the fluid level in the radiator is low, add coolant. However, adding cold liquid to the engine may cause damage. To prevent such damage, start the engine and let it run at an idle speed as you add water or coolant. Also, remember that in freezing weather or if you operate an air conditioner, you must have an antifreeze solution in the radiator. For most of the other problems that you may identify, you will probably have to call for emergency road service to have your vehicle repaired.

When removing the radiator cap, use a cloth and stand as far back as possible.

As you see, vehicle breakdowns can range from minor inconveniences to serious hazards. Proper maintenance can help you avoid such breakdowns and to handle these breakdowns if they do occur.

To Think About

1. How will proper seat adjustment help you respond to emergency situations?
2. Why is it important to evaluate off-road conditions even when there are no immediate hazards ahead of you on the road?
3. Why are "soft" shoulders a serious hazard?
4. If, in an emergency maneuver, your vehicle's brakes locked, how would you regain vehicle control?
5. If the rear end of your car began to skid toward the left on a wet surface, how would you regain vehicle control?

6. If your car's front left tire blows out, which way will your car pull? How should you respond?
7. Why is *complete* brake failure so rare? What are some clues to partial brake failure?
8. If you are driving a car with power brakes and power steering, what will happen if the engine stalls? How would you respond?
9. What is the correct procedure for changing a flat tire?
10. What is the correct procedure for jump starting a car with a dead battery?

To Do

1. Observe several drivers—including friends and members of your family—as they prepare to drive. How many of them make predriving checks and adjustments that will help them cope with emergency situations? Report your findings to your class.
2. Examine the shoulders and off-road areas of three sections of a local highway. Are the shoulders and other areas designed and maintained well? What hazards do they present to drivers? How could they be improved?
3. Survey four experienced drivers and ask them how they would respond to skids. How many of them know how to steer out of a skid? What do they say about braking during a skid?
4. Check a friend's or a family member's car. Is it equipped with a good spare tire, jacking equipment, jumper cables, and a fire extinguisher? If any of these things are missing, ask the car's owner why they are missing. Does the owner think they are unnecessary?

Driver Performance 10

After reading this chapter, you should be able to:

1. Define *impairments* and give three examples.
2. Discuss how alcohol affects a person's physical and decision-making abilities.
3. Describe how fatigue, illness, and personal feelings can affect a driver's judgment.
4. Name three visual impairments and explain how each affects driving ability.

Your ability to perform driving maneuvers depends on your mental and physical state. If you are ill or upset, or if for some reason you are not able to make sound decisions, you will not be able to drive to the best of your ability.

Anything that weakens or damages your ability to perform well or to make sound decisions is called an *impairment*. Some impairments are physical. That is, they affect your ability to see, hear, or control muscular movement. Other impairments affect your decision-making abilities. Some impairments are temporary, whereas others are permanent.

It is important for you, as a driver, to understand how impairments affect your ability to perform. You may have to compensate (make up) for these impairments. For some other impairments, you may have to avoid driving altogether.

Alcohol

It is nearly impossible to overstate the relationship between alcohol and traffic accidents. Many studies show that approximately one-half of all highway deaths are caused, at least in part, by alcohol. To put

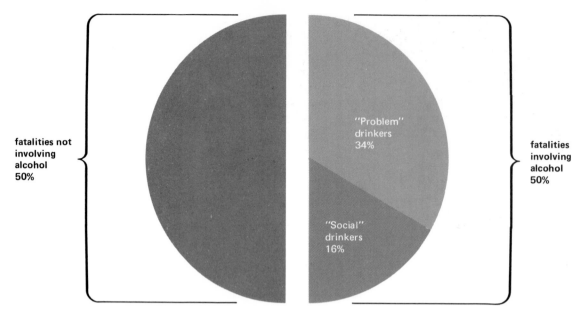

fatalities not involving alcohol 50%

"Problem" drinkers 34%

"Social" drinkers 16%

fatalities involving alcohol 50%

Alcohol is a contributing factor in approximately half of all traffic fatalities.

this in perspective, in the 11-year period, 1960-1971, 45,000 American soldiers were killed in combat in South Vietnam. During this same period, 545,000 American citizens were killed in traffic accidents. Of these fatalities, 274,000 were alcohol-related.

Characteristics of Alcohol.   Alcohol is a drug. Because of the effect it has on many people, alcohol is sometimes thought of as a *stimulant,* or something that speeds up mental and physical processes. Alcohol is, in fact, a *depressant.* It slows down mental and physical activities even when it is consumed in small quantities. It *anesthetizes,* or deadens, some of a person's senses and mental processes.

Absorption of Alcohol into the Body.   Alcohol does not have to be digested. It enters your bloodstream directly through the lining of the stomach. As a result, it affects your body very soon after drinking. The rate of absorption of alcohol into the bloodstream, however, does vary. For example, if the stomach is full of solid food, it will dilute the alcohol and slow the rate of absorption. In general, however, the absorption process is completed within 20 to 40 minutes from the time that a drink is consumed.

The rate of absorption and volume of alcohol needed to produce intoxication vary from one person to another. The research that is available, however, demonstrates that a *blood-alcohol level* (BAL) as low as 0.02 percent can adversely affect a person's behavior. (The blood-alcohol level is simply a percentage that states the concentration of alcohol in the bloodstream.) At 0.05 percent BAL, everyone is affected. The U.S. Department of Transportation believes that a BAL of 0.10

percent should be considered *prima facie* evidence of *driving while intoxicated.*

EFFECTS OF ALCOHOL ON THE HUMAN BODY

As the bloodstream carries the alcohol to the brain, it affects the *cerebrum*. This is the most critical portion of the brain, since it is where judgments and decisions are made. As the concentration of alcohol increases, the *cerebellum* is affected. The cerebellum controls muscular movement and maintains body equilibrium.

Alcohol and Vision. Alcohol has long been thought to seriously impair all functions of vision at a relatively low blood-alcohol level. This does not appear to be true. However, coordination of eye movements and the ability to divide attention between different tasks appear to be affected at low-level concentrations of alcohol. In effect, persons who have consumed alcohol tend to fix their vision on one object, rather than moving from one object to another to gather information.

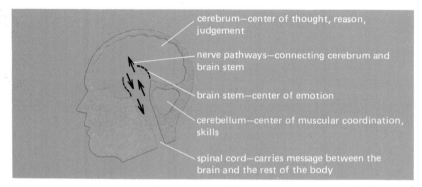

cerebrum—center of thought, reason, judgement

nerve pathways—connecting cerebrum and brain stem

brain stem—center of emotion

cerebellum—center of muscular coordination, skills

spinal cord—carries message between the brain and the rest of the body

To function well, the human body must be able to send messages to the brain and receive messages from it.

Since driving an automobile is an activity in which you must continually identify and react to many changing stimuli, impairment of your ability to divide attention among many cues can be critical.

Alcohol and Physical Response. We frequently picture a "drunk" as a person who is stumbling and having difficulty standing. Inexperienced drinkers may behave like this after consuming very little alcohol. Among experienced drinkers, however, such behavior may not appear until the individual has consumed large quantities of alcohol.

Alcohol may affect muscular control. For example, a person's steadiness may be lost. When drivers with high blood-alcohol levels are tested under actual driving conditions, impairment often becomes evident in steering, braking, and speed control. Steering-wheel move-

245

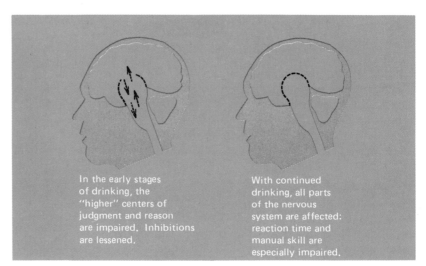

In the early stages of drinking, the "higher" centers of judgment and reason are impaired. Inhibitions are lessened.

With continued drinking, all parts of the nervous system are affected: reaction time and manual skill are especially impaired.

As a person becomes more intoxicated, the functioning of the brain is affected.

ments tend to increase and steering responses are slowed. Drivers with high blood-alcohol levels have difficulty steering through turns. They are not able to make the steering corrections necessary.

Brake reaction time under such conditions also tends to increase, as does the ability to apply the brakes smoothly or to come to a stop at a specific point. Drivers who have been drinking also have difficulty in maintaining a constant speed. They seem to speed up and slow down unnecessarily. They also make speed adjustments—either braking or accelerating—that are exaggerated.

Drivers who have been drinking often fix their attention on one object, neglecting other critical elements.

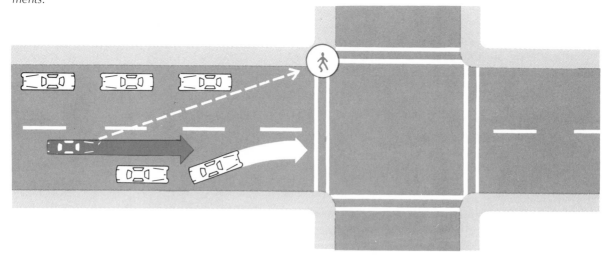

Amount of Beverage	Concentration of alcohol in bloodstream	Typical Effects		Time required for all alcohol to leave body
1 highball (1½ oz. whisky) 1 cocktail (1½ oz. whisky) 3½ oz. fortified wine 5½ oz. ordinary wine 2 bottles (24 oz.) beer	0.03%	Slight changes in feeling		2 hours
2 highballs 2 cocktails 7 oz. fortified wine 11 oz. ordinary wine 4 bottles beer	0.06%	Feeling of warmth, mental relaxation, slight decrease of fine skills, less concern with minor irritations and restraints.	Increasing effects with variation among individuals and in the same individual at different times	4 hours
3 highballs 3 cocktails 10½ oz. fortified wine 16½ oz. (1 pt.) ordinary wine 6 bottles beer	0.09%	Buoyancy, exaggerated emotion and behavior, talkative, noisy, or morose.		6 hours
4 highballs 4 cocktails 14 oz. ordinary wine 22 oz. ordinary wine 8 bottles (3 qts.) beer	0.12%	Impairment of fine coordination, clumsiness, slight to moderate unsteadiness in standing or walking.		8 hours
5 highballs 5 cocktails 17½ oz. fortified wine 27½ oz. ordinary wine ½ pt. whisky	0.15%	Intoxication—unmistakable abnormality of bodily functions and mental faculties.		10 hours or more

ALCOHOL AND THE YOUNG DRIVER

Drinking and driving appears to be a special problem among young drivers. This problem is illustrated by the fact that at least six out of every ten highway deaths of drivers between 16 and 24 involve drinking and driving. There are several possible explanations for this. One is that young drivers are generally learning to drink at a time when they are still developing the judgments and skills necessary for safe driving. Their driving skills may be less automatic. In other words, because they are less experienced, they have to think more about how they drive, and alcohol affects their ability to think clearly, logically, and quickly.

This table shows the effects of alcohol on a person of "average" size (about 150 pounds). For those weighing more or less, the amounts of alcohol needed to produce the same effects would be correspondingly more or less. In addition, each stage is diminished as alcohol is oxidized and eliminated from the body. (Developed by Leon A. Greenburg, Ph.D.)

247

Some people drink simply for the experience of feeling "high." They *want* to experience the special feeling that alcohol creates. Therefore, they may feel high after consuming a relatively small amount of alcohol. Their mental processes, however, may be impaired just as though they were truly intoxicated.

THE INFLUENCE OF ALCOHOL ON BEHAVIOR

When inhibitions are reduced, people tend to display greater anger, sadness, silliness, rudeness, or suspicion, depending on their personality and the mood they were in when they started to drink. Some people even fall asleep after a few drinks.

Because of emotional and physical differences, such as size or fatigue, the effects of alcohol differ from one person to another. Furthermore, alcohol will not affect people the same way every time they drink. A change in the contents of the stomach, one's emotional state, or the type of drink can cause reactions to vary.

DIFFERENCES IN ALCOHOLIC BEVERAGES

Many people misunderstand the effect that a single drink can have on their system. They are aware that liquors such as whisky, gin, or rum have a high alcoholic content and that wine and beer have a lower alcoholic content. (Beer is generally 4 to 7 percent alcohol by volume, wine 12 to 18 percent, and liquors 40 to 50 percent.) However, the alcoholic content of an average drink (1 ounce of 80 to 100 proof liquor), a 3- to 4-ounce glass of wine, or a 12-ounce can of beer is almost the same. For this reason, the effects of a can of beer, a glass of wine, or a shot of whisky are quite similar.

Although the percentages of alcohol in beer, wine, and hard liquor are not the same, the amount of alcohol in an average serving of each is approximately the same.

ELIMINATING ALCOHOL FROM THE BODY

Alcohol is eliminated from the bloodstream by the liver through a process called *oxidation,* in which the alcohol is broken down and removed from the bloodstream. This process occurs at the rate of about ½ ounce of alcohol per hour.

248

Since it takes such a short period of time for alcohol to be absorbed by the body, people who have three drinks within a short period of time will need about 3 hours after the last drink to eliminate the alcohol from their systems. The only way a person who is intoxicated can sober up is through the elimination of alcohol from the body. In short, sobering up takes time. *There is no way this process can be hurried.* If you try to make an intoxicated person sober by forcing him or her to drink black coffee, exercise, and take a cold shower, you will simply end up with a wide-awake, tired, and wet drunk!

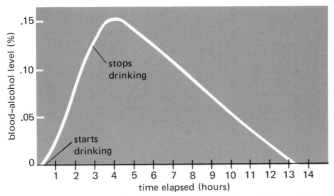

Alcohol that enters the stomach is absorbed, oxidized, and then eliminated. This process cannot be hurried. Note that the level of alcohol in the bloodstream increases even after a person stops drinking.

DRINKING, DRIVING, AND THE LAW

Because the use of alcohol so dramatically reduces the ability of a person to drive, all states have laws regarding drinking and driving. Although these laws are not always exactly the same, they are similar enough so that they can be discussed in general terms.

THE LEGAL DEFINITION OF D.W.I.

A court must decide whether a driver is guilty of driving while intoxicated (D.W.I.) on the basis of *evidence* presented by a police officer. An officer who sees a driver breaking a law and suspects the driver of being intoxicated will make an arrest and then gather evidence. This evidence must include the officer's notes about the driving behavior of the person charged, the time, the date, where the offense occurred, and usually, the results of chemical tests that determine the amount of alcohol in the blood. (These tests can be given only after an arrest has been made.)

In nearly all states, a driver who is arrested and has a blood-alcohol level of 0.10 can be charged with *driving under the influence of alcohol.* (A blood-alcohol level of 0.10 percent simply means that there is one part alcohol for every thousand parts of blood.) When the blood-alcohol level reaches four or five parts per thousand (a blood alcohol level of 0.4 or 0.5 percent), a person may go into a deep coma or even die.

Most states have a lesser offense called *driving while impaired*. A driver may be charged with this offense when the blood-alcohol level at the time of arrest falls between 0.05 percent and 0.10 percent. While a blood-alcohol level of 0.05 percent may seem low, you should remember that it takes only a small amount of alcohol to impair your driving ability. For example, a person with a blood-alcohol level of 0.05 percent is twice as likely to become involved in a traffic accident as a driver with a blood-alcohol level of 0. With a blood-alcohol level of 0.10 percent, a driver is six times as likely to be involved in a collision. This figure increases to 25 times when the blood-alcohol level reaches 0.15 percent.

CHEMICAL TESTS FOR INTOXICATION

Chemical tests consist of an analysis of breath, blood, or urine samples. The breath test is the most common and is usually administered with a device called a *breathalyser*. These tests must be administered by trained professionals.

A person who has been arrested and refuses to submit to a chemical test for blood-alcohol level may be charged under a law known as an *implied consent law*.

The implied consent law means that any person operating a motor vehicle upon a highway consents to submit to a chemical test for the presence of alcohol if arrested for driving while intoxicated. Regardless of the location (state) where the offense occurs, refusal to submit to the test can result in the person's license to be suspended or revoked.

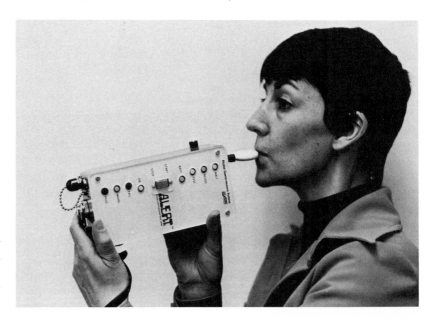

Police officers can test motorists' blood-alcohol levels after they have charged them with a violation. Police officers often carry portable testing units.

250

THE DRINKING-DRIVING DECISION

Many drivers are aware of the effects that alcoholic beverages have on their driving performance, and they avoid driving after they drink. Others attempt to modify the effects of alcohol by eating before they drink or by drinking only at meals. Still others limit the number of drinks they have, or they space their drinks so that their blood-alcohol level does not get too high.

The decisions you make about drinking must be personal decisions. No one can force you to drink or not drink, just as no one can force you to ride with someone who has been drinking. Be sure, however, to make your decision *before* you drink, because once you have started, you will not be able to make sound decisions.

Human beings make mistakes, even when they are performing at top level. Remember that consumption of alcohol simply increases the chances of such mistakes. The more you drink, the greater the risk you are taking.

Other Drugs _____

Many drugs affect people both mentally and physically, and they obviously impair driving performance. The number of accidents that have been caused by the use of drugs has not been accurately determined because of the difficulty in performing chemical tests that detect the presence of drugs. However, in one study of fatally injured drivers, 10 percent were found to have drugs other than alcohol in their bodies.

Frequently, when drug use or abuse is mentioned, people think about the so-called "hard" drugs, or *narcotics*. Actually, the use and abuse of medical drugs is just as serious a problem. Many drugs— including both prescription and nonprescription drugs—contain chemical compounds that can be harmful. They should be taken under a doctor's supervision or only after you have carefully followed the warnings and directions on the label. In addition, many drugs may effectively treat a particular illness but may also produce side effects that reduce your ability to drive.

Amphetamines. These drugs, such as Benzedrine and Dexedrine, are *stimulants*. That is, they keep the central nervous system awake. They are particularly hazardous because they may prevent people from being aware that they are tired.

Barbiturates. These drugs, such as phenobarbital and penothal, are *depressants,* or *sedatives*. They are frequently found in sleeping pills. Unlike amphetamines, barbiturates depress the action of the nervous system and slow both heartbeat and breathing. In large doses, confu-

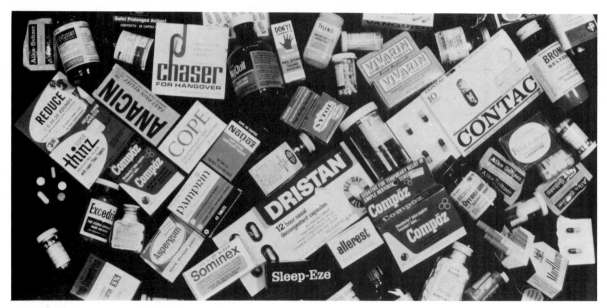

All drugs—including those that can be purchased legally—can have serious effects on your driving skills.

sion, slurred speech, and staggering may result. Barbiturates present another major problem to drivers because they also lessen the ability to concentrate.

Narcotics.   These drugs, such as heroin, morphine, and codeine, are usually used to reduce pain. They are depressants and have the same effects as barbiturates. Continued use of these drugs generally leads to addiction.

Tranquilizers.   Drugs such as Librium and Valium are used to treat anxiety, high blood pressure, emotional problems, and alcoholism. They are also depressants.

Hallucinogens.   Some drugs, such as LSD and mescaline, are known as mind-altering drugs. Medical use is presently limited to research under controlled conditions.

Marijuana.   This is a relatively mild hallucinogen with no known medical use. Evidence as to the degree of impairment induced by its use is controversial.

Nonprescription Drugs.   These are drugs that can be purchased without a prescription. They vary in strength and effect. Many of these drugs are widely advertised and consist of sprays, syrups, lozenges, aspirins, buffered aspirins, and antihistamines. These drugs should not be used when driving, unless you are sure that they will not affect your mental and physical performance. If you are in doubt, ask your doctor.

Other Factors

Fatigue, illness, personal feelings, and many other factors can all seriously affect a driver's ability to make sound decisions and to perform well.

FATIGUE

Fatigue may result from physical exertion, mental activity, stress, or lack of sleep. As fatigue increases, you become less aware of what is happening around you, and your ability to respond becomes impaired, both in terms of quickness and accuracy. For example, as fatigue increases, your normal steering responses will slow. Long periods of driving, particularly in an uninteresting environment, can cause fatigue or distract your attention from the task at hand. Fatigue may also cause eye strain or backaches. Any of these conditions will reduce your ability to perform well.

There is no good substitute for an occasional stop for rest. If you are still tired after such rests, do not continue to drive.

On long trips, stop every 2 to 3 hours to overcome some of the effects of fatigue. However, when fatigue reaches a point that you must rely on conversation, playing the radio, or singing to remain alert, you should not continue to drive.

ILLNESS

Few persons question the idea that illnesses which limit an individual's ability to complete routine tasks will also impair driving ability. Most persons will also agree that the right to drive should be restricted for persons who are subject to epileptic seizures, fainting spells, and emotional instability. In reality, many of these persons can drive safely if their condition has been brought under control and they are receiving professional attention.

Many persons, however, fail to realize the effects of common illnesses, such as colds or allergies, which cause most people to feel drowsy and inattentive. If the feeling is mild, a person may be able to adjust and carry on a normal routine. However, if you feel so bad that you avoid normal activity, you should also avoid driving. In many cases, the distraction or discomfort of an illness can be so serious that it dangerously reduces your driving ability.

CARBON MONOXIDE POISONING

Carbon monoxide gas is a byproduct of the combustion of gasoline in the engine. It is colorless, odorless, and tasteless. If the exhaust system is defective, carbon monoxide may be drawn into the passenger compartment of a car. It can cause headache, dizziness, nausea, loss of muscle control, and, if the gas is in concentrated form, death.

Carbon monoxide that leaks into the passenger compartment can make you drowsy or ill, and can cause death. It is important to keep the compartment well ventilated by opening vents and windows.

It is always a good idea to ventilate your car, either by adjusting the air vents or by opening a window to permit fresh air to enter. This will dilute carbon monoxide if it is present and reduce its effects.

AGING

As we age, our ability to see and to react tend to deteriorate. The changes that accompany old age are often due to hardening of the arteries. This in turn affects the heart, blood vessels, ears, eyes, and nervous system. It may also impair mental processes. These changes occur gradually, and in early stages their effect is minimal. They can, however, reach a point where they can make a person incapable of driving safely.

Since deterioration varies greatly from one person to another, there is no specific age at which a person should stop driving. Rather, medical observation by a physician should alert individuals to their own physical condition.

PERSONAL FEELINGS

There are some conditions that may disturb our ability to make reasonable judgments without affecting us physically. As a result, we make wrong decisions. These conditions are dangerous for us as drivers because we often fail to realize that we are being affected.

All of us have personal feelings and values. Our responses to any situation are strongly influenced by these feelings and values. These feelings and values develop over a period of years as a result of all our learning experiences. Since we are continually learning through new experiences, our feelings and values constantly change.

When we are alone, we can act much as we please. However, when we are in a group, everyone's feelings and values will not always be in agreement. We therefore have to adjust our behavior. In any group of people there must be mutual respect for the rights of others so that everyone can progress toward his or her own personal goals.

We generally learn when we are young that behavior must be regulated for the benefit of all the members of our families. Though this limits the ways we can act, most of us accept these limits. However, some people find it difficult to restrict their behavior and act aggressively anyway.

Differences in behavior are particularly important for highway users, especially when they are active members of the highway transportation system. Individual goals may be in conflict, and conflicts increase the chances of accidents.

At one time or another, all of us experience emotions such as anger, worry, frustration, love, or fear. When we drive under emotional stresses, our decisions are likely to be affected. The emotion may make us forget our primary objective—safe driving. For example, worry over a failing grade may make you lose patience. You may become frustrated and pull from a curb without looking, change lanes suddenly, or cross intersections without waiting for an adequate gap in traffic. In other words, you may let your feelings get in the way of driving safely. By driving aggressively, you will place yourself and other drivers in danger.

Generally, emotions are only temporary and will affect your driving for short periods of time. When you are angry or upset, you should avoid driving, if possible, until you are calm again. You, of course, must be the judge of your own emotional state. It is your responsibility to avoid driving if you feel you will not be able to act calmly and intelligently.

Vision and Hearing _____

You are already aware that to make good driving decisions you must have accurate information. You also know that you use your eyes to gather most of the information you need to drive safely. It follows, then, that if vision is impaired, your decision-making ability is impaired.

Good hearing is helpful in driving, but it is not as important as good vision. People with serious hearing impairments can drive as well as people with normal hearing.

Visual acuity is the ability to see clearly. If your visual acuity is 20/20, you should be able to read these letters from 20 feet.

VISUAL ACUITY

Visual acuity is the ability to see clearly. Impairment of visual acuity is the most common visual problem. If your visual acuity is not good, you may have difficulty identifying signs, signals, roadway markings, or any other object that could influence your selection of a path of travel.

Most states require corrective lenses for drivers whose visual acuity falls below a certain level. Visual acuity is described in a kind of shorthand that uses two numbers. For example, 20/20 visual acuity is the ability to accurately identify letters or objects 3/8 inch high from a distance of 20 feet; 20/40 means that you must be within 20 feet to identify an object that you should be able to see clearly at 40 feet. Some people's visual acuity, even with corrective lenses, cannot be made better than 20/70. In such cases, some states may grant these people restricted licenses, which allow them to drive only under specific conditions, such as during daylight hours.

If you do need corrective lenses, wear them. They will help you gather information and make sound driving decisions. Without them, you will have to strain to see the roadway around you.

FIELD OF VISION

Because many hazards may move from the side of the roadway into your intended path, you have to identify moving objects that appear to the left or right of the center of your vision. The area you can see—ahead, to the left, and to the right—without turning your head is referred to as your *field of vision*.

Most people are able to see or detect motion almost at right angles to either side. This means that they can see almost 90 degrees to each side. In other words, their total field of vision is about 180 degrees. Field of vision, however, varies from one person to another. Some people have a very narrow field of vision. This is called *tunnel vision*, because they see only those things directly ahead. It is almost as if they were looking through a tunnel. It is generally agreed that a field of vision that is less than 140 degrees is inadequate and should be considered an impairment. Drivers with a restricted field of vision can sometimes compensate for their impairment by glancing more frequently to the sides and by using their side-view mirrors more often. This solution, however, causes another problem: it reduces the amount of attention they give to the path ahead.

A field of vision that is less than 140 degrees requires a driver to glance more frequently to the sides.

COLOR VISION

Color attracts attention, and we can use our sense of color to organize our search of the traffic environment. For example, the color red should immediately alert you to the possibility of a traffic signal, a *stop* sign, or the brake lights of a car ahead. Any yellow sign will be a warning sign and should be given attention. On the other hand, blue or brown signs, which tell drivers about recreation areas and services available, may not be so important.

If a driver is attentive and has a well-organized search pattern, the inability to distinguish colors from one another should present few problems. Drivers should be aware, for example, that red is at the top of nearly all traffic signals and green is at the bottom. In addition, the meaning of traffic controls and warning signs are indicated by their shapes.

DISTANCE JUDGMENT AND DEPTH PERCEPTION

The ability to judge depth, or the distance between objects, is important. If you have difficulty judging distances, you may well have difficulty accurately controlling your space cushion in a stream of traffic.

Distance judgments are more difficult to make when you are moving than when you are standing still. Since accurate judgment of distance depends on both eyes working together, distance judgments are more difficult to make if one eye is impaired. It is possible to improve depth perception by learning to compare the sizes and shapes of objects at different angles and distances.

NIGHT VISION

No one can see as well in darkness as with a good light source. However, the ability to see under conditions of reduced illumination vary from person to person. The fact that you can see well in the daytime does not mean that you have adequate vision at night.

At night, all drivers are temporarily affected by glare, particularly the glare of oncoming headlights. The ability to adjust to and recover from glare is, however, an important part of safe driving at night.

Night driving is not easy. If you find it particularly troublesome—either because of glare or for any other reason—have your eyes tested. It may be advisable for you to avoid night driving whenever possible.

At night, the glare from oncoming headlights can seriously reduce vision.

HEARING

Good hearing is not as critical to safe driving as is good vision. The value of hearing is limited because it is often difficult to identify the direction or source of a sound while you are driving, particularly in a city. Sound can, however, provide drivers with information about other vehicles and the condition of their own cars. Sound can, for example, alert you to hazards such as trains, some trucks, motorcycles, and emergency vehicles that are using sirens. You may hear such vehicles well before you actually see them, and you will therefore have more time to respond to them.

People who have a partial hearing loss and refuse to admit that correction or adjustment is needed may present a problem. On the other hand, people who have experienced total hearing loss are often extra alert to visual cues.

Physical Performance _____

There are few factors that can impair your physical ability to perform certain tasks. Except when such disabilities are extreme, they do not seem to seriously affect safe driving. Most drivers with physical disabilities compensate for their disabilities with special vehicle controls or through careful attention to speed and position.

MUSCULAR CONTROL

Multiple sclerosis, polio, and other diseases affecting the nervous system may reduce a person's physical abilities. For the safety of themselves and the other highway users, people with such impairments should have their conditions checked by doctors before attempting to drive.

PHYSICAL HANDICAPS

As a result of accidents, disease, or birth defects, many people are missing hands, legs, or feet. When provided with vehicles with special controls, most of these people can become skillful and safe drivers.

In most states, people with physical disabilities are simply restricted to driving vehicles that have been equipped so that they can have full control of the vehicle when they are driving. For such people, a driver's license is especially important. It will open up job opportunities and provide them mobility that they otherwise would not have.

Impairments and Drivers' Responsibilities

With specially modified vehicles, handicapped people can drive.

All of us, at one time or another, will experience mental or physical impairments that will make it difficult for us to perform the driving task. There will be times when you will be faced with the decision of whether or not you should drive. If you generally accept high risks or if the reason for driving is important enough to you, you may make the decision to go ahead. You should remember, however, that if you choose to drive in such cases, you are increasing the risks for all other highway users without their knowledge or consent.

If an impairment is temporary, it may be best to wait. This is particularly true if alcohol or strong emotions are involved. Either results in impaired judgment and reduces your ability to make sound decisions and to respond appropriately.

If you have a permanent impairment and choose to drive, you should make every effort to minimize the effect of your disability. This might require no more than the addition of an extra mirror to your vehicle or the wearing of a hearing aid. Remember, however, that you can compensate for any disability only after you admit that you have it.

Other drivers on the road may be driving while impaired. Their impairment may not be readily apparent. However, they pose a problem for you. You have read about potential hazards, and you know that you will not always have sufficient warning that they exist. If you wait for visual evidence of danger before changing your speed or position, you may find it impossible to manage the hazard when it becomes serious. Drivers who are impaired are good examples of this problem. Unless their driving is very erratic, you will probably not be able to know that they present a serious hazard. The importance of recognizing and compensating for impairments should be obvious.

To Think About

1. Is alcohol a drug? What are some of its effects on the human body?
2. Is the effect of alcohol always the same on a person who drinks? Why or why not?
3. Is there any way to speed up the elimination of alcohol from the bloodstream?
4. Why is it difficult for people who have been drinking to judge their own driving abilities?
5. What are some of the common "remedies" for intoxication? How effective are these "remedies"?
6. How do police officers gather evidence about people they suspect of driving while intoxicated?
7. Name four other drugs, two prescription and two nonprescription, and explain their effects on driving behavior.
8. How can illnesses create special hazards for drivers? Give three examples.
9. Should people older than a certain age be prohibited from driving? Why or why not?
10. Are good hearing and good vision of equal importance to safe driving?

To Do

1. Invite local police officers and traffic officials to talk to your class about drinking and driving. Ask them what problems they encounter in trying to enforce laws relating to drinking and driving.
2. Discuss the following statement with several experienced drivers: "I drive better after I've had a drink or two." Ask them exactly how their driving becomes "better" and report your findings to your class. Do you and your class think that drinking improves driving skills and performance in any way?
3. Ask several experienced drivers about what drugs other than alcohol they take before or while they are driving. Report your findings to your class.
4. Investigate your state's rules about driver impairments. How often are drivers examined for impairments? Report to your class. Do you and your class think these examinations are adequate? Are the examinations given often enough in your opinion?

Motorcycles 11

After reading this chapter, you should be able to:

1. Describe how a motorcycle's controls differ from a car's controls.
2. Explain the importance of proper clothing for motorcyclists.
3. Describe how a motorcyclist's visual search should differ from a car driver's visual search.
4. Discuss why visibility is such a serious problem for motorcyclists.

Motorcycles, which are appearing in increasing numbers, are playing a more important role in the highway transportation system. In part, this is due to their relatively low cost, economy of operation, maneuverability, and the sense of freedom that they provide many people.

To drive a motorcycle, you must understand your vehicle and learn to master certain skills, just as you must to drive a car. Once you master these skills and understand how motorcycles work, you will be ready to drive.

Operating a Motorcycle

A motorcycle has many of the same controls as a car: accelerator, brakes, clutch, and gear selector. On a motorcycle, however, these controls are arranged and operated differently. It is up to you, the operator, to keep the motorcycle under control, and this requires learning to shift gears, brake, accelerate, and steer without giving conscious thought to manipulating these devices. At the same time, you must process more information and maintain a wider visual search than you do when you drive a car.

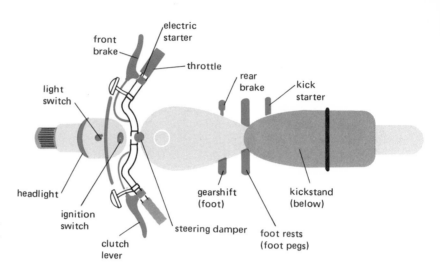

A motorcycle has many of the same controls as a car, but they are operated in a different way.

HANDLING CHARACTERISTICS

The handling characteristics of a motorcycle are different from those of four-wheeled vehicles. For example, motorcycles are particularly vulnerable to weather and road-surface conditions. Like bicycles, motorcycles are not very stable. They can easily be spilled (tipped over). A pothole that would not seriously affect a car might well cause a motorcyclist to lose control. Bumps, lane markings, dips in the road, grease, oil, and any loose material on the roadway affect a motorcycle's traction. Strong, gusting winds, especially winds from the sides, reduce stability, particularly at high speeds.

EXPOSURE AND THE MOTORCYCLIST

Motorcycle operators lack protection. They have little protection against bad weather and even less protection against injuries that might be caused by falls or by collisions with other vehicles or objects.

The physical demands on a motorcyclist are greater than those on a person driving a car. A motorcyclist is subjected to more noise and is continually pushed by wind and air resistance. Engine vibration and noise also tire out motorcyclists. (Alcohol or drugs are particularly dangerous to a motorcyclist, since even a slight lapse of attention may result in a complete loss of control.)

VISIBILITY

Compared to trucks and cars, motorcycles are quite small. For this reason, they are often not noticed by other drivers. Some drivers may not spot or even think to look for motorcyclists traveling in their blind spots.

Because of their size, motorcycles do not even come close to filling the width of a traffic lane, as most larger motor vehicles do. Because of this, other drivers tend to "crowd" motorcyclists, not realizing that they need at least as much room to maneuver as cars need.

PROTECTIVE DEVICES

Motorcycle operators, unlike operators of cars and trucks, are not protected by steel passenger compartments. In collisions and spills, they are much more likely to be injured. All motorcycle operators and riders should therefore take extra safety precautions. Proper clothing is the chief protection for motorcyclists. For this reason, it is important that you choose your clothing for its protective value.

Helmets. A helmet is the most important piece of equipment a motorcyclist can have. (A review of accident reports from throughout the country confirms that head injuries are the major cause of fatalities among motorcyclists.)

Select a bright-colored helmet for maximum visibility. The helmet should fit comfortably and should be strapped on securely so that it will not come off in a spill. The helmet should also cover your ears so that it will cut out much of the fatigue caused by road noise.

The half helmet, or "shortie," is legal, but it provides a minimum of protection to the sides of the head. Although there are several certifying standards for helmets, those that meet or exceed the U.S. Depart-

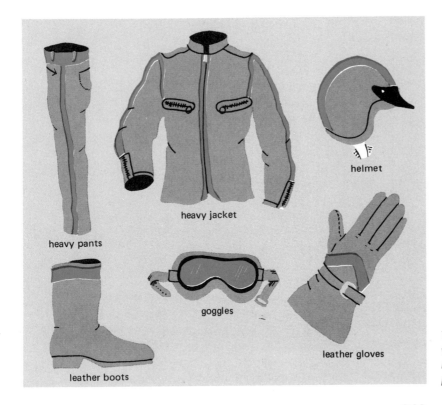

heavy pants

heavy jacket

helmet

goggles

leather gloves

leather boots

To protect themselves from the weather and possible accidents, motorcyclists should wear heavy protective clothing.

263

ment of Transportation standards are generally considered to provide adequate protection.

A helmet should not be used beyond the life specified by the manufacturer (usually 4 years). Also, it should be replaced if it is damaged in a collision or is dropped on the pavement or some other hard surface.

Eye Protection. Proper eye protection makes it easier for motorcyclists to see in glare, dust, and wind and protects the eyes from bugs, grit, and other objects. Good goggles or a face shield should be worn. For bright daylight use, gray- or amber-tinted lenses will help reduce eye fatigue. However, tinted lenses should not be used at night, since they reduce the level of light and may hide important visual cues. In addition, those who wear prescription eyeglasses should make sure that their lenses are shatter-resistant and meet state protection requirements.

Jackets and Pants. No matter how good a motorcyclist you think you are, a mistake is always possible. As a result, whenever you ride, all parts of your body should be protected. If you take a spill, you will want the best possible protection between your skin and the roadway surface. The best protection is offered by leather. Leather is not cheap, but it is the most resistant, flexible, durable material available. (If you cannot afford leather clothing, wear any heavy cotton twill, such as denim, which offers a moderate amount of protection.)

When purchasing clothing for riding, select light colors. They have the best visibility. If you have a leather jacket that is dark in color, you should also wear a reflective vest over it.

If you buy leather clothing, make sure that it is designed for motorcycle use. There should be ample room to allow for bulky underclothing in cold weather. However, the jacket should fit snugly enough so that it will not develop wind pockets and cause problems in balance when you are riding.

It is best to sit on a motorcycle in a normal riding position when trying on leather clothing. The jacket should not ride up, exposing the small of your back. The sleeves should be long enough so that your wrists are not exposed. Similar considerations hold true for pants: Are they comfortable as you sit on the motorcycle? Do the cuffs stay down at your ankles, or do they work up your legs?

Gloves. When they fall, people instinctively put out their hands to cushion the impact. Since this instinct applies to falling from a motorcycle, the need for gloves to prevent hand injuries is obvious. In addition, gloves will help keep your hands warm and flexible enough to operate the controls in cold weather. For riding in cold weather, long gloves are best; they prevent the wind from blowing up your sleeves. For warm weather, wrist-length driving gloves are sufficient.

Boots. The tops of boots should be several inches above your ankles, and the boots should have nonskid soles and heels. Steel toe and heel guards are also important for protection. Footwear with these features will protect your feet and legs from possible foot burns when stopping the motorcycle. They will also protect you from direct contact with the hot exhaust pipes or engine. Anything less than a high-cut solid leather boot could result in serious foot and ankle injuries.

Rainsuit. Because of the instability of a cycle, you should avoid riding in the rain or during bad weather whenever possible. However, if it is necessary to ride under such conditions, a rainsuit (specially designed for motorcyclists) will provide added protection. Rainsuits should fit properly at the neck, wrists, and ankles and should be large enough so that they can be worn over your regular motorcycle outfit.

PREMOUNT INSPECTION

The motorcycle should be checked out before each ride. The premount inspection of a motorcycle must be more detailed than the predriving inspection of a car. It is critical that any possible defect be identified and repaired before you get underway.

Tires and Wheels. The tires should be the best possible for the type of riding you plan to do. Check the tire pressure, look for wear and cuts, and remove small objects that may be stuck in the tread. The front tires usually wear more rapidly on the sides, while the rear tires wear more quickly in the center. A front tire with a thin side tread will greatly reduce traction on turns. A thin center tread on a rear tire will increase the possibility of a skid during hard braking or while making

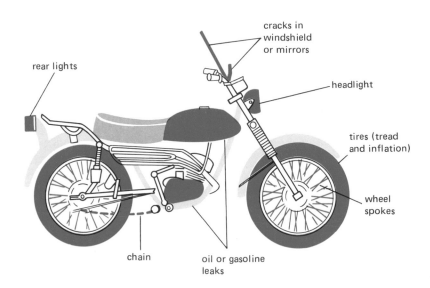

cracks in windshield or mirrors

rear lights

headlight

tires (tread and inflation)

wheel spokes

chain

oil or gasoline leaks

Make a premount inspection of all of these items each time you prepare to drive.

turns. Also, check the wheel rims for dents and make sure that all spokes are equally tight.

Control Cables.   Check all control cables, especially the clutch and brake cables, for signs of wear, loose connections, or broken strands. Lubricate these cables at regular intervals and replace them if necessary.

Brakes.   Check the front hand-brake lever and its mounting bracket for loose screws or possible cracks. If the front brake is a hydraulic disc brake, check the fluid reservoir level. The rear mechanical brake should be checked by stepping down on the brake pedal. The pedal should feel solid and should move downward only a short distance.

Gasoline and Oil Leaks.   Fluid leaks can be especially dangerous at highway speeds, since the leaking liquid will often be blown onto the rear tire, dangerously reducing traction. Check the engine- and transmission-oil levels and make sure all seals are tight.

Chain.   The chain should be properly adjusted. A chain that is too tight wears rapidly. A chain that is loose can jam around the sprocket, causing the rear wheel to lock and placing you in a serious skid. Also, the chain should be properly lubricated to prevent unnecessary wear.

Electrical Accessories.   The horn, brake, headlight, and turn signals should all be checked to see that they are working properly.

Windshield.   If the motorcycle has a windshield, check it for cracks. Even a small crack, under strong wind pressure, could result in a completely shattered windshield. Also, visibility could be reduced by any spots or cracks that are within the operator's line of sight.

Controls and Adjustments

To operate a motorcycle safely and efficiently, you will have to be thoroughly familiar with its controls. You will also have to be seated comfortably in its saddle so that you can reach for and adjust the various control devices without straining or getting off balance.

CONTROLS

In traffic, a motorcyclist must be able to observe, predict, and adjust to changing traffic conditions without having to look down at the motorcycle's controls. Skilled motorcyclists should be able to automatically

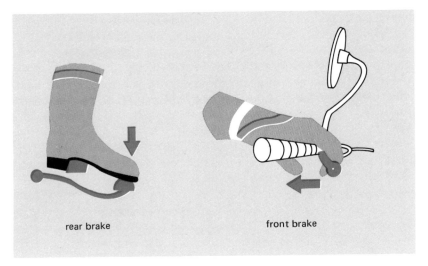

rear brake   front brake

The rear brake is operated with a pedal on the right side. The front brake is operated with a lever on the right handlebar. The rear brake should always be applied lightly just before the front brake.

operate the controls. They should not have to think about how to use the controls and should not have to take their eyes from the road.

Brakes.   The lever for the front brakes is located on the right handlebar. Since the front brake provides most of the braking power (about two-thirds of the braking effort), it should be squeezed gradually. If it is pulled up sharply, the brakes may lock, sending the motorcycle into a skid. The rear brake pedal is usually found on the right side of the cycle and is operated by the right foot. The front and rear brakes should be used together. The rear brake should be applied just before pressure on the front brake is applied.

Throttle.   The throttle is controlled with a twist grip which is located at the end of the right handlebar. Twisting the top of the grip back toward you increases engine speed. Twisting the top of the grip away from you decreases engine speed.

to increase
engine speed

to decrease
engine speed

The throttle is operated with a hand grip on the right handlebar.

267

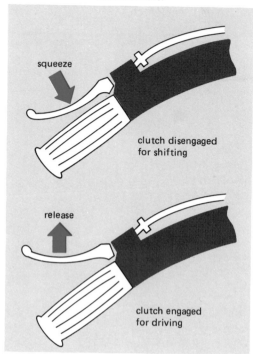

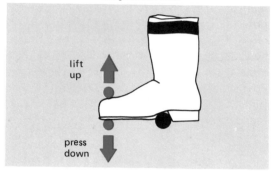

common gear patterns

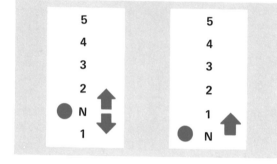

The clutch is operated with a lever on the left handlebar. The gearshift lever is usually a pedal on the left side of the motorcycle.

Clutch Lever. Most motorcycles have a manual clutch operated by a lever located near the end of the left handlebar. Closing your hand (pulling the lever toward you) disengages the clutch, allowing you to change gears. Opening your hand gradually will release the lever and re-engage the clutch.

Gearshift Lever. On motorcycles, the gearshift lever is foot operated. The lever is located directly ahead of the foot rest, on the left side. (The owner's manual will explain the gearshift pattern for a particular motorcycle.)

Ignition Switch. Most newer motorcycles have a key-operated ignition switch. Some also have a handlebar-mounted "kill" switch. This switch enables the operator to quickly cut off the ignition in an emergency. For example, if the throttle is stuck, you could "kill" the engine without removing your hands from the handlebar grips.

Headlight and Horn Button. The headlight, dimmer switch, and horn button are located within easy reach on the handlebars. You must develop the ability to use each of these without taking your eyes off the road ahead.

Mirrors. Your motorcycle should be equipped with two handlebar-mounted mirrors. They should be adjusted to give as wide a view as possible of traffic to the rear.

Steering Damper. Some motorcycles are fitted with a damper to reduce the tendency of the front wheel to kick or wobble. Screwing down (tightening) the damper makes the front wheel more stable for high speeds. Loosening the damper makes the front wheel more maneuverable for city traffic.

FITTING THE CYCLE TO THE RIDER

Control of a motorcycle requires the best riding position possible. This means that the motorcycle should be properly adjusted to the size of the rider. You should sit fairly straight, in a relaxed position, to cut fatigue and to aid balance. Your knees should be pressed gently against the fuel tank. The footrests should be adjusted so that you have easy access to the rear brake and gearshift pedals. At the same time, your legs should be bent at a comfortable angle.

The handlebars should be adjusted so that the hand grips are parallel to the ground or pointed slightly downward. In this position, your hands should rest naturally on the grips, with your elbows slightly bent. The clutch and brake levers should be positioned so that they fall in line with your forearms. (You should not have to move your hand along the handlebars to reach these levers.)

PREPARING TO GET UNDERWAY

Just as in starting to drive a car, there are certain procedures that must be followed when getting ready to drive a motorcycle. Again, a set sequence should be followed.

Starting the engine. After you have completed the premount checks, follow these steps to start the engine:

1. Open the fuelcock.
2. Straddle the motorcycle and balance it.
3. Pull in on the front brake lever to prevent the motorcycle from moving.
4. Set the choke, if the engine is cold, and turn on the ignition.
5. Check to make sure that the transmission is in neutral.
6. Open the throttle slightly, by turning the throttle grip back toward you, and either press the ignition button or kick down on the kick starter. (Use the ball of your right foot and kick all the way down to avoid injury in case of kick-back.)
7. If the engine is cold, allow it to run at idle speed for a moment. Then, gradually turn the choke off until the engine is running evenly without it.

1. Open fuelcock.

2. Straddle the motorcycle.

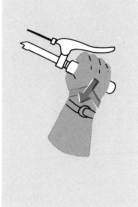

3. Apply rear brake.

4. Release kick stand.

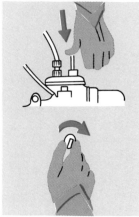

5. Set choke or prime with kick starter and turn on ignition.

6. Shift to *neutral*.

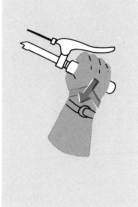

7. Open the throttle slightly.

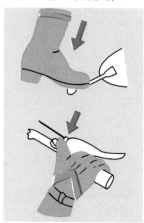

8. Start the engine with the ignition switch or kick starter.

Follow this procedure to start the motorcycle. If the engine is cold, give it time to warm up.

Putting the Motorcycle in Motion.   Again, the procedure is very similar to making a lateral movement with a car. The only changes in procedure are a result of basic differences between cars and motorcycles:

1. Signal your move into traffic.
2. Pull in the clutch lever and shift into *first* gear.
3. Place your left foot on the ground and your right foot lightly on the rear brake pedal to prevent the motorcycle from moving.
4. Check your mirrors and look over your shoulder to ensure a clear path of travel.
5. Increase the throttle slightly and gradually engage the clutch.

6. Place *both* feet on the footrests as soon as possible and shift upward through the gears without unnecessarily gunning the engine.

Gear Selection. Most motorcycles have good performance characteristics, considering the rather narrow limits of a motorcycle's engine speed. The different gears allow you to keep the engine speed at the most efficient level at all times. As in a stick-shift car, *first* gear is used for moving the motorcycle from a stopped position, for driving in slow-moving traffic, or for very steep hills. As speeds increase, higher gears should be used, with the top gear used for cruising. Downshifting may be necessary to gain more pulling power on steep upgrades, when speeds are reduced, or when bringing the motorcycle to a stop.

Shifting Up. To shift up through the gears, use the following procedures:

1. Pull in the clutch lever with your left hand.
2. Shift to the desired gear with your left foot.
3. Gradually release the clutch lever and at the same time twist the throttle grip back toward you with your right hand.

This procedure should be repeated, as speed increases, until you arrive at the proper gear.

Follow this procedure to shift into gear and move. As soon as you begin to move, put both feet up on the footrests.

1. Signal your move.

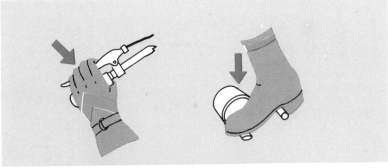

2. Pull in clutch and shift to *first* gear.

3. Apply rear brake.

4. Shoulder-check and check mirrors.

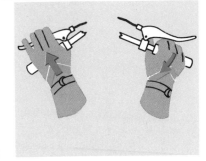

5. Increase throttle and engage clutch.

Downshifting. This procedure is the same as shifting up through gears, except that as you pull in the clutch lever you twist the throttle grip away from you (to reduce engine speed) and move the gear selector in the opposite direction.

STEERING AND MOTORCYCLE STABILITY

Steering and stability are related. Even on a straight path, a motorcycle actually moves in a series of slight curves. This explains the need for caution on slippery surfaces, even when traveling in a straight line.

A motorcycle is balanced so that it steers in the direction in which it is leaning. Steering automatically returns to the center position (straight ahead) when the motorcycle is brought back to an upright position. As with an automobile, heavy and poorly distributed loads will make a motorcycle less stable, especially if the load is improperly tied down.

CORNERING

Before driving through a curve or around a corner, estimate its sharpness. Check the available visual lead and judge whether the road surface is banked, crowned, rutted, or slippery. Such information will help you to decide whether to cut your speed and by how much. You may need to downshift. All braking should be down *before* entering a curve or corner so that you can use gentle acceleration going around it. This will make your motorcycle more stable.

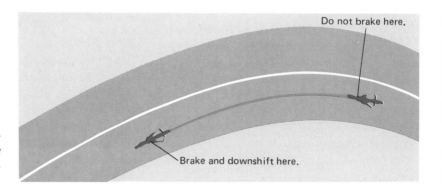

Do not brake here.

Brake and downshift here.

Apply your brakes as you approach a curve, not while you are in it. Then, as you leave the curve, accelerate.

USING THE BRAKES

Coordinate the front and rear brakes—applying the rear brakes just before the front. Increase pressure gradually to avoid losing traction. The front brake has greater stopping power, since the weight of both driver and motorcycle are thrown forward when the brakes are applied. This weight transfer presses the front tire more firmly on to the roadway surface, resulting in greater traction on the front wheel. If you use the rear brake only, you will lose most of your braking power, and the rear wheel will slide more readily. It is a good idea for new riders to spend time practicing braking in a large, clear area.

Adjusting Braking to the Roadway Surface. It is extremely important for motorcyclists to learn to adjust braking to roadway-surface conditions. If you have to slow quickly on a slippery surface, pump the brakes. Learn to scan the roadway surface ahead, and avoid braking where the surface looks slippery. If possible, choose the best surface available if it is necessary to brake hard.

Braking and Front-Wheel Position. Always brake with the vehicle upright and the front wheel pointed straight ahead. This is particularly important on a slippery surface, especially when hard braking is necessary. Avoid hard braking if the roadway is steeply banked or if the front wheel is not pointed straight ahead. Under either of these conditions, hard braking will reduce traction and tend to throw the rider away from the motorcycle.

Why must motorcyclists pay special attention to the roadway surface?

PARKING AND SECURING THE MOTORCYCLE

As applies to all motor vehicles, motorcycles must be parked in a legal parking space. Parking between two closely spaced cars, for example, is dangerous and usually illegal. It could result in damage if one of the car's drivers tries to maneuver out of the space.

When parking a motorcycle, leave it in a well-lit area. A case-hardened, heavy-link chain with an equally strong lock is a good investment. Use a chain that is long enough to enable you to anchor the frame of the motorcycle to a solid object, such as a lamp post or a street sign. A variety of alarm systems is also available and are useful in discouraging thieves.

Riding a
Motorcycle in Traffic

Once you can operate your motorcycle smoothly, your greatest challenge will be driving in traffic. You must develop the ability to protect yourself from other motor-vehicle operators by employing defensive driving tactics. At the same time, you will have to develop an expecially good visual search of the roadway surface ahead.

DEVELOPING A VISUAL SEARCH

Information processing is critical to the safe, efficient operation of a car or truck. It is a matter of life or death to a motorcyclist. A well-developed, alert visual search is essential if you are to avoid accidents.

As a motorcyclist, you enjoy a better field of vision than other motorists, since you sit higher than most of them. Further, your field of vision is not blocked by the blind spots that exist in a car or truck. You have to make the best possible use of these advantages.

Blocks to Gathering Information.   Motorcyclists are faced with certain problems that can influence their ability to gather information. For example, your vision to the rear will be poor if the rear-view mirrors are improperly adjusted, or if they vibrate too much. Eye-protection gear can also create some hazards. Tinted visors or goggles can reduce your vision, especially if the light is poor. Goggles with thick frames will tend to reduce side vision. However, you must wear goggles to keep your eyes from watering or being struck by objects in the air.

Scanning the Roadway Surface.   The best advice that can be given a motorcyclist is never assume that the roadway surface will be clear of hazards. You must learn to identify the roadway hazards, many of which would not present a problem to the driver of a car.

A skilled motorcyclist scans the roadway surface for things like oil, gravel, holes, sewer drains, bumps, and railroad tracks. Sewer drains that run parallel to traffic lanes are especially hazardous, since your front tire may wedge into the grating, throwing you off the motorcycle. If it is not possible to steer around bumps, reduce your speed and rise up on the footrests so that you will not bounce off the motorcycle when the rear wheels pass over the bump. When crossing railroad tracks, cross at a right angle to the tracks, or as close to a right angle as possible, so that the rear wheel will not spin or the front wheel get caught and make you lose control.

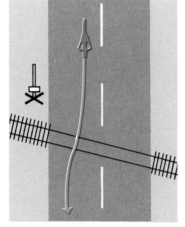

Drive across railroad tracks at as close to a right angle as you can.

OBJECTS IN THE ROADWAY

Motorcyclists have a special reason for maintaining an adequate following distance: objects that fall from other vehicles, such as mufflers or hubcaps, are especially hazardous to a motorcycle. If you cannot safely avoid objects like these or rocks, bricks, bottles, cans, tires, or broken glass, keep your motorcycle as straight as possible and go over obstacles at or close to a right angle. If you are forced to drive over sharp objects—such as broken glass or nails—get off the road as soon as possible and check your tires.

As you drive, check carefully for sand and gravel, especially at intersections, where trucks may spill small amounts while stopping, starting, or turning. Water, oil, mud, ice, wet leaves, and other slippery substances can cause a sudden loss of traction, especially if you are braking, cornering, or accelerating. Shaded portions of the roadway can be especially slippery during freezing or wet weather. Under such conditions, any adjustment of speed or direction should be made as gradually as possible.

274

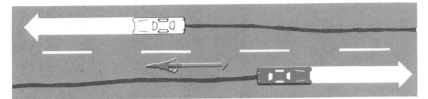

To avoid the slippery oil and grease spots found in the center of many traffic lanes, stay to the left.

You should avoid driving exactly in the center of a traffic lane, where cars frequently leak oil and water. This problem is especially bad at intersections, where stopped vehicles tend to leak the most oil. Painted lane markings, especially those that are wet, can also seriously reduce traction.

Responding to Animals. Animals, particularly dogs, can be dangerous. Try to anticipate the movements of animals. If you can do so safely, accelerate away from them. However, avoid swerving to miss the animal. Dogs, for example, will often dodge out of the way if the driver maintains a straight course. And if the animal does not dodge, you will have a greater chance of maintaining control of your motorcycle by striking the animal while you are in an upright position, rather than in the leaning position of a swerving maneuver.

SEEING AND BEING SEEN

The majority of car drivers surveyed after automobile-motorcycle collisions claim that they did not see the motorcyclist. This information emphasizes the need for motorcyclists to be visible to other motorists at all times.

Positioning To Be Seen. The profile of a motorcycle and its operator is smaller than the profile of a passenger car. It is therefore critical that you position yourself in the best location to be seen and actively search for cues to the possible moves of other drivers. It is generally best to position your motorcycle in the path of the *left* wheel of the vehicle ahead. Such a position will let the driver ahead know you are there. In addition, you will avoid the slippery center portion of the lane and have a better view, particularly at intersections.

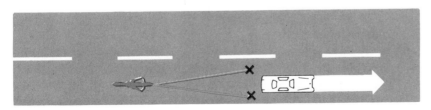

Do not get into other drivers' blind spots.

Another reason to use the left portion of a traffic lane is to ensure that a passing car will use the passing lane, rather than attempt to pass in the same lane and force you off the road.

To improve your visibility even more, drive with your headlight on at all times, and wear a bright-colored helmet and reflective clothing.

Positioning to See.   Stay out of the other drivers' blind spots. Also, stay well back from any vehicle you are following so that you can see past it and anticipate when you may have to stop. Anticipate possible danger spots where the field of vision of other drivers will be limited, especially at intersections. If you are forced to ride on the right side of the outside lane, scan for parked cars about to pull out, passengers about to open doors, and pedestrians.

Watch for oncoming vehicles that may turn left in front of you. Whenever an oncoming vehicle approaches and there is an intersection or driveway on your right, be ready in case the vehicle turns. Also, watch for vehicles approaching from the sides or backing out of driveways. Be especially alert for pedestrians, particularly children, who may dart into your path from between parked cars.

To make yourself more visible to other highway users, you should use your headlight and wear reflective clothing at all times.

SPECIAL TRAFFIC CONDITIONS

Besides making yourself and your motorcycle as visible as possible, allow ample spacing so that you will not be forced into emergency maneuvers. Moving at a steady traffic-flow speed will help reduce the number of times you or others will have to adjust speed, pass, or change lanes. When meeting a large oncoming vehicle, particularly on two-lane roads, move to the *right* side of the lane to reduce wind drafts and turbulence.

Driving in the space between lanes of cars is illegal and very dangerous. This small gap can close suddenly without warning. Drivers simply do not expect you to be there.

When driving with other motorcyclists, avoid driving side by side. Instead, drive offset, one behind the other. It is recommended that the driver on the right stay behind the driver on the left to ensure that both will have room to swerve if necessary.

Checking Intersections.   Approach intersections, pedestrian crossings, and traffic signals cautiously and at a reduced speed. Double-check side streets, oncoming traffic, and sidewalks for pedestrians and vehicles that might cross your path.

If a traffic light changes to green as you approach, carefully scan the side street in case a driver tries to get through. In any event, scan left and right a second time as you enter any intersection, in case you missed something the first time.

Watch out for drivers who may back into your path.

Turns. Give traffic to the rear advance notice by signaling and moving into the proper position well before the turn. Downshift as you approach the turn. This action will allow you to direct your attention to the roadway and the traffic ahead, rather than having to shift, signal, and steer at the same time.

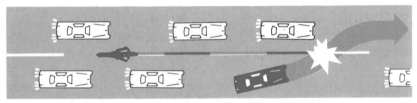

Driving between lanes of cars is illegal and extremely dangerous. A car may swerve suddenly and cut you off.

Changing Lanes and Passing. Avoid passing cars on the right, except in cases of emergencies to avoid collisions. Before passing, signal to alert traffic, and sound your horn in daytime or dim your lights at night. This will let the motorists know that you are about to pass. If you are motorcycling with a friend, pass vehicles one at a time so that you can both perform the maneuver safely.

When being passed, stay on the *left* side of your lane. If a driver is passing a car behind you, you will be more visible if you are in the left part of your lane.

Being Tailgated. If you operate a small, low-powered motorcycle, avoid high-speed roadways in which you cannot maintain traffic-flow speed. This problem is most likely to arise on upgrades.

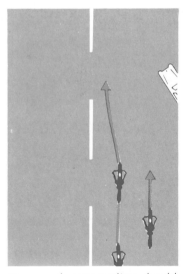

Groups of motorcyclists should drive off-set, not side by side, so that they can swerve safely, if necessary.

277

A

B

Signal and check your mirrors before you turn (A) and watch out for drivers who may not see you and cut you off (B).

If you find that you are being tailgated, accelerate slightly, if you can do so without reducing your forward space cushion. If this does not work, consider signaling and pulling off the road to let the motorist by.

Stalling in Traffic. If your engine stalls while you are moving, check traffic to the rear, signal, and steer off the road. If traffic is crowded and you cannot move off the road, warn traffic to the rear by waving your arm or flashing your brake light. Shift to *neutral* so that you can push the cycle off the road and out of traffic.

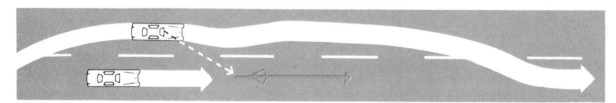

If you are being passed, stay to the left of your lane. If you move right, the passing driver may not see you.

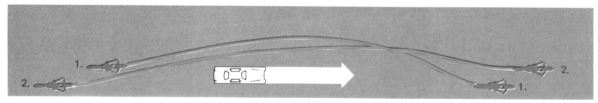

If you are alongside another motorcyclist and you want to pass a vehicle ahead, do it one at a time.

278

HAZARDOUS CONDITIONS

If at all possible, avoid driving in bad weather. Poor weather conditions make you less visible, less able to maneuver safely, and more likely to skid.

The motorcyclist is particularly vulnerable to the extremes of bad weather. Extreme cold can numb your arms, legs, and face, even when you are properly dressed. Your ability to manipulate hand and foot controls will be greatly impaired.

Rain. Rain makes road surfaces slick. Make sure that your tires have good tread and are properly inflated. Slow down and scan for obstacles, such as potholes, that may be hidden by rain puddles. Make steering, braking, and acceleration movements gradually to avoid skidding. Avoid driving through puddles of water that could cause your motorcycle to hydroplane. Do not depend on other vehicles to stop. Remember, cars also slide on slick surfaces.

Rain can also make a driver uncomfortable and, as a result, less efficient. Wear proper rain gear and face shields or goggles to stay dry and to maintain your vision. A windshield is especially helpful in rain and in cold weather. If your face shield fogs, coat the inside with an antifog solution to keep it clear.

Snow and Ice. If the roads are covered with snow or ice, do not drive. Motorcycles are simply not designed to have the stability needed for these conditions. There are many hazards that may affect your ability to control the motorcycle in such weather: blowing snow, near-zero traction, controls that ice up as you drive, gloves that freeze to the grips, iced boot soles, and foot pegs splattered with slush. Because of the wind-chill factor, the controls may ice up even at temperatures above freezing.

Night Driving. As stated previously, being seen is one of the motorcyclist's major problems. Night riding reduces both vision and visibility even further. Your speed must be reduced to adequately scan the surface for hazards.

To compensate, increase your visibility by wearing reflective clothing. Make sure that all lights and signals are clean and working properly. Be extra alert for the errors of other drivers who may be tired or who may have poor night vision. (On weekends your problems will be increased further due to the high number of intoxicated drivers on the road.)

SKIDS

Skids are a serious problem for any motorcyclist. They can be caused by slippery road surfaces, by braking too hard, by accelerating, and by cornering.

279

Braking Skid.   If the brakes are applied too hard, one or both wheels may lock, causing a loss of stability and steering. To compensate, ease off the brakes until the locked wheels roll again. Then reapply the brakes. Pumping the brakes will aid in stopping on a slippery surface without causing the wheels to lock.

Acceleration Skid.   Too much throttle will cause the back wheel to spin. This may cause the back of the motorcycle to slide sideways. To compensate, ease off the throttle immediately when you hear or feel the rear wheel spinning.

Cornering Skid.   Cornering skids are the most difficult to correct. They can be caused by driving around a curve too fast or by braking too hard when the motorcycle is leaned. All braking should be done with the motorcycle upright for maximum stability. Swerving to avoid a collision may also provoke a skid by making the turn tighter than the driver had planned.

If you enter a curve too fast, but are not yet sliding, lean the motorcycle further into the turn (for example, more to the right for a right-hand curve).

AVOIDING OBSTACLES

Under certain conditions a quick stop may not be the best response for avoiding a collision. For instance, a muffler and tail pipe might suddenly appear across your path as a vehicle ahead passes over it. The only way to avoid such an object may be a quick lateral maneuver. By turning quickly, however, you risk being hit by other vehicles. To reduce this risk, you should "squeeze" by the obstacle without leaving your lane. This demands that you respond quickly and it is one time when the size of your motorcycle is an advantage. Even if the obstacle is large, make every effort to pass it while staying in your lane. Only under extreme conditions should you change lanes without first checking for other vehicles.

TOURING

Touring by motorcycle requires advanced planning. Preplanning includes checking things like clothing, spare parts, tools, and the motorcycle itself. The motorcycle you select should be sufficiently large and have an engine large enough for long-distance touring. (Remember, if you are going to load the motorcycle with gear or a passenger, you will decrease its steering, braking, and accelerating capabilities.)

For the typical high-school-age driver, a motorcycle with a 300- to 400-cc (cubic centimeter) engine will generally be satisfactory. For a 6-foot, 180-pound person, however, something in the 400- to 500-cc engine range would be more realistic. A 100- to 200-cc engine, for example, is much too small for carrying two passengers or for touring on high-speed roadways.

The Experienced Driver. Any driver who carries a passenger should first have had solo driving experience under various traffic conditions. The driver should be aware that, with a passenger aboard, the motorcycle's acceleration and handling capabilities will be impaired. As a result, speed should be reduced and all maneuvers should be performed more gradually and smoothly.

If the passenger has never been on a motorcycle before, the driver should not only explain the proper procedures, but should practice driving with the person before a tour is started.

The Informed Passenger. A passenger should be dressed in the same way as the driver. The passenger should sit still, avoid distracting the driver, keep both feet on the passenger foot pegs, and grip the passenger hand holds. It is also important that the passenger lean with the driver when making turns. At all cost, the passenger should avoid leaning in the opposite direction or more than the driver, since this may cause the motorcycle to lose its stability.

How to Pack the Motorcycle. The load should be evenly distributed and placed as low and as far forward as possible. Avoid overloading the rear end of the motorcycle if you have a rear-mounted luggage rack. Consider a tank-mounted bag or saddlebags.

If you carry anything on the luggage rack, mount it securely with heavy-duty adjustable stretch cord.

Tools and Spare Parts. Because motorcycles frequently require repairs, you should always carry pregapped spark plugs, a set of points, headlight bulbs and other bulbs, fuses, replacement control cables, a variety of nuts and bolts, a spare chain, and a master link.

Loosely packed luggage could shift during cornering. This could cause a serious loss of stability.

To perform repairs, you should have electrical tape, a chain breaker, a tire patch kit, a tire pressure gauge, special tools needed for changing oil, tools for setting the ignition, and an assortment of screwdrivers, pliers, and open-end wrenches. A first aid kit is also an essential item.

HIGH-SPEED OPERATION

Motorcyclists are confronted not only by the same problems that confront operators of other motor vehicles, but also by unusual problems created by wind and fatigue.

Wind. A strong side wind can have a marked effect on the control of a motorcycle. The influence of these winds increases as your speed increases. The only way to compensate is to reduce your speed to the point at which you can maintain full control. This is particularly true when being passed by or meeting trucks, which first create a buffer and then a high wind turbulence as they pass.

Fatigue. Some people feel that motorcyclists are less subject to fatigue than the operators of cars or trucks, since the wind is blowing on their faces and keeping them awake. However, the brisk feeling cyclists get from the wind may hide the fatigue and impaired reflexes caused by long hours in the saddle. Your best safeguard is to compensate for fatigue by making a rest stop at frequent intervals (approximately every 1 to 1½ hours).

TRAIL RIDING

For many people, trail riding represents the real world of motorcycling.

Required Equipment. An off-road motorcycle should have good ground clearance, knobby tires for traction, and a spark arrestor to reduce the possibility of fire. For the new driver, a lightweight bike of modest size and power is recommended. A helmet, gloves, sturdy boots, and other protective equipment are essential in case of a spill.

Selecting an Off-Road Area. When exploring areas or when going off well-traveled paths, take a companion along—preferably an experienced driver who can break you in gradually to the skills of off-road driving. Choose the driving location carefully. Avoid going off marked trails. If you want to drive on private property, ask for the owner's permission. You will probably get permission if previous drivers have not worn out the welcome by being inconsiderate.

Make sure that you know the terrain over which you are traveling. Blasting along at a high speed over unfamiliar terrain is a sure way to run into abandoned pits and machinery, trash piles, wire fences, and many other objects obscured by high grass and shrubs. In other words, use common sense.

PURCHASING A MOTORCYCLE

It is extremely important that you consider the type of driving that you expect to do. If you intend to drive only on the street, your best purchase is a motorcycle that will give you better handling on the street—not an off-road motorcycle with knobby tires.

For local use, a motorcycle with a 100- to 200-cc engine will generally provide ample power. Motorcycles with smaller engines, or even a 100- to 200-cc engine, may not be a good choice if you drive in hilly areas. If you intend to do much touring, to carry passengers, or to do much high-speed freeway traveling, a larger (350- to 500-cc) motorcycle will probably be more suitable. Consider accessories, such as luggage racks, saddlebags, or windshield.

If you plan to buy a used motorcycle, shop carefully and have it inspected thoroughly by a competent motorcycle mechanic. Avoid motorcycles with modifications, which might impair handling capabilities.

INSURANCE

Although a motorcycle is relatively small, it can cause considerable damage. Check any insurance policy to make sure that it covers passengers. If it is available, buy coverage for medical payments. (Motorcycle accidents are more likely to result in injuries to drivers and passengers than are automobile accidents.) Motorcycle coverages and rates vary. It is smart to comparison shop to find the best coverage.

NOISE

Motorcycles require the good will of motorists to survive in traffic. One of the surest ways to offend other highway users is to make unnecessary noise. It is only common sense, then, to avoid using modified exhaust systems that increase noise levels. In addition, avoid high engine speeds in urban and residential areas, especially at night and early in the morning.

To Think About

1. In what ways is operating a motorcycle different from driving a car?
2. Describe good motorcycling clothing and explain why it is needed.
3. Why does motorcycling require especially careful positioning in traffic?

4. Why is scanning the roadway surface even more important for motorcyclists than it is for other motor-vehicle operators?
5. What are the obligations of a motorcycle passenger?
6. What special visual problems do motorcyclists have? Do they have any advantages?

7. How can motorcyclists compensate for the fact that they are especially vulnerable to weather conditions?
8. How can you control a motorcycle that begins to skid?
9. Why is it better to have some packs or bags mounted up front rather than having them all at the rear?
10. Why do motorcyclists often suffer from fatigue?

To Do

1. Report on the regulations for owning and operating motorcycles in your state. How do these regulations differ from those relating to automobile ownership and licensing?
2. Ask local motorcycle dealers and mechanics about important maintenance checks and procedures that motorcycle owners often overlook. Summarize your findings in a report.
3. Observe and report on motorcycling practices in your area. How many of the motorcyclists that you see are properly dressed? How many seem to adjust their speed and position to maintain safe space cushions? Do other highway users seem to cooperate with the motorcyclists?
4. Survey some licensed motorcyclists in your area to find out how they learned to drive. Ask them questions 1, 3, 4, and 6 from the "To Think About" section.
5. Invite a local police officer to talk about motorcycle use in your area. What does the officer think are the major causes of accidents involving motorcycles?

Career Opportunities 12

After reading this chapter, you should be able to:

1. Identify and describe careers in each of the five occupational areas of the highway transportation system.
2. Explain how driver education programs improve the highway transportation system.
3. Describe ways in which engineering can help motorists, pedestrians, and bicyclists.
4. Give examples of ways in which service-industries careers can improve the highway transportation system.

You have read about how the design and maintenance of motor vehicles and the highway environment are critical to vehicle control. In this chapter you will read about careers in the maintenance and management of the highway transportation system.

The importance of the highway transportation system to our national life is hard to measure. However, we do know that within the labor force, approximately one out of every seven workers has a job that is related to meeting the needs of this system.

Maintaining and Improving the System _____

A properly managed highway transportation system contributes to the economic and social well-being of this country. It makes possible the movement of people and goods that is essential for our social and economic growth. For the system to work effectively, people and goods must move swiftly, conveniently, economically, and especially, safely. The system's safety is essential to its efficiency. An unsafe system wastes time, money, and goods. More important, an unsafe system wastes our most important resource—people.

Occupations related to the highway transportation system fall into five broad categories:

1. Education
2. Engineering
3. Motor-vehicle administration
4. Police traffic services
5. Service industries

Within each of these categories, the necessary occupational skills range from those requiring little or no special training, to internship and apprenticeship programs, to those requiring highly specialized preparation and, in a number of cases, advanced university degrees.

Education

Education, in its broadest sense, is critical in improving the efficiency of the highway transportation system. People usually think of driver education only as it relates to courses in public schools or private driver-training schools. Such courses are important, but they represent only a small part of the effort. There is, for example, an expanding need for instructors who specialize in the preparation of drivers of heavy construction equipment, buses, and trucks.

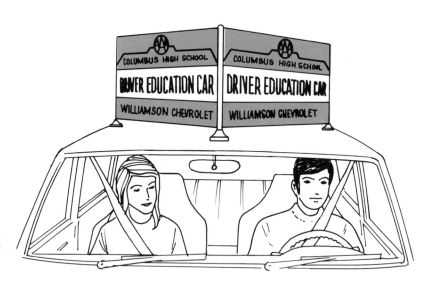

Driver education at the high school level includes in-class and on-road teaching.

PUBLIC INFORMATION

There are many people working for insurance companies, automobile manufacturers, tire manufacturers, oil companies, and agencies like police departments, departments of motor-vehicle administration, the National Safety Council, and the American Automobile Association who devote some or all of their effort to public education and highway safety. These activities include public information and support for programs such as safety-belt use, vehicle care, pedestrian safety, and alcohol safety programs. For example, the alcohol programs and other similar programs are directed at rehabilitating problem drivers. In addition, driver-improvement programs designed for the general public are gaining increased attention.

JOB REQUIREMENTS
In some situations, a high school diploma in addition to work experience in the field will meet the educational requirements. In other programs, a few specialized courses are necessary. A high school driver-education teacher, for example, must have a college degree, with specialized course experience in driver education. People teaching in the field of traffic and safety education at the college and university level and those directing research activities must have advanced degrees in their fields.

Professional positions in business and industry usually require preparation beyond high school. However, many technical and supportive jobs that do not require extensive training are available. For example, defensive driving courses and alcohol safety programs are sometimes conducted by people who do not have college or advanced degrees. With specialized course training, well-developed materials, and a back-up professional staff, teachers without college or university degrees have been quite successful.

Police officers and traffic officials may take part in driver education programs at local high schools.

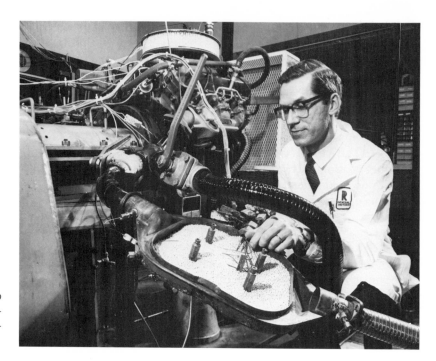

Automotive engineers develop and test new products. This engineer is checking the exhaust-emissions levels of a new engine.

Engineering

Engineering plays an important role in all aspects of the highway transportation system. Engineers design and supervise the construction of vehicles and roadways. There are three areas within the broad field of engineering that are directly related to the highway transportation system: automotive, highway, and traffic engineering.

AUTOMOTIVE ENGINEERING

In general, automotive engineers are concerned with the design and manufacture of motor vehicles and related equipment. They design and develop vehicles that meet certain federal standards. These vehicles may range from the most powerful construction equipment to the most efficient subcompact cars that can be produced. Automotive engineers must also try to design vehicles that can be manufactured at the lowest cost possible.

Automotive engineers must consider safety, styling, the availability of materials, and durability as they design new equipment or make changes in existing equipment. Before any new motor vehicle or piece of equipment is made available to the public, its safety and reliability must be determined. This is accomplished through extensive performance testing. Automotive engineers are closely involved with this phase of production. They monitor and test each type of vehicle or piece of equipment before it is made available to the public.

288

Related Occupations. Persons in other occupations work closely with the automotive engineer in the design, testing, and construction of motor vehicles and parts. Assembly-line workers, test drivers, and even racing-car drivers often supply valuable and necessary information that contributes to a safe, efficient, and economical product.

After the public sale of a motor vehicle or piece of equipment, a valuable contribution is made by people involved in repair and maintenance. With the ever-increasing complexity of vehicles, there has been a parallel increase in the demand for competent vehicle repair and maintenance personnel. This group of highly trained technicians provides valuable feedback information that can be used by engineers and designers in developing new vehicles or in modifying existing vehicles. These technicians may provide information that can improve the safety and durability of products which are already on the road.

HIGHWAY ENGINEERING

The highway engineer is involved with overseeing the planning, construction, and maintenance of streets and highways and coordinating them with other modes of transportation (such as pedestrian and bicycle paths or railroads). In their work, highway engineers attempt to develop the most safe and efficient roadways, with the minimum amount of disruption to the environment. In addition, highway engineers, like automotive engineers, must work within guidelines and standards set down by federal, state, and local governments.

Modern highways need constant maintenance and improvement. New signs and roadway markings are an important part of this program.

289

Construction projects require clearing a right of way, preparing a subgrade or base, laying the roadway surface, and then installing curbing, guardrails, and off-road areas. The highway engineer works together with various contractors and agencies in this construction process.

Related Occupations. The variety of jobs and activities involved in the construction of a highway involves large numbers of people—even for modest projects. Heavy-equipment operators, drainage specialists, construction-materials workers, surveyors, landscape architects, traffic-control personnel, truck drivers, and draftsmen are just a few of the kinds of workers involved in a typical construction project.

Once they are built and in use, highways must be maintained, repaired, and sometimes improved. Maintenance activities include identifying hazards, diagnosing and correcting guide-sign problems, snow removal and salting, and periodic roadway repairs and resurfacing.

TRAFFIC ENGINEERING

Traffic engineers are directly concerned with the safe and efficient movement of vehicles and goods in the highway transportation system. They are often involved in the design of roads and highways, supplying information about such things as the traffic flow and parking requirements for new residential communities, housing sites, and shopping centers.

Accident spot map

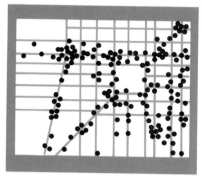

Collision diagram

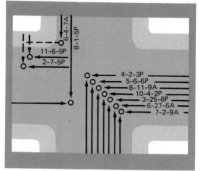

Traffic engineers use maps and diagrams like these to keep records of when and where accidents occur.

The traffic engineer uses all available technology to promote safety and to reduce congestion on streets and highways. An important part of the job is learning to use the many techniques of gathering data about traffic flow and traffic problems. This includes counting the number and types of vehicles passing certain points in the highway system, keeping

Traffic engineers can use the data they have gathered to suggest changes in the traffic flow, the signs, signals, and markings, or the roadway itself.

accurate records of all kinds of accidents, and predicting changes in the number of vehicles using the streets and highways. With this kind of data, traffic engineers can make recommendations for changes in traffic flow. For example, they might recommend converting two-way streets to one-way streets, widening streets, removing parking facilities, installing or removing signs or signals, or adding special turn lanes.

Related Occupations.   Traffic engineers are assisted by various technical personnel and public agencies. Traffic technicians, for example, are used in investigating accidents and conducting traffic studies. They are often involved in the design and installation of traffic-control devices. Police, public works, and city planning departments work closely with traffic engineers.

Some expressways are now surveyed with television monitors at a central location. Information about accidents or traffic tie-ups can then be relayed to the police or other motorists.

Traffic engineers also benefit from, and work closely with, citizens and citizen groups. Many traffic problems are brought to their attention by citizens. And in many cases, traffic engineers may have to go before citizen groups to explain their reasons for certain actions or to ask for responses to a proposed project.

Motor-Vehicle Administration _____

Motor-vehicle administration is a general title under which are grouped many occupations dealing with motor vehicles and the driver. Motor-vehicle inspection, driver licensing, vehicle registration, traffic courts, accident records, and driver rehabilitation programs are the main areas that fall within this category. Specialized preparation and training requirements vary greatly among these occupations.

MOTOR-VEHICLE INSPECTION

Motor-vehicle inspection requirements vary from state to state. Vehicle inspection is carried out by independent or state-operated garages in some states, while in others the police may stop vehicles on a random, spot-check basis. The complexity of the inspection and the equipment required have increased over the last few years. With this change, the amount of training required of inspection personnel has also increased. (In some states, for example, the procedure now includes chemical tests of vehicle exhaust emissions.)

Some states require motor-vehicle inspection at regular intervals. These inspections may take place at state-operated or state-licensed facilities.

DRIVER LICENSING

Driver licensing makes up a major part of a state's motor-vehicle-administration work. Examination of drivers requires administering tests for vision, knowledge of traffic laws and control devices, and tests of driving skills. The large number of new and renewal licenses processed by the states have resulted in computerized license records and, therefore, the need for people with training in computer technology.

MOTOR-VEHICLE REGISTRATION

Motor-vehicle registration, like driver licensing, has become computerized to meet the needs of the increasing numbers of vehicle owners and the increased demand for registration information by other agencies. Because registration and licensing are often carried out in one location, the same equipment and personnel are sometimes employed for both jobs.

Licensing and registration personnel sometimes also do work related to taxation. In some states, motor vehicles are taxed as personal property. This requires that information be retrieved from registration records. In addition, local governments may also charge residents with an additional registration fee as a source of revenue.

TRAFFIC COURTS

The traffic courts in a state work closely with the police and the driver-licensing and registration agencies of a state's motor-vehicle administration. Information gathering and record-keeping are essential to the courts in carrying out their duties. The degree of legal training required for court employees is as widespread as the variety of positions available. Judges, lawyers, legal secretaries, and clerks are just a few of the many different occupations included in the traffic courts.

TRAFFIC RECORDS

To ensure that appropriate data on accidents, drivers, motor vehicles, and road systems are available, traffic-records systems have been established. Such systems provide objective data sources for predicting trends in the number and kind of traffic accidents. Records of individual drivers are also kept. These records must also be readily available for law-enforcement agencies and courts.

DRIVER REHABILITATION PROGRAMS

State and local governments often conduct driver rehabilitation programs for traffic offenders. The most common program requires that drivers who are guilty of a certain number of traffic violations attend classes. The classes teach safe driving practices and remind unskilled and negligent drivers of the consequences of unsafe driving.

Driver rehabilitation programs in some communities are aimed at improving the skills and attitudes of experienced drivers who have committed a number of offenses. A court may refer a driver to such a program.

Federal, state, and local governments have only recently realized the potential benefits of driver rehabilitation programs for drivers with alcohol-related offenses. In the job opportunities in these programs, there is a need for educational and psychological training, as well as a knowledge of safe driving practices. People involved in the alcohol rehabilitation programs must also have some formal training in the mental and physical effects of alcohol and the social problems involved with its use.

Police Services

Traffic laws have been developed to provide a set of guidelines for all motor-vehicle operators. Unfortunately, not all drivers follow these guidelines. As stated in previous chapters, there are a number of reasons why such behavior may occur. These include inattention, lack of knowledge, or, in some cases, deliberate disobedience. The primary function of the police is to discourage violations and to encourage adherence to laws and ordinances.

Some police officers are specially trained in traffic activities. Specialized or on-the-job education might include training in high-performance driving, alcohol (DWI) surveillance, and the conduct of tests for the presence of alcohol in a driver's bloodstream.

Another area of police traffic work that is receiving great attention is accident investigation. With the increasing awareness that accidents often result from a combination of driver, vehicle, and roadway failures, these investigations are increasingly complicated. Such inves-

Some police officers specialize in traffic activities.

tigations are sometimes conducted by a team of specialists from the fields of law, medicine, automotive and highway engineering, and others. These teams carefully investigate and try to understand the causes of accidents. They do not simply try to uncover violations of traffic law. By attempting to get at *all* the causes of accidents, these teams work toward preventing future accidents.

The enforcement of traffic laws is an important part of a police officer's work.

Some police officers are involved in community-relations programs.

Job Requirements. The majority of police agencies require a high school diploma or its equivalent. However, many new jobs in police traffic work require advanced training. The development of specialized activities, such as community relations and driving-while-intoxicated countermeasures, may require professional and advanced degrees.

Service Industries

Critical to the operation of the highway transportation system is a group of occupations that can best be described as service industries. Foremost among these are the hundreds of occupations within the corporations that manufacture vehicles—from the smallest cars that travel our highways to the heavy earth-moving equipment used in construction.

Construction companies which build and maintain roadways and off-road areas are an important part of the service industries that maintain the highway transportation system.

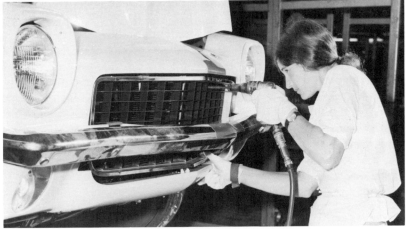

The corporations that manufacture motor vehicles make up one of the largest groups of service industries that contribute to the well-being of the highway transportation system.

In addition to the manufacturing industry, there is a vast service industry that provides everything from electronic diagnosis to vehicle maintenance, repair, and emergency road service. Some facilities may specialize in the repair of air conditioning, radiators, brakes, front-end alignment and wheel balance, or electrical and ignition systems. Automotive repair centers that specialize in body repair and painting represent an industry with a continuing high demand for skilled mechanics and cost estimators. In addition, parts manufacturers, distributors of petroleum products, and automotive-parts wholesalers and retailers all provide essential services.

Other services and occupations that may be less obvious are those involved in the maintenance of the roadway itself. These include industries involved in roadway resurfacing. The research, manufacture, and installation of efficient guardrails, crash barriers, lighting systems, and off-road fencing are also part of this industry. Other companies and agencies are involved in the development of improved paints and equipment used in roadway signs and pavement marking. All these activities contribute to the maintenance and improvement of a safe, efficient highway transportation system.

Another critical service is that provided by emergency medical services. Among the people involved in activities of this kind are vehicle operators who drive or fly ambulances, airplanes, and helicopters to the scenes of accidents; paramedics and interns who provide medical attention to victims at the scene of an accident; and highly trained professionals at trauma centers who administer complete emergency medical services, including surgery. Such services, patterned after military medical evacuation teams, have proved highly effective in reducing the number of deaths resulting from accidents.

It is obvious that the number of career opportunities that exist within the highway transportation system is huge. The occupations that have been discussed in this chapter do not, by any means, represent a complete picture of the activities essential to the operation of the highway transportation system. They should, however, suggest to you the size and complexity of the cooperative effort necessary for the design, construction, maintenance, and improvement of all parts of the system.

Emergency medical and mechanical teams attempt to provide prompt aid to drivers at the scene of breakdowns and accidents.

There are many workers in the industries that maintain and repair motor vehicles.

To Think About

1. Why is the proper management of the highway transportation system important to the economic and social well-being of the United States?
2. Should driver education programs be aimed only at people who are learning to drive for the first time? Why or why not?
3. List three kinds of driver education programs other than high-school courses. Explain the importance of each.
4. Explain the differences between careers in automotive engineering, highway engineering, and traffic engineering.
5. What kinds of records does the motor-vehicle administration in your state keep?

Are these records important? Why?

6. Are driver rehabilitation programs important? Should some drivers be required to enroll in such programs? Why or why not?
7. When they investigate an accident, do the police in your area do more than find out who was at fault or who broke the law? Why?
8. Describe the emergency medical services that are available in your area. Do you think they are adequate?

To Do

1. Make a poster that illustrates how the highway transportation system is related to

the social and economic well-being of the United States. For example, show how the system is related to the farming and recreation industries.

2. Invite a local police officer or traffic official to discuss with your class educational or public-information programs and campaigns in your area. Ask the officer or official if there are programs or campaigns relating to alcohol abuse, pedestrian safety, and bicycling. Do you think the programs and campaigns are adequate?

3. Find out how motor-vehicle inspections are carried out in your state. What special equipment and skills are required to complete these inspections? Report your findings to your class and discuss whether or not you feel the inspections are adequate.

4. Discuss with a local traffic official or police officer some of the problems of rehabilitating drivers who have repeatedly been found guilty of serious driving offenses. Discuss your findings with your class.

Index

Credits _____

All photograph credits are listed in clockwise order, starting from the top and right of each page:

Page 2: Pro Pix/Monkmeyer, Cranham/Rapho Guillumette, Sequeira/Rapho Guillumette, Greenberg/Photo Researchers; page 3: Rogers/Monkmeyer; page 4: DeLellis/AAA; page 5: Gerster/Rapho Guillumette, Stack/Black Star; page 6: Neubauer/Rapho Guillumette; page 8: Davidson/Magnum; page 9: Natali/Rapho Guillumette, Lanks/Black Star, Lisl/Photo Researchers; page 11: Wilson/Black Star, Uzzle/Black Star (center photograph), Mahon/Monkmeyer, Stock/Magnum, Forsyth/Monkmeyer; page 143: The New York Auto Club, the Ohio Department of Transportation; page 154: Wilson/Black Star; page 155: DeLellis/AAA; page 158: DeLellis/AAA; page 159: DeLellis/AAA; page 167: Massar/Black Star; page 168: Westveer/Black Star, DeLellis AAA; page 211: Erick Kroll; page 213: Siteman/Stock Boston; page 214: Roberts/Rapho Guillumette; page 217: Bayer/Monkmeyer; page 219: Zalesky/Black Star; page 222: Ski-roule, Ltd.; page 223: Mulvehill/Photo Researchers; page 250: Hennepin County (Minnesota) Alcohol Safety Action Project; page 252: Peter Vadnai; page 258: Guss/Black Star; page 259: Roberts/Rapho Guillumette; page 276: 3M Company; page 287: DeLellis/AAA; page 288: General Motors Company; page 289: Alcoa; page 291: Rogers/Monkmeyer; page 292: Shackman/Monkmeyer; page 295: St. Louis Post-Dispatch/Black Star, Baker/Monkmeyer; page 296: Freed/Magnum, Rogers/Monkmeyer; page 297: Brock/Black Star, General Motors Company; page 298: Barad/Monkmeyer, Munroe/Photo Researchers; page 299: Strickler/Monkmeyer.

The table on page 247 is adapted from "What the Body Does with Alcohol," a pamphlet by Dr. Leon A. Greenberg. Copyright 1955 by the Journal of Studies on Alcohol, Inc., New Brunswick, New Jersey, the Center of Alcohol Studies at Rutgers University.

6 7 8 9 10 DODO 84 83 82 81 80